SEO Secrets For 2012

Search Engine Optimization

Mike Monahan

The Internet.
140 million domains.
59 billion URL's.
...and counting.

Royal House Publishing

SEO Secrets for 2012

The material contained in this book are not sponsored by, endorsed by, or affiliated with Microsoft Corporation, Google.com, Bing.com, Yahoo!, MSN, Live, SEOAudits.com, AccuQuality.com, WebsiteSubmitter.org, SubmissionComplete.com or any other search engine and or products, code, or software shown herein. All logos are trademarks of their respective owners.

ISBN-10: 0985100001
ISBN-13: 978-0-9851000-0-1

Royal House Publishing has attempted whenever possible throughout this book to distinguish proprietary trademarks from descriptive terms by following capitalization and style used by their respective owners.

The authors and the publisher have used their best effort to prepare this book and content based on the final release of the product. Portions of this book/manuscript may be based on prerelease versions of the software supplied by the manufacturer. Royal House Publishing and its author(s) make no representation or warranty of any kind as to its completeness or accuracy of the content and accept no liability of any kind as to the performance, merchantability, fitness for any purpose, or any losses or damages of any kind related caused or alleged to have been caused directly or indirectly from the use of this book.

Royal House Publishing accepts no responsibility from the opinions expressed in the book to any entity and the opinions expressed are those of the authors and not of Royal House Publishing, its publisher, or assigned.

Cover images licensed for print from Fotolia US.

Patience is an SEO's best friend. If people would stop long enough to let the good, basic SEO items work they'd be so much happier. The problem is we're all human beings and we cannot help but try to watch the plant grow and add more fertilizer, water, poke our fingers in the soil, or adjust the sunlight until it dies.

We desire so much to get great quick results from SEO that after planting a seed, watering it, and fertilizing it we just want to keep going back to the pot to watch the plant grow. Stop and let it grow. Good SEO can take 6 months to a year to start growing. SEO works best without interference.

--Jason McCormick

2010. Author of SEO Made Simple For 2010, 2011, and 2012

Create a website easy on the eyes, that can compete with your competition, and rank well with the search engines. Your business can't help but be successful.

--Sean Odom

1998, Author and the founding father of Search Engine Optimization.

... Amazing how the same principles endure today.

About the author – Mike Monahan

Mike Monahan is the Chief Technology Officer at his own company, Mike Monahan SEO (MikeMonahanSEO.com). For 15 years he has taken on the toughest URLs and keywords for some of the nation's largest companies to bring their websites to the top of the major search engines.

He is a master of search engine optimization techniques, using mathematical equations and test applications to determine the exact algorithm each search engine is utilizing to place rankings for each individual keyword.

Acknowledgements

Also I have to acknowledge a few really great friends and customers. Joe Smith and Bruce Winkel from the Matheson Gas, Mindy Morgan at LocalNewsDay.com, Ken Gregg at Sliding-Thru Productions, Neal Ice at A Bobcat Excavations, and author . Most of all I need to thank Tim Thomason at Royal House for the belief he has in me and the chance he has given me to be a published author.

TABLE OF CONTENTS

CHAPTER 9-SOCIAL MEDIA 178

CHAPTER 10-SETTING SEO GOALS AND MAKING A PLAN 185

CHAPTER 11-SEO TOOLS 198

Chapter 1 – What's New For 2012?

I am in the real business of SEO using current and up to the minute (sometimes) techniques to optimize websites. I use real analytical results, real research, and real client websites. I have a team of 6 full time employees dedicated to nothing but figuring out what Google is doing so I can apply the correct principles to every clients websites and obtain the best possible results. So this book is based on actual current results of our own research and not from what I have read on the Internet and haven't confirmed through actually applying trial and error.

Sometimes it frustrates me when I see reviews of my books that say something to the fact I stated the keywords are no longer used by the search engines but my book says to put them on the website…etc." This is just one example of many. The fact is the person misread somewhere that Google doesn't read the Keywords Meta tag for determining the keyword, it uses the title instead. Every other search engine still uses the Keywords Meta tag. This is just one example of the wrong thinking people have when reading my book. The fact is, many of the things that were changed year after year come back and go. It is an ever changing science. Google wants to change things up frequently to keep ahead of SEO. If it didn't and everyone applied SEO and got on page 1, why would they need Pay-Per-Click their main money maker?

When reading this book, I need you to forget everything you learned last year and everything the years before. Every year SEO is a brand new ball game. This year it is an exceptionally changed environment and I waited an extra two months to put this book out so it would be completely up to date.

If you have never read one of my SEO books and have never met me, nice to meet you. My name is Mike Monahan and I have been the bestselling SEO author since 2009. But for years before that I have taken not only my own websites, but my clients which were transparent on the Internet and made them very successful in Internet marketing terms.

This year is somewhat different than any other year. Instead of working for the other guy and not making much money on all of my talent and efforts, I have gone out on my own and started my own SEO company. I am calling it Mike Monahan SEO (MikeMonahanSEO.com). Cleverly disguising the true brains behind the operation.

As most know Sean Odom is credited by most of the Internet as being the creator of the Search Engine Optimization (SEO) by being the first to write articles on directory placement in 1993 and calling it "Optimization For Indexes and Search Engines". Later he called it "Search Engine Optimization" in his book in 1995. I have not only met Sean Odom but have worked side by side with him for many years.

So what is Search Engine Optimization also known as SEO? To make it easy, virtually no one uses the telephone book anymore. A vast majority of the planet turns to the Internet and to be a successful business in the year 2012 your business needs to show up page 1 or 2 of a Google, Bing, or Yahoo! search or you might as well not exist at all. You might be surviving now as a business by using other advertising or word of mouth, but you're missing out on a lot of business and probably in a few more years without SEO your business will most likely be out of business.

I user *AccuQuality.com* which is a major ranking and website auditing company because they are always accurate and I trust them. Each year they provide SEO's with two semiannual reports on Internet usage and trends and three interesting statistics really stood our this year. I wanted to share these with you as some interesting changes are evolving.

From AccuQuality.com's Internet Usage Report 12/15/2011:

> *"Less than 5% of the Internet uses professional SEO services, however, those companies that use professional SEO services garner over 86.8% of all organic clicks."*

If you think about it, that's probably pretty accurate. The another one I thought was very interesting:

"Most 1ˢᵗ page clicks now come from positions organic positions 2, 3, 4, and 5."

This is a new trend which I thought was very surprising as every business owner who calls me wants to be 1ˢᵗ on page one of a Google search for their key terms. Why has this trend changed? There were many reasons given in the report. The most common reasons given were the searcher thought position one was the most expensive, they thought that the space on position one was part of pay-per-click, and some just said they never click on position one because it is usually not the most relevant to their search criteria. It is a major trend shift in search engine use.

The third item I want to address from the report is the most interesting and it is more of a statement than a trend.

"It is almost impossible to get first page placement of your website on Google, Bing, or Yahoo! without implementing a majority of modern SEO techniques."

This means that getting on a Google search accidentally only happens now for words in your domain name or unlikely to be searched for terms without using current SEO techniques.

As you read this book you need to remember that what you do on-page, (coding, wording, Meta tagging, keyword density, etc.) only accounts for about 35% of where your website is placed by the major search engines. The other 70% or so is what you do off-page. Everything from social media, links, and much more as you will see in this book.

As I was writing this page I got interrupted by a prospective client for my SEO company who told me a yellow page advertising representative just told him that no one really needs SEO. I hear this almost weekly. The yellow page salesperson stated the all the client needed was his yellow page advertisements. They will not only be in the book but also on the web. The cost? $4,200 a month was his quote. I asked him, when is the last time you did a search on the Internet and saw a yellow pages ad? I haven't even finished this paragraph and my email just showed me I got his signed contract for services. Long silence on the phone is all I got by the way. The fact is Google wants to be the phone book. It will never rank yellow page listings highly or more organized than Google Places.

Let me change topics here. When you first started your website did you think there was some sort of magic on the Internet and after you created your website, Google and the other search engines would magically tell people about your website? That Google and the other search engines would magically know when people searched for whatever product, service, or information your website would come up instantly in a search? I got news for you, it's not magic. It's called search engine optimization that tells each of the search engines what your website is relevant for and the search terms you should be found for and it IS AN EXACT SCIENCE.

In my personal opinion I am the only trusted source you should listen. I will never steer you wrong unlike the 20,000 websites saying they are SEO's from India, Pakistan, and Nigeria who will gladly take your money and never do a thing. I have to note that not all of them are con artists, but 9 out of 10 are according to *SEOAudits.com*. I will also note that *SEOAudits.com's* latest statistics show that 98% of all articles found on the Internet regarding SEO are outdated and misleading. That means that for every 100 articles you find about website optimization on the Internet, only 2 of them have correct or current information. That is tragic and why so many website owners are steered in the wrong direction and give up on SEO all together.

This book has a lot to digest and it goes in a very specific chronological order. Just like if I were to take a new website and optimize it myself. I go through these same steps. So don't miss chapters or sections and read them in the order I have written them.

It takes a lot of work to master every part of search engine optimization. After you have read this book you should know SEO well enough to make adjustments when your website won't go up in the rankings or positioning because of the competition in your industry or you're competing with a number of other competitors who have good SEO companies. It gets tougher as you increase the size of your intended audience. Local campaigns are easiest but when you go to a national or international campaign level the competition is even more challenging to overcome.

In the end, I teach you everything you need to know in this book. However, my company and I are here to help you if this is overwhelming or too much for you to grasp or handle on your own. You can call me at 714-398-8175 or visit my website at www.MikeMonahanSEO.com. I can help you with everything you read here. Now let's take a look at what is new and important to know in 2012 which are:

- The Panda Updates
- Google's Search Plus Your World.

The PANDA of Google's Algorithm

Many of my personal clients began to experience dramatic declines in their overall website visits and positioning on Google.com beginning at the end of August. Most of these drops can be attributed to some recent changes to the algorithm that Google uses and changes caused by what the industry calls the "Panda Updates". Here is a brief explanation of the changes to Google called the "Panda Updates and the actions you need to take on your websites to combat the effects of the new algorithm changes on Google.

The New Panda Updates

I know many of you have been waiting and some dreading to read this section of the 2012 book, knowing that there has been a major changes to Google's algorithm nick named the "Panda Updates". What many of you do not know is this has been a series of updates and new versions as well as changes. So many in fact that we now classify the version being used as version 3.6 as does most of the professional SEO industry. Keeping up with these changes as well as gaining verified research has been a challenge in this case and has taken longer than most updates. In the meantime some of you have really taken a hit on your positioning waiting for this information.

The Goal Of Panda

If you understand the goal of the Panda update, you can understand what you need to do to combat its effects. The goal appears to be this, "Google wants a brand new original Internet." Meaning Google wants to see new and original content.

How Do I Modify My Site Pages That Have Dropped Due To Panda

The changes are simple to describe but less easy to implement. Before you read the following information, remember I am the consultant not the creator. In other words, don't shoot the messenger.

1. Content created before September 1, 2011 needs to be dramatically updated. Not just minor changes but needs to be republished and plentiful with information and focus on just one keyword per page in a readable format.

2. You need to make sure that you check each URL with **copyscape.com** to make sure that your content is original and not copied or that the content is similar to any other content on the Internet. Rumor has it that Google is now date stamping content that it indexes. In the past if you were complaining that your content was stolen from you and caused your page rank to drop because there was duplicate content on the Internet this will hopefully not be a problem again on the Internet.

3. Make sure that your website is compatible with all browser including **Android, IPAD, IE9**, and **Google Chrome** for sure. (To make sure you are compliant in all respects you can get either an *AccuQuality.com* or *SEOAudits.com* Website Report to check this issue.)

4. Make sure all pages render in under 10 seconds. You can use Google's speed test to make sure. **https://developers.google.com/pagespeed.** If your website does not get a score of 70 or above you need to read the suggestions given from the report you receive or find better hosting.

5. Anymore than two broken links on a page can be detrimental to that page! **Fix all broken links!** (To make sure you are compliant in all respects you need to get either an *AccuQuality.com* or *SEOAudits.com* Website Report to check this issue.)

6. Google has changed the *Keyword Density* requirement from 7% to a more reasonable 6-6.5%. This means that your each of your pages should focus on one keyword. Each page should also contain 300 words minimum and your keyword should appear at least 6 times for every 100 words on the page. If you have 300 words on the page, your keyword should be on the page 18 times at a minimum. You can use the keyword density check tool at **http://www.gorank.com/analyze.php** to check your keyword density and learn other places you can place keywords on the page.

How Does Google Search Plus Your World Effect You?

Two buttons. What do they do?

Personal Results   **Hide Personal Results**

Google's Social Media Attack

Google struck another blow in the social media war with the launch of "Search Plus Your World", their enhanced algorithm for personalization in your SERPs.

This change will have far reaching impacts on a variety of things, including SEO. One of the most notable things that came out of this change is that pages on Google+ which relate to your searched topic come up first. And there is a serious lack of integration with Facebook and Twitter.

Amit Singhal, who currently oversees Google's ranking algorithms, had this to say about the omission of Facebook and Twitter in the new results:

> *"Facebook and Twitter and other services, basically, their terms of service don't allow us to crawl them deeply and store things. Google+ is the only [social media website] that provides such a persistent service. Of course, going forward, if others were willing to change, we'd look at designing things to see how it would work."*

SEO and Social Media have now been literally joined at the hip thanks to Search Plus Your World. You now cannot run a successful SEO campaign without integrating it heavily with social media.

Even with the new addition of Google+ in late 2011, up until the 15th of January, most of the focus of SEO social media efforts had been on primarily focused on YouTube, Facebook and Twitter.

Google knows it is the most influential search engine on the Internet and Google is clearly integrating and favoring results coming from people's Google+ and social media circles making Google+ the most important social media outlet to focus on from an SEO perspective.

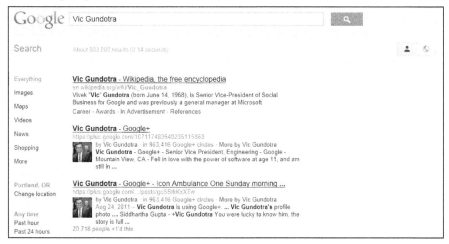

By default Google's Search Plus Your World displays personal results which as you can see from my results searching for Google's vice president's name above.

One of the new features of Google pictured on the next page if you try to create a Google account from Google's homepage, you'll notice that Google redesigned the page to create your account. You cannot just create an account using any email address. Now you'll have to create a Gmail account, a Google Profile and you now automatically join Google+.

The redesigned information gathering form includes the new fields: name, gender (required for Google+) and a mobile phone number (not required).

Your Google Account is more than just Search.

Talk, chat, share, schedule, store, organize, collaborate, discover and create. Use Google products from Gmail to Google+ to YouTube, view your search history, all with one username and password, all packed up all the time and easy to find at (you guessed it) Google.com.

Take it all with you.

A Google Account lets you access all your stuff — Gmail, photos, and more — from any device. Search by taking pictures, or by voice. Get free turn-by-turn navigation, upload your pictures automatically, and soon even buy things with your phone using Google Wallet.

Share a little. Or share a lot.

Share selectively with friends, family (may be even your boss), on Google+. Start a video Hangout with friends, text a group all at once, or just follow posts from people who fascinate you. Your call.

Work in the future.

Get a jump on the next era of doing, well, everything. Watch as colleagues or partners drop in a photo, update a spreadsheet, or improve a paragraph, in real-time, from 1,000 miles away. Google Docs is free with a Google Account.

Two SEO Strategies

In terms of SEO, two strategies need to now be running concurrently with each other. The first is the "personalized or social media" strategy, and their "normal" strategy which gives regular organic results for those not logged in to Google or who click on the World icon which hides personal results.

Your "normal" SEO strategy will not change your social media strategy. What is going to change will be the need for developing a strategy for building your content on Google+ and gaining social approval and trust in order to create an organic environment of sharing knowledge. This will have an impact on how that network's personalized results and how they will be displayed

Chapter 2 - Let's Talk About What SEO

Lately I have been hearing from a lot of my clients that they have been told, "**SEO is dead**". Every time I hear it, I have to say…"Are you kidding me???" The rumor is so rampant that two of the webmasters that do website work for my customers told them that they would stay on the first page of Google without SEO services. All they had to do was just keep adding to their blog.

Both have since returned as customers. The only bad thing is that it is taking their website months to get back to their coveted place on Google and Bing and have cost them thousands in sales and customers. I wanted to laugh and tell the clients I told you so but when they think they are talking to a trusted person. It is hard to sway their thinking.

The truth is though, Google's algorithm gives you imaginary points (Meaning they find your website more relevant.) if you have a blog linked from your website than if you didn't have one. But that is only one part of about 130 different things you have to do each month to stay competitive even for keywords that have an average competition level. The explosion of social media especially Google+ and how Google is displaying results. now gives little weight to entries in blogs and now you rarely see blog entries come up on indexed searches. In fact Google now ranks blogs separately from their respective websites and not very well.

The "SEO is Dead" claim is based largely on the specter of mounting algorithmic complexities, rising barriers to overcome, the advent of personalized and local search, integration of social usage data signals, and a perfect mechanical website both on the human side and the digital side.

One nice thing Google's did for us this year was have their own Matt Cutts' who is the head of Google's Webspam team has become the official information disseminator between Google and SEO's stated that "**SEO is a way of getting relevant information in to searches.**" So it is here to stay. **SEO is becoming a staple of many marketing plans for businesses and getting more embraced and more familiar to business owners, the colloquial 'SEO' shorthand is being used more often than the formal term 'search engine optimization.' "**

If SEO is so dead, choose any industry and type in the keywords they would focus in on for their business. Every single website that comes up on the first two pages regardless of industry has some kind of professional SEO help. Even at the local level.

Compare SEO to Other Channels

So this got me thinking about examining more query trend activity to see how well SEO fares against other online marketing channels, like Pay-Per-Click (PPC) marketing for instance. I have my own opinion about how SEO fares against PPC in the marketplace. In my experience, I see that PPC's popularity is dropping quickly. It shows that the cost per click actually dropped 8% last month on Google. There are less people bidding on PPC.

Website Submitters conducted a recent survey of over 500 business owners and marketers. An overwhelming majority (338) plan to reduce their PPC spending and increase their SEO spending in 2012. All but two stated they felt PPC purchased through a bidding war was becoming too expensive and that "Click fraud" was becoming too rampant. Click fraud is when someone clicks on your purchased pay-per-click ad and not intending to buy or learn anything. Such as if your competitor clicked on your ad to increase your costs.

This happens frequently. I won't name the website, but there is a website that finds work for U.S. companies by hiring off shore labor from India, Pakistan, and other such countries. Currently if you search for jobs to perform "Click Fraud" there are 3,318 jobs available just to click on other competitors ads all day. Some pay by the hour, others pay by the job. I just looked at two focusing on clicking on competitors "dating ads" nationally and "roofing ads" in the local Chicago market.

Back to the survey from Website Submitter. Over 82% of participants in the survey said they see SEO as more instrumental in their businesses growth in 2012 than in 2011. This is a 7% increase from last year.

What are the driving forces for SEO in 2012?

There are a lot of variables in SEO but several have much heavier weights than others. Last year it was good linking that took first place. This year linking is virtually off the radar. Linking still needs to be done and I wouldn't ignore it much other factors are much more important. I have addressed these in the order of importance which are:

- Social Media Drives SEO
- Local SEO Is Taking Over
- Google+ And Community Building
- Original Quality Content
- Invest Real In Your Website
- Make Sure You Have Good Coding
- Realize You're Now In The Marketing and Publishing Business
- Schema.org, Microformats and Rich Snippets
- The Term SoLoMo
- Do Something Not In This Book?

Social Media Drives SEO

The traditional on-page SEO factors will still hold true since it's all about making your content search friendly, but what we'll see in 2012 is nothing like how social media factors in to SEO results like never before. This past year Google pushed to integrate social results into its SERP's (and launched Search Plus Your World this alone will make Google+ a huge part of SEO and 's not forget the Facebook-Bing partnership.

Local SEO Is Taking Over

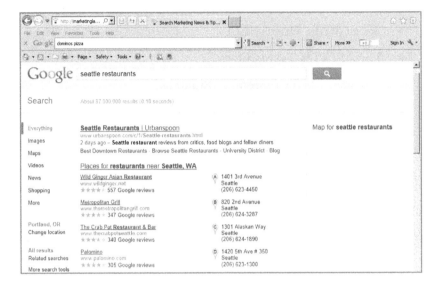

There's a good probability that a large percentage of the Google searches you perform will display Google Places listings. Consumers are noticing as well. Accuquality.com has tracked eye movement and clicks and found that when those are displayed they are clicked on a much higher percentage than even organic results. The results show that users heavily gravitate toward any of Places' listings, whether they're mixed into organic lists.

If your business relies on local listings, concentrate on creating a listing at Google Places. You can do this by using:

- **Citations**: Ensure that your correct business information is listed in as many (reputable) sources as possible around the Internet.

- **Google Places page optimization**: Just like your website, make sure your Google Places page is properly optimized. Include categories that match exactly, and point your Places page back to a city-specific landing page if applicable. Also notice you have to choose a category from Google's list but you can add up to 5 others or choose 5 other keywords to be found in.

- **Reviews**: Google will only display reviews from Google, but getting reviews from aggregators like Yelp, CitySearch, Superpages or Trip Advisor. This will help increase your notice as well.

Google+ And Community Building

Google will aggressively roll out new features to Google+ this year which will make Google+ pages more business-friendly. The biggest advantage Google has is its integration with other Google services, Google Search plus Your World, search engine results pages, in paid search ads, Google Reader, Blogspot.com, YouTube, etc.

As Internet marketers get sophisticated with planning and measuring their SEO campaigns, you will see businesses paying close attention to their existing community members. An increased emphasis will be placed on building an engaged community as opposed to simply amassing numbers of followers. This means in social media you must energize your community members as well as engage members for a variety of things like product or service reviews, development, market research, and special discounts, to name a few.

Community building and management is all about people, content, and consistency. This tactic will be widely adopted and used throughout 2012.

Original Quality Content

Most of us appreciate good original quality content. Especially content that is engaging, relevant, and helpful to the person finding what they were looking for. A good content writer is now the key to good SEO. Google is so good at finding paid and spam links even in content. For the most effective long-term SEO strategy, move the focus back to great ORIGINAL content, both on your website and across other sites. Invite guest blogging or some other incentive to get good content to get ahead of your competition.

I have seen so many companies cut corners and slash costs from their budget using software, copy content then modify it slightly, with the sole purpose of creating content just for SEO and not human beings. If you read a few pages earlier you know what now is happening to all the poor souls that were doing this thanks to Google's Panda updates. So, in retrospect, Panda was a timely and much needed update from Google. The only sad part of this as when content is copied from one place to another, Google had no way of knowing who was the originator of the content. One of the bad things is that if you were the originator and your content was copied. You are caught up in the mess the Panda Updates have caused and it may be you who is suffering with bad positioning on Google right now.

What we'll see in 2012 is a more structured approach by businesses to create content that focuses on providing more unique and high value original content to the visitors on their websites. This will require and result in higher engagement levels with their community members. We'll see a more holistic approach from businesses with better content , whether it's text, videos, how-to content pieces, or other types of content.

Schema.org, Microformats and Rich Snippets

Search engine rarely work together but the "Big Three" (Google, Bing and Yahoo!) have worked together to develop shema.org which is a set of website standards that will tell search engines what your site is about, making it easier for those engines to read the site's data and index accordingly.

By using rich snippets, for example, you're able to tell Google what information to feature in SERPs: product reviews and prices, upcoming events, and more as shown below:

Lakers Tickets	Los Angeles **Lakers Tickets** - Barry's Tickets Service
www.barrystickets.com/lakers/
Lakers Tickets. We have **Lakers Tickets** and Los Angeles Lakers Schedule ...
Sun, Jan 22   Los Angeles Lakers vs Indiana Pacers
Tue, Jan 31   Los Angeles Lakers vs Charlotte Bobcats
Fri, Feb 17   Los Angeles Lakers vs Phoenix Suns

The added data will increase your click-through rate because users are able to preview more about the link before they commit to the click.

Invest Real In Your Website

Don't pick your websites designer out of a hat especially if you run a focused business. Hire a design firm that designs easy to comprehend websites and knows current SEO or admits he doesn't and is willing to work in yours or your SEO's guidelines. Make sure he also knows the differences from designing a local focused websites as opposed to a national or globally focused website. These are completely different. Your website must be easy on the eyes for a human visitor, compete with your competition, and rank well with the search engines. Be prepared to make a serious investment in an excellent of just not money but more so your time.

Make Sure You Have Good Coding

Google's algorithm has really taken a strong look at how well a website is designed and coded. So much so that if your website has a large number of broken links, it is almost impossible to get ranked well. There are more deal breakers with Google as well such as are your pages too big over 180Kb? Is your website compatible with all the new browsers including Chrome, Ipod, IPhone, and Android browsers? How do you find out if you have problems?

Every client I take on gets a SEO Audit by an independent authority. There are only two that I trust. Those are **SEOAudits.com** and **AccuQuality.com** which provide SEO Audit Reports. These two companies provide the most comprehensive reports for the money. I highly recommend that every website have an audit initially after the design is completed and every year at a minimum. Standards change and their reports keep up with the latest standards. Secondly, if changes you make to the website create broken links or links change from your websites to others, they can be effecting your search engine rankings and you will never know it!

If you have ever got to WebsiteGrader.com report you get a report only on your homepage using a dozen or so tests to give your website a grade. AccuQuality.com and SEOAudits.com test every page of your website and each of them do over 400 tests per page and give you a huge online report complete with links to explain how to fix each item. The tests they perform give results on everything from broken links, W3C compliance, browser compatibility, search ability, and much more. They both even spell check your entire website and deliver a huge report online.

Not only do they do a complete comprehensive website report on your entire website, but the report also identifies the line in the code on each page with an issue and instructions on how to correct every issue that the report identifies. For every issue the report identifies, if it is not fixed you lose those imaginary ranking points toward getting ranked well. If the SEO audit companies can see the issues, you can be sure Google does as well.

Realize You're Now In The Marketing and Publishing Business

If you own a website and you're doing SEO, it means that you are trying to market either information, a product, a service, or many variations of all of those. Whether you realize it or now, you're in the marketing and publishing business. A fact so many business owners fail to realize.

From the title of your website, to the text people see, to the business listing you make, to the blog articles you create...you are marketing your website and publishing information. I write books and I have a complete arsenal of nouns, verbs and adjectives to describe what I do and how to do it. If you don't know how to communicate in written form well, then you need to invest money and hire a copywriter who does. Not just any copywriter though. One who knows your business from the inside and out and knows how to write with a good keyword density. Focusing on just one keyword for each page that the copywriter creates. Google has made it a requirement that if you want good rankings, you must keep the words flowing on your website, social media, your profiles, your reviews, and more.

The Term SoLoMo

This is a new term to apply to what is important in 2012. It combines the social, local, and mobile environments in to SEO. These are the items that will really take hold in 2012. Integrating your SEO campaigns by combining social media with local offers involving mobile devices and compatibility with your website essential. Mobile content has the potential to boost brand loyalty, and this can boost sales for on-the-go shoppers.

Top daily deals sites like Bing Deals, DealOn, Groupon and LivingSocial are perfect examples of this where they using deals to drive local sales. Foursquare is perfectly positioned for this SoLoMo tactic.

W3C Validation

If you have had a year of website designers and developers making continual changes to the site. You may have major problems with your coding. If you haven't been continually monitoring errors, run a W3C validation to ensure your code is still clean as well as page load tests to assess any page elements dragging down load time.You can check this by employing **SEOAudits.com** or **AccuQuality.com** to do an SEO Report.

Do Something Not In This Book

The tips in this book are standard as well as best-practice advice. Being creative is something I love to hear about and can take you to the next step in SEO. If you do something no one has ever thought of before, wither online or off, to put your business on the map or in the public's mind, I want to know about it. If I use it in my next book I will send you a nice electronic device. This year I gave away over 25 IPOD Touches for ideas I used here in this book. The fact is, good new ideas sell and persistence is rewarded.

If you have an idea or something you have done to promote your business let me know! Email me at **Mike@MikeMonahanSEO.com**.

Chapter 3 – The Coding You Don't See

Keywords in Meta tags are no longer a requirement for Google, but they are helpful on other search engines. Google scans the actual relevant content that is on all the pages on your website (with correct linkage that is.) and places more weight on the words placed in the <Title> tag.

> **WARNING:** *We already touched on this a little but for websites that have their relevant content or words mainly in pictures or in Flash the search engine crawlers cannot read this. This is why the most Flashy and spectacular looking websites are on page 284 of a keyword search.*

Now I said that having Meta tags on Google was not a requirement, but, I wouldn't leave them out. If you were looking at this from points prospective, your description, keywords, and other information in your Meta tag all give you more points if they match the content actual website page of your website as well as the title bar. It all adds up to what the search engines see as relevant content.

In this section we will look at how to properly format meta tags to allow prime optimization, allow the bots, spiders and crawlers to visit more than your landing page, how to make them relevant to your keywords, add location based meta data, and much more!

Choosing A Keyword

As I said earlier, keywords in your Meta tags are just one of about three dozen elements that are taken into consideration when search engines visit your website to collect information about your website. But choosing those keywords, correctly placing those keywords on your websites landing pages and matching them to the Titles and Meta tagging of your website absolutely is necessary.

Some keywords absolutely have value; and more important, keywords can cause damage to your websites reputation and make it almost invisible if not used properly.

Choosing Quality Keywords

Targeting your trophy keywords is absolutely important!

It's complicated I know. As I said earlier, keywords in Meta tags are no longer a requirement. When I say it is not a requirement, I see companies with a ranking of one or two on Google all the time that do not have a single Meta tag, nor a list of keywords and no description either.

Their domains longevity, linkage, and relevant content sped them along in the process to get ranked. But it won't get them much farther in the ranking process. Each stepping stone that you make on the list gets you a little higher in the ranking process.

I always like to explain it to customers that each item you do equals a point value to the major search engines.

- Have a website that has been online for a long period (Years), add points.
- Have your website registration paid so it expires in 5 years or more, add points.
- Create your website in WordPress get points. (Google seems to love WordPress more than any other web development platform.)
- Have it expire in less than a year, subtract points.
- Have Meta Tags, add points.
- Have relevant content, add points, have quality and relevant links, add points.
- Have an SEO company that is a Search Engine Ambassador, add points.
- Have a good hosting speed add points. (You can check at **http://pagespeed.googlelabs.com**. A passing score is 70 or more.)
- Have a homepage that has is smaller than 180KB get points.
- Have news articles published about your website on websites that are determined by Google to be "Official News Sites" such as LocalNewsDay.com, DailyTrib.com, ChicagolandNewspaper.com, FoxNews.com, etc., add a lot of points.
- Have links from .gov and .edu sites, adds points.
- Have a good website quality score, add points. (You can check this by employing **SEOAudits.com** or **AccuQuality.com**.)
- Do well on all 137 factors I outline here in this book, get higher rankings!

The higher the point values, the higher the rankings can become. The more points needed is based on a number of factor, including the industry you're in, the competition you have, competing companies with SEO vying for the top spots, local or national campaigns, traffic to your website, two way links, and much more, but obviously not based on your keywords alone. In fact, it barely has an impact on rankings.

Now this imaginary point's scale I have created to explain to clients and you how rankings work have nothing to do with the quality scoring, which I will talk about in later in this book. However, deciding on your keywords has a major impact on this score.

Weights Of Keyword Placement

Now, knowing that overall the keywords in the Meta tags we decide to use only has a small overall percentage in relevancy and rankings on search engines, it does have a more noticeable impact if we use those keywords in different places of our website to make our word density higher and our website seem more relevant to the search engines. In fact here is a chart we have put together to show just how much of an impact on relevancy placing our keywords on our website can be:

Keyword in the Title Tag(6%)

Keyword in the Root Domain Name (e.g. keyword.com)(6%)

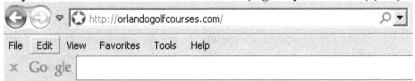

Keyword in the H1 Headline Tag(5%)

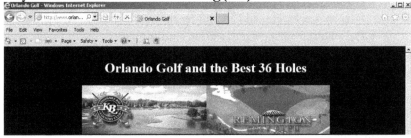

Keyword in Internal Link Anchor Text on the Page(4%)

PARTNERS:

Bethesda Maryland Counseling | Best Senior Medical Alert Devices| Medical Alert DevicesCell Culture Products | Kissimmee Golf
Best Medicare Supplement Insurance | Great Medicare Supplemental Insurance | The Aesthetic Surgeon | Best SEO Services | Orlando Golf

Keyword 3 times in the first 100 words on the page(4%)

Golf Orlando today! That is what I try to tell everyone that I know this time of year as I am absolutely a golf enthusiast. November through April is my favorite time of year to go to go on an Orlando golf trip as well. Why? It's the best time of the year to escape the cold and dreary days in the upper hemisphere and go down below and get some sun near Disney World with an Orlando golf trip. There are a couple of courses I really love during my Orlando golf trip which are both located just 10 minutes from Orlando. Just a quick 10 minute drive and you get better Orlando golf greens and you save alot of money. You just can't beat turnpurtures in the 80's almost everyday and a nice cool ocean breeze and not a single cloud in the sky.

The course conditions at these two courses owned by Remington Golf courses are excellent, the greens are nice and friendly staff are my personal favorites. . Then there is there slogan, "All you can, practice, play and eat at one price, less than $60. Making this an is an experience like no other **Orlando golf** course can offer. For the price of a normal greens fee in Orlando we had a breakfast, a hot dog for lunch and soda's at every turn and when we got back to the clubhouse we had a great lunch all for one proce. It was the most affordable "ALL YOU CAN" experience and I have no idea how this Orlando golf course can afford to do this. I give this Orlando golf trip and this Orlando golf course five stars.

If I can go back to the management team I have to say they were great! I was treated great by all the staff and they were all smiles. Not only that the courses are public and open to everyone which is not very common anywhere near Orlando. One thing that stood out is that we were greeted in the parking lot before we ever stepped foot in the club house. Then we were helped to the pro shop, received our first bucket of unlimited practice balls to warm up, and were treated to the food! At the club house It's not a buffet style either. Your order it from a real person, then it gets cooked to your order. I must say I personally really enjoyed this Orlando golf club and the "ALL YOU CAN" Orlando golf experience! I can't leave out mentioning how freindly the staff in the lounge were as well at both courses. There was a girl from Wisconsin working there who really explained everything and the pitfalls of some of the 36 holes we were going to experience that day. She was very knowledgable. It was warm on the course, and that beverage cart seemed to be everywhere we were. When were we done all four of us in the party enjoyed the great atmosphere at the bar, and we learned that just about everywhere you go at the Orlando golf course, everyone really knows how to have fun.

Keyword in a subdomain (3%)

Keyword in the page name URL (3%)

Keyword in image ALT text(3%)

```
46
47  <body>
48  <div align="center">
49      <table width="200" border="0">
50          <tr>
51
52          <td><div align="center">
53              <h1 class="style1">Orlando Golf and the Best 36 Holes </h1>
54              <img src="OrlandoGolfLogo.gif" alt="Orlando Golf Course Logos" width="598" height="114" /><br>
55                  <script src="http://h1.flashvortex.com/display.php?id=3_1270324983_9276_151_11498_957_37_6_44" type="text/javascript"></script>
56              <br>
57                  <table width="939" border="0">
```

Keyword repeating in the HTML text on the page(3%)

Golf Orlando today! That is what I try to tell everyone that I know this time of year as I am absolutely a golf enthusiast. November through Apr my favorite time of year to go to go on an Orlando golf trip as well. Why? It's the best time of the year to escape the cold and dreary days in th upper hemisphere and go down below and get some sun near Disney World with an Orlando golf trip. There are a couple of courses I really lo during my Orlando golf trip which are both located just 10 minutes from Orlando. Just a quick 10 minute drive and you get better Orlando go greens and you save alot of money. You just can't beat turnpurtures in the 80's almost everyday and a nice cool ocean breeze and not a single clo the sky.

The course conditions at these two courses owned by Remington Golf courses are excellent, the greens are nice and friendly staff are my perso favorites. . Then there is there slogan, "All you can, practice, play and eat at one price, less than $60. Making this an is an experience like no of **Orlando golf** course can offer. For the price of a normal greens fee in Orlando we had a breakfast, a hot dog for lunch and soda's at every turn a when we got back to the clubhouse we had a great lunch all for one proce. It was the most affordable "ALL YOU CAN" experience and I have idea how this Orlando golf course can afford to do this. I give this Orlando golf trip and this Orlando golf course five stars.

If I can go back to the management team I have to say they were great! I was treated great by all the staff and they were all smiles. Not only that courses are public and open to everyone which is not very common anywhere near Orlando. One thing that stood out is that we were greeted in parking lot before we ever stepped foot in the club house. Then we were helped to the pro shop, received our first bucket of unlimited practice b to warm up, and were treated to the food! At the club house It's not a buffet style either. Your order it from a real person, then it gets cooked to order. I must say I personally really enjoyed this Orlando golf club and the "ALL YOU CAN" Orlando golf experience! I can't leave out mentio how freindly the staff in the lounge were as well at both courses. There was a girl from Wisconsin working there who really explained everything the pitfalls of some of the 36 holes we were going to experience that day. She was very knowledgable. It was warm on the course, and that beve cart seemed to be everywhere we were. When were were done all four of us in the party enjoyed the great atmosphere at the bar, and we learned just about everywhere you go at the Orlando golf course, everyone really knows how to have fun.

Keyword in image names on the page (orlando-golf-swing.jpg)(3%)

Keyword in <b> or <strong> Tags(2%)

The course conditions at these two courses owned by Remington Golf courses are excellent, the greens are nice and friendly staff are my personal favorites. . Then there is there slogan, "All you can, practice, play and eat at one price, less than $60. Making this an is an experience like no other **Orlando golf** course can offer. For the price of a normal greens fee in Orlando we had a breakfast, a hot dog for lunch and soda's at every turn and when we got back to the clubhouse we had a great lunch all for one proce. It was the most affordable "ALL YOU CAN" experience and I have no idea how this Orlando golf course can afford to do this. I give this Orlando golf trip and this Orlando golf course five stars.

Keyword in List Items <li> Tag on the page(3%)
- Orlando golf training class.
- Orlando Golf Tee Times

Keyword in <i> or <em> Tags(2%)
Orlando Golf

Keyword in the Meta Description Tag(2%)

```
<title>Orlando Golf</title>
<Meta name="keywords" content="orlando golf, orlando public golf, orlando golf public course" />
<Meta name="description" content="Orlando Golf's best two courses with 36 holes of excitement. Come try
our ALL YOU CAN Practice, Play, and Eat for one low price." />
```

This is average relational information I have gathered and target Google's results from my latest experimenting just two weeks ago prior to publishing so it is accurate. These percentages typically change throughout the year but for the most part don't differ enough to worry about. Just make sure these are applied to each page of your website..

Long-Tail Keywords

Long tail keywords are a type of keyword phrase that have at least two, and some times as many as five words in the phrase. Long tail keywords are used to refine search terms to the web page, as well as when the searcher is looking for something rather specific. Like normal keywords, long tail keywords are used to define what is on the web page and what the publisher wants to be found under in search engines and on search engine results pages. These keywords are highly specific, and draw less traffic for the website, but tend to draw more quality traffic, in turn leads more conversions than normal keywords. Long tail keywords can also be used by the website creator and visitors in different ways.

When the website creator uses long tail keywords, they are searching to corner a market that might be smaller than normal, but has just as much potential as other, larger, more exposed markets. Using long tail keywords can also be less expensive when it comes to pay per click bidding, and other paid inclusion methods, as there are less people attempting to place bids on those keywords for pay per click ads on search engine results pages.

Visitors use long tail keywords to narrow down what they are searching for. When a visitor is looking for "Los Angeles welding supplies" it makes more sense. Especially, if you only sell welding supplies in Los Angeles.

Working with long tail keywords successfully means that a website creator needs to know which long tail keywords actually get hits or are searched for on the major search engines. Research is the only way to know if long tail keywords will work or not, and that if the smaller investment will still pay off at the end of the publishing campaign.

Keyword Stuffing In The Keywords Meta Tag

There is a fine line for keyword stuffing. I can see what you are thinking right now. As a website owner you're probably jotting down a list of every word you can think of as a keyword for someone to search with to find your website. I had a roofing contractor who came to me for SEO services that had more keywords in his Meta tags on one page than he had on his whole website. When we were done deciding on the eight keywords he would be using, we didn't even use one of the keywords he had on his list before he came to me.

His list contained every city in the state of Texas, with every possible part, board, nail, or roofing type spelled out. It was probably close to a thousand keywords and is an extreme example of what is known as, "keyword stuffing".

There is a defined science to finding and using the right keywords on your website. When I get done with a website I have eight to twelve keywords I focus on and I call those words, "Trophy Words". I use these words to improve your site's ranking.

As a consultant I spend countless hours finding and applying the right keywords for my customers and working with those who design websites for my customers. Finding the most effective keywords is a fine science and I have to weigh using popular and effective keywords on a website while weighing those keywords against the amount of competition. Let me give an example. I do the SEO for a website that does relationship counselor in Bethesda.

The keyword, "couple counseling", is a term that is searched on about 2,700 times per month in Bethesda. But, there are 1,222,500 counselors with websites that are competing for the same keyword nationwide. On the other hand there are 6,800 searches per month in Bethesda for, "bethesda couples counseling" but only about 100 therapists with websites competing for that term. A lot less completion. This is a small example but you can see I would choose the second keyword term over the first even though there are fewer searches. Only, after I took into consideration the site rankings of the competition which we will discuss later in this chapter.

Determining Your Best Keywords

Well we have talked about the keywords and what they can do for you, but picking the right keywords is, well, the holy grail.

If you are a small-business owner, you will want your website to be readily visible on each and every search engine for the right keywords. In fact using the right keywords in your website's content can mean the difference between being listed as one of the first 20 sites returned from search engine results (which is good) or being buried under other websites forty pages into the results (which means hundreds of results are returned before someone sees your site).

There have been many studies showing that searchers rarely venture past the second page of searches and majorities choose websites on the first page of the results when looking for something online.

Per Page Keyword Focus

Now this is worth all the money you paid for this book because it is a major change that happened in mid 2011. You want to pick only 1 keyword per page as your trophy keywords if you are optimizing for Google.

The smaller the keyword focus (meaning focus on one keyword) the better. Why? "Google Instant" started in late 2010. Google Instant turns search into a real-time stream of results which flow onto your screen as you type your query letter by letter. With each letter you type, a whole new set of results flash by. This is important for several reasons. First and foremost a suggested term is now selected 60-70% of the time. Next you see many more search results than you would have by typing in your search query and just pressing enter. One thing you cannot ignore is that Google gives suggested keywords and they like to change those slightly within every 6-8 month period or so for many keyword. This means you must be constantly alert for changes.

Google Instant had an immediate effect on a users search pattern and causes people to shy away from doing a click through to the second page or more of the search results. Google's average user behavior and keyword usage hasn't changed much as a result of Google Instant but there are some keys to how you should optimize your pages.

At the basic level there are many things as a website owner or SEO guru you should know. Including the fact that Google Instant only affects a portion of Google searches.

There are several limitations and Google Instant functionality is turned off in the following circumstances:

1. If you are not logged in to a Google account.
2. If a user types a search query directly into a browser or toolbar.
3. If you are located outside of the US, UK, France, Italy, Germany, Spain or Russia.
4. If your browser is outdated.
5. If you choose the deactivate Google Instant.

NOTE: *It is definitely worthy to note that not all searches are at Google.com. They are in search bars such as in Firefox or in the URL bar in the case of Google Chrome.*

So how do I modify my website's SEO practices to help me with users search pattern changes in optimizing my website? Do I just optimize pages for parts of keywords? The answer surprisingly is 'no'. Google definitely hates websites with bad mechanics. Spelling issues are a problem with gaining relevance on Google so that is definitely not the answer.

SIDEBAR: What is the purpose of Google Instant?

For this answer you need to know a little bit about the history of Google and really understand a major driving force behind this change in their search engine results pages (SERPS). As recently as 2008, you could optimize a page and find relevance for 15 to 18 keywords. In 2009, it became smaller. For most websites to find good rankings website developers needed to concentrate on less than 5 to 8 keywords in 2009. In 2010, it became 1 to 3 keywords. In 2011, it is now 1 keyword per page with some exceptions. This new indexing method makes it really one page optimized for one keyword.

Why would Google do this? Well only less than 5% of the websites on the Internet employ any type of purposeful SEO techniques. Out of those, only a small number of those actually use updated or good SEO techniques and of those only a small fraction get professional SEO services that keep them up on the techniques. The rest of those website owners do not know how to make multiple landing pages, get indexed correctly, stay up on the latest SEO principles, or understand site maps so they can focus on multiple keywords.

What this means is that the average website not employing the latest SEO techniques **to** focus on multiple keywords has to pay money to stay competitive for more than one keyword. For Google this money goes primarily to AdWords and this has been an extra billion dollars per month in Google' pocket. The fewer the keywords you can stay competitive for, the more you need AdWords to stay on the first page of Google. Google know this.

So getting back to the topic of this chapter, Meta tagging and keywords. You probably have the question now of what do I need to do to stay on top and be found with users new search behaviors? Through our testing of Google Instant we have determined that a majority of the time Google is looking at the first word of the characters in the domain name, Title tag, and the words in the Meta description tag to decide the most relevant pages to display. You should modify your web pages or add pages so that your singular keyword search term on your pages contain only the individual key search term and its plural form which is the longer keyword goes first. Here is an example:

<title>NBA Sports Shirts | NBA Sports Shirt</title>

You will have to create pages and optimize them for other keywords you have in secondary or later positions to remain competitive for those keywords. Don't forget you need to modify your Meta Keyword and Meta Description tags to include your keyword as well using your first keyword in the Meta Description tag as well.

For most website owners these changes will be a burden and require many new pages, but the sooner the changes are made, the sooner you will reap the rewards.

More about keywords

Let us do a few examples to help your understanding of how to pick your keywords correctly. Let's say that you own a convenience store and you put a list of products you carry as keywords such as coffee, sodas, fountain drinks, bottled drinks, ice drinks, etc. You would be stuffing your keywords on the page.

How Keywords Are Used

It helps to decide on keywords if you understand how people search for your products or services and not how you, being in your own industry search for them. It is usually different. When you go to a search engine and want to find a place that sells welding supplies, you open a search engine such as Google and you type in, "buy welding supplies" and click search. You get about 60,000 results but none of them are places you can go locally and get a welder. You are not likely going to order a large welder online. The shipping would cost as much as the welder.

Are you going to go searching through the 64,000 results for a local place to buy one? No. You're going to refine your search down to something less broad like, "los angeles welding supplies" which will have better results.

If I sell welding supplies in Los Angeles, I would make one of my keywords "Los Angeles Welding Supplies". I would have less of a chance if my keywords in my Meta tagging are "los angeles, ceritos, anaheim, welding, supplies, supply" as these words individually are more broad and have less relevance to the search. Each one is treated by most search engines as an individual search term. Los Angeles is a city, welding could refer to any number of items, how to weld, welding stories, training schools, metal fence welding, etc. I typed in just "welding" into Bing and on the first page was a job listing working as a welder to build cruise ships. The point I am making is that users are now educated to refine their search. We can keep going on but I think I have made the point here. Using the exact phrase people will use as a search term in your keywords can make all the difference on whether your site will show up on a search engine search.

Keyword Research Tools

There are many tools on the Internet to help you find the exact keywords to use for your website. The trick is understanding how keywords work, which you should use, and the best ways to use them. If you choose the most relevant keywords and properly design your site using those keywords you will have a highly visible and successful website.

At a basic level, keywords capture the essence of your website. Keywords are the words or phrases, a potential visitor to your site enters into a search engine to find websites. Only websites related to the specific subject matter in which they are looking for. If you went to Google, did a search and had to go through 30 pages of content to find a website that matched what you were looking for, you would stop using Google and go back to the telephone book, or choose Yahoo! instead. That is why choosing keywords that match your websites content is so important. The keywords that you choose are used throughout the optimization process applied to your website. If you do not choose to use them in this way then I would not expect to have anyone find your website, unless they know the exact URL.

Figure 3.1

So let's ask ourselves some questions:

1. What words best describe my website content?
2. How do I know which keywords to use?
3. Where do I find help in deciding?
4. Once I know my possible keywords, where do I see how many people search on those keywords?

All of these are great questions and knowing the answers to these questions will save you a great deal of time when creating a website.

First off you can go to Google and start to type words that apply to your site. The most commonly searched terms will populate for you as shown in Figure 3.1, where I began to search for "Mike Monahan".

There are five hundred software packages, books, and website out there to help you determine your keywords. One of the best, if you want all the work done for you is www.WebsiteSubmitter.org.

However, if you do not want to spend the money, do what I do. Have Google do the work for you. "Say what? Google can do the work for me?" you ask. Who wrote this book? He must have been drinking while he was writing this.

Figure 3.2

No really. Google has a little known website tool for determining keywords. They advertised its existence to Google Ambassadors but it is generally unknown to most website owners or the general public. Let's take a look at what this tool can do for you.

If you go to the URL of:

https://adwords.google.com/select/KeywordToolExternal

(You will find this tool as shown in Figure 3.2.)

Notice you have a couple of options. You can put a generalization of your keywords or, if you already have a website, you can choose to have Google crawl your website and decide the words that will work best.

The search reply that you get back will be incredibly long and many of the results will most likely apply to your website. But the ones that do, you can see how many searches there were on a average on a local level or on a global level. Not only that, but a measurement of how hard the competition is for each keyword!

Why don't we take a look at both options in detail.

Google's Keyword Search Tool

Now, it is not called the Google General Keyword Search Tool but I had to have a descriptive name in the title. I am fortunate enough to have a very large alternative news site as a client, and so I will use the search terms "alternative news" as shown in figure 3.3a.

Figure 3.3a

Figure 3.3b

In Figure 3.3b you see Google's Keyword Search Tool.

The results in Figures 3.4 shows search results from Google's Keyword Search Tool. Figure 3.5 shows the same search results from Google's new Keyword Search Tool.

Keywords	Advertiser Competition ⑦	Local Search Volume: September ⑦	Global Monthly Search Volume ⑦	Match Type: ⑦ Broad ▼
Keywords related to term(s) entered - sorted by relevance ⑦				
brand new alternative press		Not enough data	36	Add
alternative news		18,100	27,100	Add
alternative news media		Not enough data	390	Add
alternative press news		Not enough data	58	Add
alternative news papers		Not enough data	28	Add
alternative news paper		58	58	Add
alternative daily news		Not enough data	590	Add
alternative news magazine		Not enough data	91	Add
alternative news weekly		Not enough data	320	Add
alternative news magazines		Not enough data	36	Add
alternative news headlines		Not enough data	16	Add
alternative weekly news		Not enough data	320	Add
alternative news sources		1,000	1,300	Add
alternative newspapers		Not enough data	1,900	Add
alternative newspaper		5,400	5,400	Add
alternative independent news		Not enough data	91	Add
alternative news source		210	390	Add
alternative news sites		590	590	Add
alternative news blogs		Not enough data	28	Add
alternative news links		Not enough data	36	Add
alternative news website		Not enough data	58	Add
the alternative news		Not enough data	170	Add
alternative news blog		Not enough data	46	Add
alternative news websites		Not enough data	210	Add
alternative news from		Not enough data	140	Add
alternative news online		Not enough data	720	Add
alternative news site		46	110	Add
alternative news network		Not enough data	73	Add
alternative news video		Not enough data	73	Add

Figure 3.5

Notice in Figure 3.4 and 3.5 is merely suggestive keywords. Also the list can be downloaded in either a text, or .csv (for excel)to review later. You will notice to the right a new field that shows by month how many searches have been made for that keyword over the last year.

Figure 3.5

Now let's look at what happens if I let Google crawl the site and come up with search terms.

Google's Keyword Search Tool

Again, the title of this section is not an official name for their search tool. Now, I am going to use one of my customer's websites called www.localnewsday.com. I have not asked their permission to be in the book, but I do a good enough job that I don't think they will care, and since they are reeling over the fact that they had over 16,000 unique hits last month, my competition will have a hard time wooing them as a client.

So let's use them. In Figure 3.6, I chose to have Google crawl the site to determine the best keywords to use.

Figure 3.6

Now that it is done let's take a look at figure 3.7 to see what the differences are.

☐ medical and dental insurance	🔍		9,900	8,100	
☐ health insurance portland	🔍		2,400	2,400	
☐ private medical insurance	🔍		27,100	8,100	
☐ medical health insurance	🔍		74,000	60,500	
☐ travel medical insurance	🔍		135,000	49,500	
☐ medical indemnity insurance	🔍		2,400	880	
☐ medical liability insurance	🔍		12,100	9,900	
☐ dental insurance portland	🔍		390	390	
☐ insurance broker portland oregon	🔍		480	390	
☐ insurance portland oregon	🔍		4,400	4,400	
☐ pre existing condition medical insurance	🔍		9,900	6,600	
☐ medical insurance companies	🔍		110,000	74,000	
☐ aetna insurance	🔍		90,500	90,500	
☐ get medical insurance	🔍		4,400	3,600	
☐ maternity insurance	🔍		40,500	27,100	
☐ cost of medical malpractice insurance	🔍		1,600	1,600	

Figure 3.7

You will notice that some of the keywords don't fit. Like "health insurance" this caught me off guard until I went to the website and saw that there was a news story related to health insurance, as shown in Figure 3.8.

Figure 3.8

Deciding On Keywords?

Well we have collected the information we need to decide on our trophy keywords for our website but not which ones to use. We know the possible keywords, the number of local and global searches, and an estimate of how much competition there are for those keywords.

As I said before, as a consultant I spend countless hours finding and applying the right keywords for my customers and working with those who design websites for my customers. Finding the most effective keywords is a fine science and sometimes it's an experimental process.

Many times I will add, subtract and reorder my Meta tagged keywords based on what is working and what is not on my customers websites. I can tell a lot about how well a keyword is working by tracking a Pay-Per-Click (PPC) campaign. But we will discuss that later in this book.

Now that I have my possible keyword list from Google, from the last section, I have to weigh using heavily searched on keywords against the amount of competition I have. If I have a high Google ranking I can compete against whoever I want for the keywords, but if I am just starting out and my ranking is low on Google, I have to choose words that have less competition.

If I went right out for the search term "daily news" as shown in figure 2.7 for my customer LocalNewsDay.com it would be a big mistake. Sure, there are 2.7 million searches a month for that term but there are 600 sites ranked higher than LocalNewsDay.com's site and it would wind up on page 43 of any Google search for that term.

However, if I went for the search term "portland daily news" on the other hand, there is a good chance that even with a low ranking I will wind up on page 1 or 2 with basic optimization in a few months because there is less competition for that search term.

Meta Description

The description is what most people see on the end of a Google search, right under the link to the website page is the Meta tagging description. Now that we have decided on our keywords, we now need to formulate the keywords into the description using complete sentences. This is not as easy as it sounds.

If you use long tail keywords you must use them in the same order in your description and you need to keep you descriptions to 155 characters or less. This is the number of characters most search engines will display.

Here are some keyword examples:

los angeles excavating, los angeles excavation, los angeles dump truck, los angeles tight access excavating, los angeles residential landscaping, los angeles track hoe

Now the description should be:

We are Los Angeles excavating professionals who can handle any L.A. area excavation job needing a dump truck, tight access excavating. Whether you are doing residential landscaping or clearing a site we come with a full size dump truck, track hoe and the loader all at one great price.

Meta Title tags

The title that you see may be one of the most important parts for any website as shown at the top of figure 3.9.

Figure 3.9

Remember those keywords we decided on? We want to use as many of those and in the same order as you can. Google allows up to 66 characters (including spaces) for title tags, whereas some others look at up to 120 characters. The numbers change frequently and last year the general rule was don't put more than 70 characters.

If your title tags exceed those limits, they'll be truncated to fit into the maximum space allowed. To ensure that you are getting the most value for the character limitations of title tags, the World Wide Web Consortium (W3C) recommends that website designers keep their titles to 64 characters or less in length. In the next section I will show you how to configure the Title as well as the rest of the Meta Tags.

> **TIP:** Google finds a page more relevant if it focuses on only one keyword in the Title Tag.

Search engine crawlers, bots and spiders use the title tags as one of the main sources for determining the web-page topic. Spiders, bots, and crawlers examine the title, the words used in it then uses this information as a key source to determine the topic of the page. It's always best to use your keywords in your page title, and to use them as close to the beginning of the title as possible.

There should also be a unique title tags for every page of your website which creates relevancy and distinguishes the difference in content. Make the title as descriptive as possible and use the most important keywords you have decided on for the page. Words you use in your Title tag will appear in the reverse title bar, or the tab title, of your web browser, as well.

The Science of Meta Tagging

Did you know that search engines don't usually send their creepy crawlers to index your site without your permission? This is one of the biggest mistakes website owners make.

I can see many of you reading this have your eyes wide open, asking yourself if you have done this part! It is a good question to ask because I would say 7 out of 10 people desperate for my SEO help do not have this done and anything else they do to help doesn't make a difference.

There are two ways you can allow spiders, bots and crawlers to come index your site. You can include a file called robot.txt with permissions (we will talk about this later in the book.) or you can use the Meta Robots tags to do this which is the most efficient way. If you haven't done this, well you might see your landing page on a website, but you will never see a good ranking and none of your other pages will get indexed.

Sidebar: The Meta Robots Tag

This gives you the ability to specify whether search engine bots, spiders, and crawlers should index that page or follow the links appearing on that page.

The following is the Meta Robots tag which should be on your landing page. (You will learn where to put your Meta tags in the next section.) I add it to every page of the website:

<meta name="robots" content="index, follow">

There are other syntaxes you can use instead of "index, follow" which are:

- **index:** This allows the spider to index that page.

- **noindex:** This instructs the spider not to index the page.

- **follow:** This instructs the spider to follow the links from that page and index them.

- **nofollow:** This instructs the spider not to follow links from that page for indexing.

- **all:** This is identical to "index, follow".

- **none:** This is identical to "noindex, nofollow" telling the search engines to ignore the web page.

The other acceptable tags:

```
<meta name="robots" content="noindex, follow">
<meta name="robots" content="index, nofollow">
<meta name="robots" content="noindex, nofollow">
<meta name="robots" content="all">
<meta name="robots" content="none">
```

Keep in mind you only use one of the tags. They are not used in combination with each other.

Meta Tags Creation

We already learned earlier in the chapter that that our Meta tagging starts with determining our keywords. Also, known as our "long tail keywords" because they are not usually a single word. I could go section by section here but let's go and analyze the keywords all at once. I think you might understand it better if I just show you what the keywords should look like and then break it down tag by tag.

So our imaginary business will be called "Los Angeles Excavating Contractors". I did a Google search to make sure it wasn't really a business. Of course, in my last book, I created an imaginary company and someone took the name, started a company and is using the exact Meta tagging I created. So I guess for this one it will be first come, first serve again.

Anyway, our imaginary business provides a tight-access track hoe and loader to dig pools, create retaining walls and any other residential or commercial work which might need our 1 track hoe as shown below in Figure 3.10.

Figure 3.10

I already did the research and my long tail keywords are:

- Los Angeles Excavation Contractors
- Los Angeles Excavating Contractors
- Los Angeles Excavating
- Los Angeles Excavation

> **Note:** *I actually came up with about 40 more keywords but these are the most basic. Also I would concentrate on the same keywords but replace the city name with every local city around Los Angeles. These would be Anaheim, Hollywood, Etc.*

So let us take a look at what I came up with for the title and Meta tagging for this website.

```
<HEAD>
<Title> Los Angeles Excavating Contractor | Los
Angeles  Excavating</Title>
<Meta http-equiv="Content-type" content="text/html;
charset=ISO-8859-1">
<Meta name="keywords" content="los angeles
excavating contractor, los angeles excavating">
```

```
<Meta name="description" content="We are a Los
Angeles Excavating Contractor with a tight access
trackhoe and loader for your Los Angeles excavating
needs.">
<Meta name="googlebot" content="index, follow" />
<Meta name="robots" content=" index, follow ">
<Meta name="Revist-After" content="7 days">
<Meta name="city" content="Los Angeles">
<Meta name="country" content="United States
(USA)">
<Meta name="state" content="CA">
<Meta name="zip code" content="90011">
<Meta name="subject" content="Los Angeles
Excavating">
<Meta name="author" content="Sean Odom">
<Meta name="copyright" content="Los Angeles
Excavating Contractors">
</HEAD>

<Body>
(This is where the visible portion of your website is configured.)
</Body>
```

Take a look at each one of these in the next sections.

Configuring the Keyword Meta Tag

So I am going a little out of order but I need it to make sense to you
and reiterate what I have been trying to explain through this entire
chapter. That is, keywords are IMPORTANT. You shouldn't even
think about the Title tag or the Description tag until you have
decided on your keywords!

In the last section I showed you the keywords I decided. If you
don't know how I determined my keywords, I taught you this a few
pages back. So the tag is configured like this:

```
<Meta name="keywords" content="los angeles excavating
contractor, los angeles excavating">
```

I made keywords bold for this example. The keywords are not
bolded in the configuration. You might notice something else. All
the keywords are in lower case. Why? Well Google doesn't care,

but we need to think about all the search engines. Some search engines are case sensitive and most people don't capitalize their word searches. They just type in their keywords to search.

Configuring the Meta Title Tag

The title tag is located somewhere in between the opening <head> tag and before the closing <\HEAD> tag. It doesn't really matter where it is, but most people put the Title above the Meta tags.

Now remember our keywords? Notice that I used the first 3 which are my main "trophy words" in the Title.

<Title>**Los Angeles Excavating Contractor | Los Angeles Excavating**</Title>

Configuring the GoogleBot and the Robot Tags

Here is the Meta Robots tag that we discussed a few sections back in a sidebar. You might notice another tag though. Google really likes it when you put its own Meta tag in your website and tell them what to do. That tag is called "googlebot" and the instructions are similar to the Robots tag as shown:

index: This allows the GoogleBot to index that page.

noindex: This tells the GoogleBot not to index the page.

follow: This allows the GoogleBot to follow the links from the landing page and other pages it finds and index them.

nofollow: This instructs the spider not to follow links from that page for indexing.

Noodp: Prevents the search from using the page's description.

The tags are easy and should be in any website you have. Also, you never know what users or links Googlebot or other creepy crawlers arrive from and so these should be in the Meta tags of every page in your website.

<Meta name="googlebot" content="**index, follow**" />
<Meta name="robots" content=" **index, follow** ">

Configuring the Meta Revisit Tag

Google and other major search engines typically visit your site once per month on average. But let's say your website's content changes more frequently such as a news website? How do you tell the search engines spiders, bots and crawlers to visit more frequently? The "Revisit-After" Meta tag is used just for this purpose.

<Meta name="Revist-After" content="**7 days**">

Configuring the Meta Location Tags

These tags are really important to search engines to help identify the geographical locations. In a few sections we will look at a new GPS type of geographic location tool and add the Meta tags as well. In the example below, we add the city, country, state, and zip code, just as if you were mailing yourself a letter as shown below:

<Meta name="city" content="**Los Angeles**">
<Meta name="country" content="**United States (USA)**">
<Meta name="state" content="**CA**">
<Meta name="zip code" content="**90011**">

Configuring the Meta Subject Tag

This tag arguably has very little influence with the major search engines but it does have some with smaller ones. I typically place the first long tail keywords in my Meta Keywords tag here which should be the most important subject of our website as shown below.

<Meta name="subject" content="**Los Angeles Excavating**">

Configuring the Author and Copyright Meta Tags

These two tags do very little to enhance your search engine rankings and have more to do with identifying who owns all the hard work you put in to your website. I see parts of my books in other books and on the Internet all the time. Most have the common sense to give me credit, but when they don't, I get upset. I spent blood, sweat, and tears to get this done. Not to mention the time I didn't get to spend with my family because I was writing and doing other things.

The "author" tag is the person or company name that created the content in the website. The "copyright" tag identifies who owns the copyright. I will remind all the readers that Los Angeles Excavating Contractors, Inc. is entirely bogus and at the time of this writing didn't really exist.

> <Meta name="author" content="**Mike Monahan**">
> <Meta name="copyright" content="**Los Angeles Excavating Contractors, Inc.**">

Meta Redirect Tag

Have you ever wanted to redirect someone to another site when they got to a page? Say you changed your websites URL. Well you can with just one line! Let's take a look at this one liner:

> <Meta http-equiv="refresh" content="**5**;url=**http://www.losangelesexcavatingcontractors.com/newpage.html**">

Now the "5" indicates the number of seconds to wait. If you don't want search engines to ding you as if it is a doorway page, which we will discuss later in this book, then it needs to be set to 5 seconds or longer. The last part is the URL that you want to redirect the page to. In this example I chose the page to be the blog.html page.

> **NOTE:** *There are many other not so important Meta Tags. You can learn them all at: http://www.metatags.info*

Now let's take a look the new geographical Meta tag that is really catching on using GPS and longitude and latitude.

Adding yourself to GeoURL

Figure 3.11

Identifying your businesses location in your Meta tags is jumping up in high tech, Google and other search engines are catching on. GeoURL has started a new Meta tagging system to identify where your business is located.

This helps the search engine identify how close you are to a customer and give proper mileage. If you are a retail establishment such as a store or restaurant, doing this can actually help you show up on GPS device searches as well. Take a look at GeoURL in Figure 3.11.

First you need to identify where you are. If your website is about your business you will need the coordinates for your businesses location.

You can go to *http://geourl.org/add/helper* to not only get your coordinates for your tag but to generate your tags as well if you are in the U.S.

Remember my fictitious company in the last section. I have made up an address and entered it in to the GeoURL Head Generator and it actually gave me the tags that I need to use with the GPS coordinates for my business. The GPS coordinates are actually that of Disneyland's parking lot.

GPS coordinates are in the form of a latitude and longitude, separated by a comma. Remember that minutes and seconds are in 60ths, so if something is X degrees, Y minutes, and Z seconds, the decimal equivalent is $X + Y/60 + Z/3600$.

So why don't we add our new tags to our website in the next section.

Configuring Meta GeoTags

You can go to the GEOTags.com website to get the following Meta tags to add to the <head> section of your web page:

> <meta name="ICBM" content="**XXX.XXXXX, XXX.XXXXX**">
> <meta name="DC.title" content="**THE NAME OF YOUR SITE**">
>
> <meta name="ICBM" content="**41.657006, -70.271763**">
> <meta name="DC.title" content="Los Angeles Excavation Contractors">
>
> **Note**: *If your site uses frames, you must add the meta tags to your* **top-level** *page which contains the <frameset> tag.*

Figure 3.12

Above in Figure 3.12 I will also index *http://www.geotags.com* style
"geo.position" meta tag as per their documentation at:
http://geotags.com/geobot/add-tags.html

The reason it is called the x is that this was actually used for
generating geographically-correct maps. This became known as a
company's ICBM address or missile address, and some people
include it in their sig block with that name.

Here is an example of the entire Meta Tag we created:

```
<HEAD>
<base href="http://www.Los AngelesExcavatingContractors.com/" />
<Title>Los Angeles Excavating Contractor | Los Angeles Excavating</Title>
<Meta http-equiv="Content-type" content="text/html; charset=ISO-8859-1">
<Meta name="keywords" content="los angeles excavating contractor, los angeles excavating">
<Meta name="description" content="We are a Los Angeles Excavating Contractor with a tight access trackhoe and loader for your Los Angeles excavating needs.">
<Meta name="googlebot" content="index, follow" />
<Meta name="robots" content=" index, follow ">
<Meta name="Revist-After" content="7 days">
<Meta name="city" content="Los Angeles">
<Meta name="country" content="United States (USA)">
<Meta name="state" content="CA">
<Meta name="zip code" content="90011">
<Meta name="subject" content="Los Angeles Excavating">
<Meta name="author" content="Mike Monahan">
<Meta name="copyright" content="Los Angeles Excavating Contractors">
<meta name="geo.region" content="US-CA" />
<meta name="geo.placename" content="Los Angeles, CA" />
<meta name="ICBM" content="41.657006, -70.271763">
<meta name="DC.title" content="Los Angeles Excavation Contractors">

</HEAD>
```

A Quick Review

These on-page search engine optimization tips will assist you in setting up your pages with the appropriate title, meta tags, headers, text elements and alt attributes.

Title Tag

The *Title tag* is used to define the title of a web page, with the Title tag placed between the <head> and </head> tags in the html of the page. Search engines will recognize the Title tag as the title of the page. Each page should have its own distinct Title tag.

Title Tag Fundamentals:

- The Title will be displayed within the browser at the top of the browser window or tab.

- When a user searches for a specific word or phrase, Google will return a link to the website, and the Title tag will be displayed as the anchor text for the website link.

- The text in the Title tag is one of the most important relevancy factors influencing search engine ranking algorithms.

- Using your most important keywords or key phrases in the Title tag will have a dramatic effect upon your page's ranking for those keywords.

Recommendation: It is recommended that you keep your Title short, preferably between 10 and 64 characters, 70, at most. Over 70 will not contribute any weight as part of the document.

Use of irrelevant words (not found on the page) in your Title will dilute the impact on your targeted keywords. Use of irrelevant words can also trigger the spam filters of the search engines. Place your most targeted keyword phrases as early as possible in the Title. Try to minimize the use of stop words, such as a, an, of, on, etc., as they consume character count and offer no value.

Description Meta Tag

Used to provide a brief description of a Web page, the Description meta tag should clearly describe the purpose of the page, for both the user and the search engines.

- The importance of the Description tag as an element of the ranking algorithm has decreased significantly over recent years, but some search engines may still support this tag.

- The search engines will often display the Description along with the Title in the SERPS (search engine results pages).

The maximum length of a displayed description varies between search engines, so wherever possible, try to place your most important keywords early in your Description tag, in case the search engine truncates the results.

Keep your Description between 50 and 149 characters, including spaces, whenever possible. Google will display 154 characters, but other search engines display less. Longer descriptions are of little value, as most search engines place little to no importance on this tag.

In extreme circumstances, the Description can be as long as 200 characters (including spaces), but understand that there is a high probability of truncation. As is the case with the Title, the use of irrelevant words can trigger the search engines' spam filters. Avoid adding text that is not found within the visible text of the page.

Description Meta tags are not intended for the search engines, they exist for human users. Therefore, the text should be written to attract the user and convert them to a buyer, achieving the best ROI for your SEO efforts.

Keywords Meta Tag

This tag lists the words or phrases that are descriptive of, and found within the contents of the page. This tag provides some additional text for crawler-based search engines. However because of frequent attempts to abuse their systems, most search engines now ignore this tag.

Similar to the Meta Description tag, there is a limit to the number of captured characters within the Keywords Meta tag. Keep the tag to between 4 and 8 keywords or keyphrases, separated by commas.

Syntax: *Keyword1,Keyword2,Keyword3,Keyword4*

All keywords listed in the Keywords Meta Tag should appear at least 4% in your content (body), or they may be considered to be irrelevant spam. You should also avoid repetitions, to prevent penalization by the search engines for keyword "stuffing". The most important keywords should be listed first, to increase their prominence for the search engines that still consider this tag in their determination of your pages' rankings.

Chapter 4 - Submitting Your Website

Let's assume that you, as most people, had a web developer design that is a completely awesome site but he or she who designed the site didn't have a clue about SEO. Some of my customers have spent thirty thousand dollars on a website and it didn't even have a single Meta tag on it!

We already talked about matching the title, Meta tags, Meta descriptions, Meta Keywords to the root pages of your website and having all the same appear in all those areas, right? (If you didn't catch that and you are about to submit your website(s) please go back to the last!)

If you are done with that, then you are ready to go to the next step!

First Stop, Google.

Why Google? Well, about sixty percent of all web searches happen right on Google, which means that although there are other major search engines, you want to make Google happy first.

> **NOTE:** I will include a step later where you go to http://www.SubmissionComplete.com and submit your website to the 200+ little search engines for about $35.00. This will save you about 100 hours of your precious time, if not more.

First off, you will want to go to Google and create a Google account for Google Webmasters.

Step 1 - Add Your Site to Google Webmaster Tools

Google's Webmaster Central as shown below can be used to notify Google of the existence of a website, verify with Google that you have control of the website (Webmaster), identify the site map location for a website, access keyword research tools, verify the Robot.txt file, and locate any errors within a website.

To add your website to the Google Webmaster Central, do the following:

1. Go to **http://www.google.com/services** as shown in Figure 3.1. Then click on the Webmaster Central Link.

2. After you have created the account you should be able to access Google Webmaster tools. Right in the middle of the page should be an icon that says, "Add site".

3. You can then place a Meta tag which Google gives you on your website or upload an HTML file. This is used to verify that you truly are the webmaster. Once Google confirms it has verified your website URL, the next stop is Google Analytics.

   NOTE: *Later we will add a Google Sitemap.xls to the website to help Google index all of your pages.*

Step 2 - Add your site to Google Analytics

1. Go to **http://www.google.com/services** as shown in Figure 3.2 below. Then click on the Analytics link. You should already be logged in but if not, log in using the same account you used for the Google Webmaster Central.

2. After you have accessed Google Analytics, again right in the middle of the page should be an icon that says, "Add New Profile".

3. Then add the website URL as shown below and click Finish:

NOTE: *If you want your business to be seen in the Local Places results on Google, see Google Local Places and Bing Local Business Listings in the next chapter.*

Step 3 – Setup Google Places For Your Business

Google Places Quality Guidelines

For Google the local business listings are added at the Local Business Places as shown in Figure 4.1 at the following and configured at:

http://www.google.com/local/add

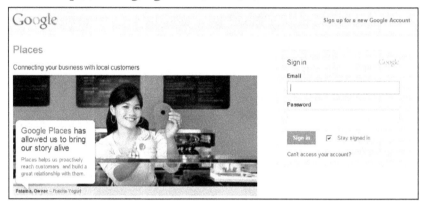

This is really in-depth and configuring this is taken step by step in the next chapter. For almost any website, even ones that focus globally, Google Places can be one of your best friends. If you have questions beyond this book I would search Google for the

Step 4 - Submitting your site to Yahoo!

At the time of this writing, you can still submit your website for free to Yahoo.com at: **http://siteexplorer.search.yahoo.com/submit**. But that is expected to change as Yahoo is now going to get its results from Bing.com.

Submitting your site for free to Yahoo! (as shown in Figure 3.3):

1. Create a **Yahoo! ID at http://www.yahoo.com**
2. Go to: **http://siteexplorer.search.yahoo.com/submit**
3. Enter the website URL and press Submit URL as shown below.

Figure 3.3

Step 5 - Submitting your site to Bing

Bing.com is gaining an incredible market share—especially since they are owned by Microsoft and the engine is used to perform searches not only on Bing, but on MSN, Live, and many other smaller sites. And guess what? Now, some Yahoo! results as well as a deal was made to allow Bing to provide the results and advertising on Yahoo! as well.

To submit your website to Bing.com, follow these instructions:

1. Go to the URL of: **http://www.bing.com/docs/submit.aspx**

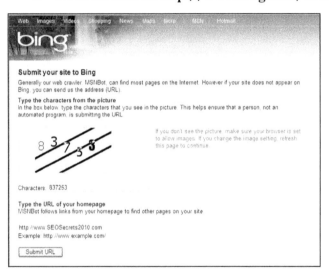

2. Enter the verification characters.
3. Enter the URL of the website you want to submit to Bing.com and then click "Submit URL".
4. You get a message thanking you for submitting your site to Bing.

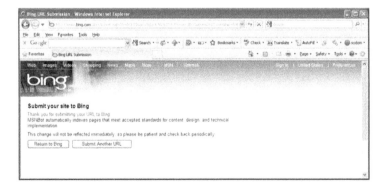

Bing's Webmaster Center

Bing's Webmaster Center, as shown below, can be used to notify Bing of the existence of a website, verify with Bing that you have control of the website (Webmaster), identify the site map location for a website, access keyword research tools, verify the Robot.txt file, and locate any errors with a website.

The Bing webmaster console as shown above can be found at: **http://www.bing.com/webmaster/WebmasterManageSitesPage.aspx**

Since I have a new client who is an author of travel guides, let's add their newest website to the Bing Webmaster Console.

In the figure below you will notice that I have added their website address, the address of the site map I have created, and the email address. Since I do their SEO services, I enter my email address as the Webmaster's email.

Bing then gives you a screen which makes me authenticate the website. I can either add an additional Meta tag to the tags I have created or upload a verification file to the website to verify that I am the owner or webmaster of the website. I usually download the file as you never know what will happen to the landing page of the website in the future.

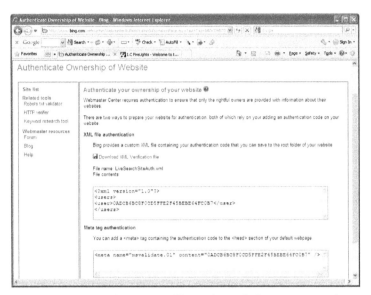

In the next screenshot, you will see the website amongst other websites I have verified. It shows the website name and on the right it shows how I authenticated the website. The middle characters are the verification code assigned by Bing.com.

Step 6 - Submitting to Alexa

Submitting your website to Alexa is important as this is another site that helps demonstrate your website's importance to major search engines. To add your website, do the following:

1. Submit to Alexa as shown below. Alexa has a lot of weight with Google and other search engines.

2. First go to **http://www.alexa.com/edit**

3. Once you submit the URL it will give you the option to update the URL information as shown below.

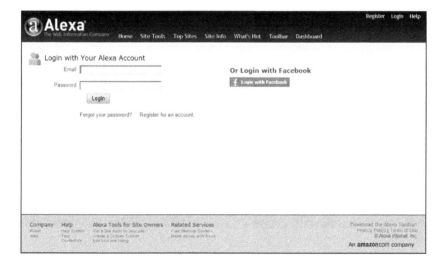

4. After you have completed the entry it will give you two options to verify the information: It can either e-mail you a confirmation or give you an info.txt file to place at the root of your websites FTP folder.

5. Once you have entered an e-mail or uploaded the info.txt file, press one of the confirmation link buttons.

Step 7 - Submitting to AllCanSee

Adding your site to AllCanSee.com couldn't be easier. To add your website to AllCanSee.com, do the following:

1. First go to this URL: **http://www.allcanseek.com/add/**

2. Enter a verifiable e-mail address.

3. Enter your sites URL and press submit as shown in the picture below:

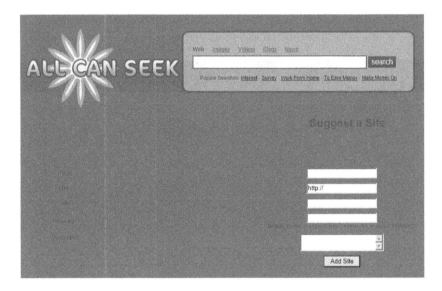

Step 8 - Submitting To Jayde For Business Websites

Jayde is a specialized search engine catering to businesses only. To add your website to Jayde, do the following:

1. Go to the URL of: **http://www.jayde.com/submit.html**

2. Enter your email address.

3. Enter the URL you are submitting and press Submit your site.

4. It should return with a message:

"Thank you for submitting to our directory"

Step 9 - Enlisting your URL and company on Merchant Circle

Merchant Circle is one of those websites that didn't seem like much when it first started but then caught on quickly. If you have a web presence on the web you should join and list your business there. It creates a link to your website as well as generates local and national advertising for your business.

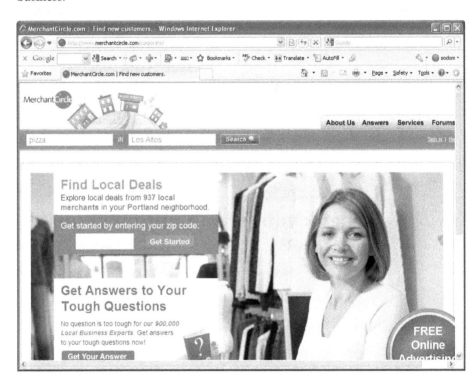

Step 10 - Enlist your URL on WhatUSeek

WhatUSeek.com is a search engine used by businesses on the Internet. To add your website to WhatUSeek.com, do the following:

1. Go to the URL of: http://www.whatuseek.com/addurl-secondary.shtml

2. Enter your websites URL.

3. Enter your email address, check the appropriate boxes, and press submit URL.

   NOTE: *Listing your company is free. However, the next screen will give you paid options which are not required.*

Step 11 - Submitting To Social Media

That was just a start in the previous steps. Now you need to create accounts on the following social media websites and provide the following at a minimum:

1. Add your title.

2. Add your website's URL.

3. Add a description that includes at least the first three keywords in your keyword's Meta tag.

4. Add your name and email address.

5. The category and a description of your business.

To the following websites.

- ✓ **Google Plus**: https://plus.google.com (Google)
- ✓ **Blogspot:** www.blogspot.com (Google)
- ✓ **CitySearch:** www.citysearch.com
- ✓ **Crunchbase:** www.crunchbase.com
- ✓ **Delicious Bookmarks**: www.delicious.com
- ✓ **Digg:** www.digg.com
- ✓ **Twitter:** www.twitter.com
- ✓ **MySpace:** www.myspace.com
- ✓ **Facebook:** www.facebook.com
- ✓ **LinkedIn:** www.linkedin.com
- ✓ **Merchant Circle:** www.merchantcircle.com
- ✓ **StumbleUpon:** www.stumbleupon.com
- ✓ **Reddit:** www.reddit.com
- ✓ **Yelp:** www.yelp.com
- ✓ **YouTube:** www.youtube.com

Using Submission Complete to Make the Rest of the Job Easy

There are literally thousands of other smaller search engines and directories, as well as major search engines for other countries. You never know when someone is going to use one of these smaller search engines; since you are competing with a lower number of sites, your chances are higher, that the smaller number of users will find your website a greater percentage of the time.

You might have figured out that getting your site included in search engines and directories is no easy task. It takes a lot of time, research, and if you don't follow all the directions to the letter, you risk the chance of being refused for listing on websites.

There are submission websites which use custom tools that are automated software programs and applications that remember the repetitive information that must be provided in order to get your website listed in hundreds of search engine and directories.

Many submission tools try to scam website owners by promising to submit their site to thousands of search engines and directories for one low fee. The problem with that claim is that most of those search engines are either nonexistent or mostly worthless to your site.

You absolutely need help in submitting your website to the smaller search engines and directories as there are hundreds of them. It would take you months to add your site to every one of these sites on your own. However, for about $15.95 you can have a company that specializes in submitting websites do it in just a few days.

We highly recommend Submission Complete as seen on the next page at **http://www.submisssioncomplete.com**. It's the engine that I personally use as well as many other SEO companies. They are reputable and always get the job done right.

There are many packages that you can choose from as shown above. If you are doing your own *search engine optimization*, the bigger the package you get, the less you have to do on your own. In fact the high end packages actually helps you decide your keywords, create your Meta tags, and scan your site of optimization problems. Most of the important work is done for you.

Chapter 5 – Local Business Listings

Local Business Listings help consumers find retail locations. If you have a local business or a business with local store locations you can list those stores in the Local Business Listings on either Google or Bing. Keep in mind that by listing the business on Bing you are listing the business on MSN, Live, and most likely Yahoo as well.

One of the great things about the local listings as shown in figures 5.1 and 4.2, is that they automatically appear at the top of the listings. And your retail location shows on the map that is provided as well.

Let's take a look at the Local Business Listing results for "portland pizza" on both Bing and Google starting with Bing in figure 5.1.

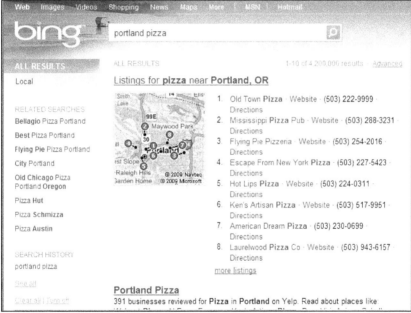

Figure 5.1

Next let's look at the same search on Google in figure 5.2.

Figure 5.2

They are very similar. Again, there are some differences. Google usually wants to see relevance to the search term such as "portland pizza". Bing not only wants to see relevance but also that your address is the closest to Portland Oregon. If your business is in Oregon City and you come up first in the organic listings for the search term, "portland pizza" you did a great job optimizing your website making it relevant to the search term.

On the other hand, your businesses physical address is not in Portland, so other companies that are in Portland or closer to Portland will show up on Bing's Local Business listings before your company does.

There is also one other factor that helps in this situation. Each listing allows you to click on it and get more information on both Google and Bing Local Business listings. Each gives you the ability to see more information on the business and give reviews. It's these reviews that have some weight as to whom is shown on the listings.

A good recommendation is to give your customers a suggestion either by email or some other advertising form encouraging them to leave positive reviews if they like your product or services. Both Google and Bing are pretty good at identifying false reviews. Especially if you leave more than one from the same login or IP address.

So let's take a look at adding your business to the Local Business listings of both Google and Bing, starting with Bing in the next section.

Adding a Local Business Listing To Bing

First off you need to know where to go. And for Bing the Local Business listings are added at the Local Listing Center as shown in figure 5.3 at the following address:

https://ssl.bing.com/listings/ListingCenter.aspx

Figure 5.3

I can go ahead and add a new listing and create a login. I already have a login, so I will login and it will immediately show my current listings as shown in figure 5.4.

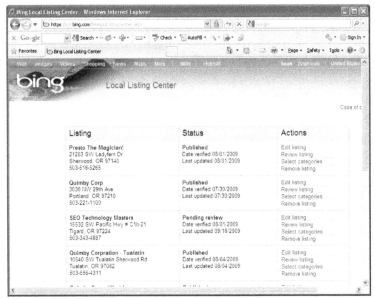

Figure 5.4

Now, I will use ICFireLights as an example and add them by clicking Add New Listing to the Bing Local Listings Center starting in Figure 5.5. All this information is public information so there is not any confidential information here.

Figure 4.5

You will notice I only added the required name, and email address to get started. They don't have a public address so that was not shown on the screen. I also check the option to not display the address on the Local Listing. The next screen I get in figure 5.6 is the hours of operation. Since they sell online 24 hours a day I selected the first option stating that they are "Open 24 hours a day". I also clicked on all the forms of payment that their website is willing to take by checking each option.

Figure 5.6

The next screen you get in Figure 5.7 allows you to enter the year they were established, a tagline, business description, brands carried and any specialty items or services the business provides.

Figure 5.7

The next screen shown in Figure 5.8, allows you to choose the predefined categories that your business falls under. You can choose up to 6. Choose the best keywords relevant to your company based on the keywords you came up with earlier in the book.

Figure 5.8

Once you have entered all the information in the previous screens, Bing outs all the information together to let you verify it as shown in Figure 5.9

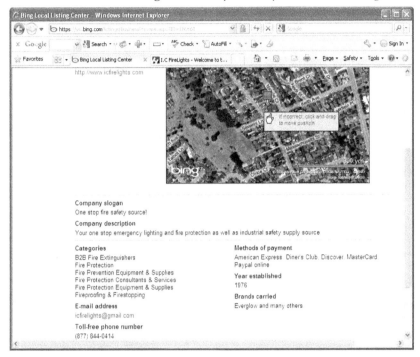

Figure 5.9

Next step is to verify that your business really is at the location you specified. Bing will send you a post card with a pin number to the address you entered. When you come back to the listings shown in Figure 5.4 a few pages back, the Status column allows you to enter the Pin number from the card when it arrives in the mail as shown in Figure 5.10 below.

Figure 5.10

Adding a Local Business Listing To Google Places

First off you need to know where to go. For Google the local business listings are added at the Google Places as shown in Figure 4.11 at the following address:

http://www.google.com/local/add

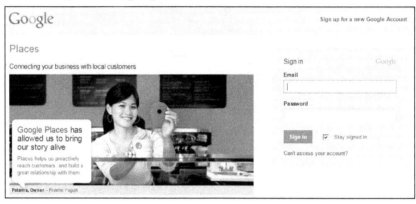

Figure 5.11

If you are already logged in to Google and you have been here before it will list all your current business listings as shown in figure 5.12.

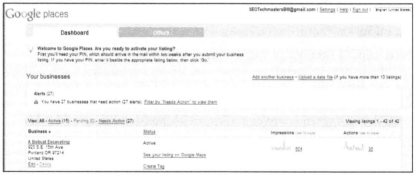

Figure 5.12

You will notice from Figure 5.13 that there are a few more options than we saw on Bing's version. Also you see how many times your business was shown on the listings and how many people clicked on it. Only recent information is shown. Notice the option to "View Report". This will show you legacy information and give you a more accurate view.

Since we are focused on adding your business lets click on the Add New Listing option and begin as shown in Figure 5.13 and 5.14. I had to make it two figures because the screen was so large.

Figure 5.13

Figure 5.14

Then next screen you see appears in Figure 5.15 below. This screen allows you to enter the hours of operation and the payment types that your business accepts as shown below.

NOTE: *Google has a complete guide to Google Places at:*
http://www.google.com/support/places/?hl=en&rd=1

▼ Hours of operations

Make sure your customers know when you're open!

- ○ I prefer not to specify operating hours.
- ● My operating hours are:

Mon:	9:00 AM ▼	.	5:00 PM ▼	☐ Closed ⇩ Apply to all
Tue:	9:00 AM ▼	.	5:00 PM ▼	☐ Closed
Wed:	9:00 AM ▼	.	5:00 PM ▼	☐ Closed
Thu:	9:00 AM ▼	.	5:00 PM ▼	☐ Closed
Fri:	9:00 AM ▼	.	5:00 PM ▼	☐ Closed
Sat:				☑ **Closed**
Sun:				☑ **Closed**

Are your hours split during a single day, such as 9-11am *and* 7-10pm?
☐ I'd like to enter two sets of hours for a single day.

▼ Payment options

Specify how customers can pay at your business.

☑ Cash	☑ American Express	☐ Visa
☑ Check	☑ Diner's Club	☐ Financing
☐ Traveler's Check	☐ Discover	☐ Google Checkout
☐ Invoice	☑ MasterCard	☑ Paypal

Figure 5.15

The next screen allows you to add a logo, picture, and even video describing your business as shown in figure 5.16.

Figure 5.16

Lastly in figure 5.17 you have the option to add brands you carry and other details about your business.

Figure 5.17

The last screen shown in figure 5.18 sums up all the information you have entered. You will see in the figure my customer, Dr. Gil Mintz's information on Google Local Business Listings.

Figure 5.18

The last thing we have to do is choose how we want Google to verify our business. Google allows you to either verify the phone number by calling you and giving you a pin number over the phone. Or you can verify the address by waiting for them to send you a pin number by mail as shown below in figure 5.19.

Figure 5.19

Verifying by phone is the quickest, but if you do, have the phone sitting right next to you because it is less than 10 seconds sometimes before the phone rings to give you your pin number which you enter in on the main listing screen which lists all the businesses you have listed on the Google Business Listing's as shown in Figure 5.20.

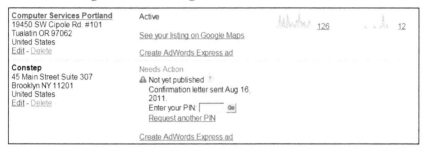

Figure 5.20

One more really interesting thing you can do in the Google Places is offer coupons. If someone clicks on your local business link next to the map on searches you can offer them a coupon. Once your business is verified go click on the Offers Tab and choose "Add new offer" as shown below in Figure 5.21 which shows a coupon offer I have already entered for a Free Network Analysis from one of my SEO customers.

Dashboard			Offers

Offers

+ Add new offer

Offer	Status	Valid at locations	Actions
Free Service Call	Expired - not showing Aug 1, 2011	**6 locations**	Edit - Pause - Delete

Figure 5.21

So let's sum up this chapter. We entered our local business listings with Bing.com and with Google. Learned how to verify our company information so we can start being listed in the both search engines Local Business Listings, how to increase our relevance by having customers give good reviews of our business, and add coupons to our listings in Google.

Adding Multiple Locations For The Same Company

The store code is a unique ID that you can assign to each of your businesses. A store code must refer to the exact same store across multiple versions of a bulk upload. These codes can help you identify your businesses at a glance.

Examples:

store1, store2
location: NY, locationFL, locationCA
101, 102, 103

> **Note:** *The store code must be under 60 characters in length and not contain any leading or trailing whitespace.*

For additional information on Google "Google Places Quality Guidelines" or use the link below:

http://support.google.com/places/bin/answer.py?hl=en&answer =107528

> WARNING: Determining your business' eligibility for inclusion in Google Places, the number of Places Pages you are allowed to have and how to avoid committing what seems to be the most common violations are all explained in this simple page of guidelines.

Google Places Reviews

Don't forget that after you create your Google Places submission that you need to get customers to submit positive reviews for better placement. If you are an honest business person and don't want to accidentally create was Google views as SPAM please consult the Review Guidelines at this URL:

http://support.google.com/places/bin/topic.py?hl=en&topic=165 6749&parent=1656875&ctx=topic

This page explains who can leave reviews of your business, how to incentivize reviews, whether or not reviews removed, and much more.

Adding Your Local Listing To Yahoo!

Yahoo is still in the top 3 search engines and with their partnership with Bing.com, you can bet their share of the search engine market will only grow. Here are the instructions to add your website to the local business listings of Yahoo!.

1. Go to local listing to add your business at the following URL as shown in Figure 5.22: (You will need a Yahoo! User I.D.)

http://listings.local.yahoo.com/csubmit/index.php

Figure 5.22

Enter in all your pertinent information for your business including your business hours, phone numbers, and the types of payments you take as shown in Figure 5.23.

Figure 5.23

1. After you have completed entering all your information including the year and history and verification information press submit and you are done as shown in Figure 5.24.

Figure 5.24

Other Local Listing Sites

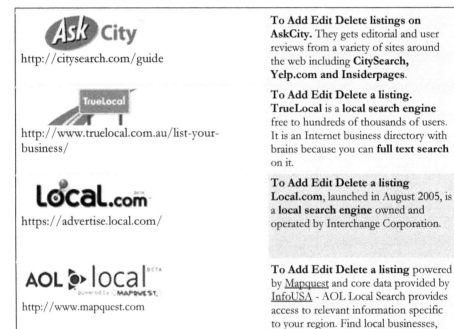

http://citysearch.com/guide

To Add Edit Delete listings on AskCity. They gets editorial and user reviews from a variety of sites around the web including **CitySearch, Yelp.com and Insiderpages**.

http://www.truelocal.com.au/list-your-business/

To Add Edit Delete a listing. TrueLocal is a **local search engine** free to hundreds of thousands of users. It is an Internet business directory with brains because you can **full text search** on it.

https://advertise.local.com/

To Add Edit Delete a listing Local.com, launched in August 2005, is a **local search engine** owned and operated by Interchange Corporation.

http://www.mapquest.com

To Add Edit Delete a listing powered by Mapquest and core data provided by InfoUSA - AOL Local Search provides access to relevant information specific to your region. Find local businesses, breaking news and other information for your area.

Chapter 6 – SEO Design & Website Usability

Very often a new clients comes to me and says, can you just optimize my website. I will just pay you by the hour. Sometimes this is possible with what I am given and other times I just cringe. It is sometimes disheartening when a website owner hears, "We need to reorganize or rebuild your website." Especially when the websites owner just paid a small fortune to get the website made and it won't rank well for anything unless major changes or a redesign is done. The fact is, SEO works best if it starts from the design going forward.

Saying that you know SEO without understanding searchers goals and behaviors is like saying that you understand math without knowing how to add or subtract. Many people believe that SEO is simply optimizing a website for search engines with some meta tags and some keywords. In reality, SEO is optimizing a website for people who use search engines, placing items that intrigue search engines, and then building an online reputation through many things such as social media, links, reviews, etc.

Many people also mistakenly believe that website usability is simply making a website easy to use. Easy to use for whom? The visitors? The website owners? Search engine optimization has fundamental building blocks but much more. Website usability comes down to how your content is laid out in front of the potential visitor and how they navigate through your website.

Content Delivery

Organization of the content is especially important. Whether you have a single product or you have multiple products to market. Let me first show you a couple of websites before and after pictures. The first is a website for a very good relationship therapist. His original website can be found on the next page on Figure 6.1.

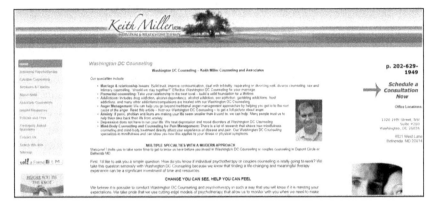

Figure 6.1

No I ask you, that do he do? Sell books? It is hard to tell because the message is embedded in too much text and not enough simplicity. Let's take a look now after the redesign for usability in Figure 6.2.

Figure 6.2

Notice how in my redesign I focused on a much simpler message which is easy to digest quickly.   Let me show you one that I did for a company that provides home building products with lots of lines of products. Here is the before website in Figure 6.3:

Figure 6.3

Without seeing the redesign on the next page there is no way you could ever tell all the product lines the client has without seeing the website. Let's take a look at the after in Figure 6.4.

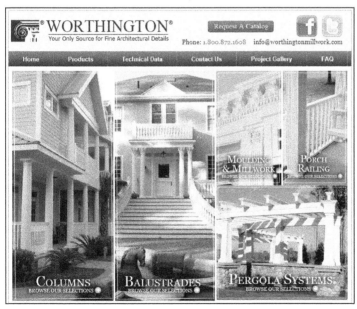

Figure 6.4

As a usability professional, I have to evaluate how quickly and easily searchers learn what your website is about and how to use your website the first time they encounter it. I review and evaluate every webpage for the ease of message deliver, meaning how easily your website announces what you are selling and how easy it is for newcomers to navigate through your website.

If your website visitors have to spend time learning how to use your website or trying to figure out what the products, services, or information is that you have to offer, they are spending less time on achieving their search goals. If a website is too hard to learn, then searchers hit the little red X at the top.

Visitor Satisfaction

Overall it comes down to visitor satisfaction. The search experience of the actual user. In other words, whether or not the website visitor is able to achieve their goals and complete their search task efficiently. If searchers encounter too many steps or roadblocks and do not find their desired content or a call to action, the total usability experience is low.

It is not about you as the website personals opinion. Usability is about achieving objectives. So when search usability professionals measure the effectiveness of a website, you should be able to answer the following questions positively:

1. Can searchers achieve their objectives and complete specific tasks using only a search engines organic results and your website?

2. Can searchers easily find their desired information, destination, or activity by landing on any indexed page on your website?

3. Can any pages, steps, or roadblocks be eliminated or minimized on your website to increase the user experience and still deliver the pertinent information?

4. How quickly can site visitors perform each specific task on your website? Is there a way to speed up the process?

5. What elements on your website discourage or prevent searchers visitor attaining their search objectives or get to a call to action?

6. What errors do visitors a make or encounter?

7. How frequently do these errors occur?

There is a general 3-Click Rule which basically states that every piece of content on a website should take no more than three clicks to complete.

SEO professionals should be careful about over-generalizing efficiency. Even today, I still hear and read SEO professionals reinforcing the 3-Click Rule. However, if you can give the visitor all the information they need and the call to action on one page. The better.

The last items are errors and some errors are deal breakers. Such is the care with missing content, missing pages, broken links, etc. Some errors are very infrequent and not so severe that they need to be addressed before you have your next meal. You can get help by monitoring data from web analytics, Google Webmaster Tools, site search analytics, SEO audit reports, etc.

SEO In The Design

So we covered usability but actually we should have covered the design first. For the rest of this chapter that some of you will look at some of the designs that make my clients cringe. Usually because they spent tens of thousands of dollars on this all Flash-based or picture based, super great looking website that will do nothing to get you better rankings and not anything that will make your website standout to the search engines.

I often hear similar things from prospective customers when I tell them their old site won't work: "What do you mean? My site looks great. It's all flashy and things move here and there, etc.

Well, let me tell you a true story. Last night before I started working on this chapter I met with a new client who is starting his own business doing psychological counseling. He paid an out-of-country guy to design his and his business partner's website.

Apparently there were disagreements on the design and layout; the site they came to a consensus on (below, in Figure 5.5) is one large picture. (I don't want to identify the site so I am only placing a little snippet of the site. There is some text underneath and above in the picture.)

Figure 6.5

It's a nice clean looking site with a spectacular picture on the first landing page. When I started discussing that he needed to have relevant readable text, RSS feeds, links, video, social media items, and more to increase his rankings, he stated, "Do whatever you want, but don't change the look."

Remember way back earlier in the book when I explained that Google and other search engines can't read pictures? Here is what Google sees of this website (Figure 6.6):

Figure 6.6

That pretty picture on their website in Figure 5.1 is great, isn't it? Not at all! Why? Because search engines cannot look at the text on pictures and index the information. They can't look at Flash or video either. Now here is the odd part. Having a little of each of those, including relevant text, pictures, video, and Flash, does increase the point ratio that increases your website's rankings on many of the major search engines.

So, am I going to turn a company that approaches me away for not allowing its website to be changed to optimize it? No. I am going to consult with them and tell them how to make their website increase its rankings, which is what I am paid to do. Then I am going to take their money and spend it wisely. I am an expensive person and if someone pays me for advice I am going to give it to them. If they choose not to use my advice, which others find very valuable, I will have no problem taking their money. They got what they paid for.

Also, this is something new that never came up before until this week. If you pay an SEO company to optimize your site during a site redesign, don't change the names of the pages that are indexed with the search engines. When a person does find you and the site file names have been changed, when they click on the link to your site, it won't work. There is a process to doing this if you really want to do this later in this chapter.

What should come first, SEO or the design?

This really is the chicken and egg question of the internet marketing age. Depending on who you ask will determine the actual answer you receive.

A graphic designer will argue that in a majority of cases the design comes first, of course. Without an aesthetically pleasing design, a visitor will bounce off your site within a matter of seconds. Not so fast. How did they get to your website in the first place? A great-looking website is nothing if there is no one to look at it.

Even if you intend to employ Google AdWords, you will soon realize you are spending a fortune to make your sales. That is usually when the SEO expert gets called in because of some research someone did to see how to properly market a website. Then you learn from your poor design that it will take 6 months or so for the major search engine marketing campaign to try and rescue your website rankings.

Is this really the best way to go? The thousands of business owners that have been through this exact cycle will certainly argue that it most definitely is not the way you should go, especially when the owners of these sites realized when it was too late. There was too high an amount of profit, potential, and clients lost because the design looked great to humans but was invisible to the search engines.

What is really laughable, though, is that if you actually read the sales pitch on any one of the myriad of web design companies that own websites, many of them blatantly claim to be SEO experts as if it is a badge of honor or perhaps a must-have tick in the box. However, a quick check of their portfolios soon reveals that if they are search engine marketing experts, then it is clearly evident that their clients are definitely not on the receiving end of any claims they make.

Can you implement site optimization into the design before you launch a website? Yes! The web design and SEO should go hand in hand. The thought process of optimizing a website and SEO-friendly website design should form the foundation right from the outset, so ultimately the content and design will capture free organic search engine traffic and also mark the website as a potential authority on the product or service.

You should remember that search engines do not care about what the site looks like: it is what's behind the scenes that makes the site so much more relevant to them. However, if we go back to the example above, my new client's initial chance to make the best impact on the search engine when the site first got indexed was wasted. In contrast, the extra time and money spent on predevelopment SEO, including the keyword research and SEO copywriting, gives an outstanding return on the investment of the website. This also gives you a far better chance of getting good website ranking from day one and even, in some cases, a page-one result faster than you might think.

If a web designer is not promoting web design SEO as part of your initial client brief, then they are selling you short. Now that you have read this book, even if you have only read Chapter 1, you know how to see the rankings of their referral sites to see if they know anything about SEO. If your web developers are not SEO experts or if they are not showing results in 6 months in terms of better rankings, the best practice would be to team up with an SEO professional to work with your web designer.

If you are implementing your own SEO, you need to set some SEO design goals for your website. Let's take a look at the different design or redesign goals for your website in the next sections to best design your website for both search engines and visitors.

Site Design Goals

If your website is a business, then your website most likely details the sales aspect of your business. Whether a visitor can buy right there online or has to contact you in other ways, this has to be addressed in the design. So when you design your website, optimizing your website is one goal, but making your website easy to navigate, getting more visitors, and getting leads are another.

Sidebar: Optimizing For Mobile Devices

I picked up early that Smartphones , Android, IPODs, and IPADs were going to be big so I started optimizing websites for mobile web devices. I haven't even seen this addressed in any books yet. But, as most companies are aware, the mobile Web is becoming more and more important in your web building efforts, which should translate into your SEO efforts as well.

As a company we have been doing Mobile Web SEO for larger enterprise companies for quite a while. As we have researched how to accomplish this, we have collected links on how to make your website mobile-ready:

- o **Bing Mobile:** discoverbing.com/mobile
- o **Google Mobile:** http://www.google.com/mobile/
- o **Google Mobile Sitemaps:** www.google.com/support/webmasters/bin/answer.py?hl=en&answer=34627
- o **Google Mobile View:** www.google.com/gwt/n
- o **Mobile Search Marketing Guide:** www.mobilesearchmarketing.com/guide.php
- o **Tappity:** www.tappity.com
- o **Technorati Mobile:** http://m.technorati.com
- o **Windows Mobile 2003 Smartphone Emulator:** www.microsoft.com/downloads/details .aspx?familyid=8fe677fa7-3a6a-4265-b8eb-61a628ecd462

Add your mobile-optimized site to search engines and let retailers know here:

- • **Abphone:** http://www.abphone.com and http://m.abphone.com
- • **Bing:** http:// discoverbing.com/mobile
- • **Bango:** http://www.bango.com
- • **Crispy:** http://www.crispyweb.com/submitmobile.htm
- • **Dotmobi**: http://mtld.mobi/sitesubmit
- • Google: Uhttp://www.google.com/addurlU (Put "Mobile" in comments)
- • **Medio:** http://medio.com/partners/addyourmobilesite/
- • **Mobiseer**: http://www.mobiseer.com

- **Nokia:** http://europe.nokia.com/A4568518
- **Taptu:** http://taptu.com/a/submit?ps=Q1A9b
- **Sprint:** https://developer.sprint.com/site/global/home/p_home.jsp

You should focus on the results you want: more visitors, leads, and customers. Every decision you make should be focused on fulfilling those goals. Keeping that in mind, you might spend a bit less time worrying about the exact shade of blue on the callout background, and more time worrying about things that will improve your marketing results and keep visitors directed toward your goals.

There are countless ways a website design can negatively impact your results. In fact, I would say that more often than not, website designs done without an SEO professional tend to have a negative impact on marketing results.

Another problem occurs when you attempt to implement too many strategies in your SEO. For one, you won't be able to tell which of your strategies are successful and two, search engines don't like it when you lose focus. Most major search engines like to see each of your website landing pages centered around one topic.

Implementing one strategy at a time allows you to determine which strategies are working and which strategies are not. SEO campaigns are most successful when you concentrate on one effort at a time.

> **NOTE:** *One of the first things that attracts a search engine's attention is the actual design of your site. The Meta tags, links, navigational structure, and relative content are all focused on a single topic.*

If you have an existing website you usually have a lot of material that has accumulated over time. These items help your prospects find your website and help you turn them into leads and customers.

> **WARNING:** *When you do a site redesign, make sure you use the same links and file names for your new site. If you don't, the links that are on search engines will become useless. The proper way to change the site is to create the new pages with new file names. Use the Robot.txt file to tell search engines not to index the old links. In a few months you can get rid of the old files as they will no longer show on the search engines.*

The general rule is, the more content you have the more visitors you will have and the longer they will stay. This will in itself grow your business faster. A 100 page website will beat a 10 page website 90% of the time on search engine rankings. And a 500 page website is even better. If some of those web pages were written recently, that's even better. But remember, always keep the focus of each page as close as you can to a single topic and optimize that page, the Meta Tags, Title, and keyword density to that topic.

A little known rule that helps add to your imaginary point standings with search engine rankings is that the more often you update your content (while keeping it relevant to your website subject matter), the better.

NOTE: *Blogging makes creating new and updated content easy.*

You want your website design to attract new visitors and increase your conversion rate and the number of leads you get from your website. Over time you should constantly improve the effectiveness of your conversion tools, including your landing pages.

If you build a completely static website and have to go to a web designer, every time you want to set up a new landing page or to change an existing page, you are limiting your ability to quickly experiment and improve on the design. You should have a website that lets you edit content and build landing pages without having to know website code unless you know HTML, PHP, or XML well.

One of the rules you should live by is that you should spend money on resources and relevant content that attracts and converts as well as optimizes your site. You should not overdo a design that limits you to only one type of code, such as websites that include Flash. The code should be dynamic and easy to change. Of course, sometime the easily changed part costs a little more upfront, but not at the end.

If you follow the rules set forth in the last paragraph, you should be able to create ongoing content with a building strategy. When you have more content, you can grow your website. This will help you increase your visitors and grow your business faster.

When you have finished your website, you should constantly have conversion experiments. The key to driving your conversion rate and the number of leads you get from your website over time is to constantly improve the effectiveness of your website. Several sites can be used to test your website:

Website Grader (www.websitegrader.com) – Has a useful tool for measuring the marketing effectiveness of your website.

HubSpot Internet Marketing Blog (blog.hubspot.com) – Has articles about business strategies and inbound internet marketing. This site also has internet marketing software that helps you get found by more prospects and generates more qualified leads and sales.

The Basics in Our Design

We have already hit on the points here, but they fall into this chapter as well. So let's make sure our design or redesign has these points covered:

- Meta and HTML Tags

- Header Tag Content
- Body Text
- Links
- Alternative Tags
- Header Tag Content
- Other Items You Should Make Space For
- RSS Feeds
- Other Valuable Content
- Other Tips

Meta and HTML Tags

Meta tags are HTML tags; they just appear in very specific places on a web page. There are two Meta tags which are given more weight than the others on most search engines. Those are the keyword tag and the description tag.

Most of the Meta tags are also given some weight on less major search engines and directories. However, not all search engines take keyword and description Meta tags into consideration because in the past, these tags have been overloaded with keywords that were irrelevant to the website.

Header Tag Content

This is a simple attribute but about as commonly overlooked by web designers as the Meta tags are. The *header tags* are a bit different from other tags discussed earlier in this book. These are the attributes that set up the different levels of headings and subheadings on your website. There can be as many as six different levels of headings but typically search engines only look at the first four.

Figure 6.8

To help you understand this, the title or topic of a web page should be the H1 title that the human side can see. Subheading of the topic should be tagged with the H2 tag and so on–kind of like a tree (as shown in Figure 6.8).

110

So let's say you have a website page that sells motorcycle helmets. The heading hierarchy in this example should look like this:

> H1: (Page Topic) Motorcycle Helmets
> H2: (Main Topic) Buy Motorcycle Helmets and Accessories
> H3: (Sub Topic) Motorcycle Face Shields
> H3: (Sub Topic) Motorcycle Custom Straps
> …and so on.

If there is a new sub topic such as there is in the example, you would start again with an H2 tag.

> H2: (Main Topic)

Headings denote important information and enable users to quickly skim the page to find the information they are seeking. The search engines use this in their scanning of web pages to determine what's vitally important.

Header tags on a web page should contain your most important keywords in a contextually appropriate manner. Specifically, search engine spiders, bots, and crawlers take into consideration the text within a header tags. Looking at the different levels of headings, first-level headings should contain the most important keywords on your web page.

> **NOTE:** *You should use your most important trophy keywords in the level-one heading, then lower-level headings (levels two through six) should contain decreasingly important keywords.*

The heading tags are similar in format to other tags that you've examined to this point and used after the <Body> tag of the website:

> <H1>Header 1</H1>
>
> <H2>Header 2</H2>
>
> <H3>Header 3</H3>
>
> <H4>Header 4</H4>
>
> <H5>Header 5</H5>
>
> <H6>Header 6</H6>

> **WARNING:** *Search engines are smart enough to know when your keywords are the same shade or color as your back ground and will penalize you for hiding the H1 tags or text that contains your keywords.*

Header tags should be included before the body-text tags of your website, and the text of the header goes in between the opening and closing tags.

Body Text

Like the Header tags, the *Body text* is also text that is visible to human readers of your site. When you look at the pages of this book, for example, the text that is between each of the headings would be the body text – the same way as it is for a web page.

The body text is another place where you want to include your keywords. A good rule of thumb is to use your keywords once in every paragraph as long as it makes sense to a reader.

Sidebar: Keywords in Text

Having your keyword strategically placed in your text on every page is one of the most important elements of any website. Of particular importance are the trophy keywords which we determined in Chapter 3. The trophy keywords need to be placed throughout the text on your primary landing page. It is of particular importance where those keywords appear and how often they appear on the page.

The keywords you choose must match the words and phrases that potential visitors will use when searching for the products or services your website provides.

You can also use additional tags to indicate special formatting in text. Those tags are as follows:

Bold
Italics
Strongly Emphasized
Emphasis
<li>New Line in List</li>

Each of these special tags indicates special formatting for the word or phrase in between the opening and closing tags, and the special emphasis makes a search engine crawler take notice of those words.

NOTE: *You should try to use keywords within the special tags if possible. Only use keywords where appropriate, and avoid stuffing keywords into your site simply to improve your search engine rankings. If you use those tactics, they will most likely fail and may even get your site banned from some of the search engines.*

Sidebar: Things to Avoid

To make your website's body text visible to spiders, bots, and crawlers, avoid the following:

- Text embedded in JavaScript applications or Macromedia Flash files cannot been read.

- Text contained in images such as those with extensions .jpg, .gif, .png, and .bmp cannot be seen.

- Text that is accessible only on a submission form is not readable.

Most of these things make your site look flashy and cool. Site designers struggle with these issues and sometime choose looks over site optimization on purpose to make the site owner happy. There are only about 8 different fonts that can be used on a website without pictures because of the standards. Also, certain text styles cannot be indexed by search engines.

If search engine spiders, bots, and crawlers can't see your website text, then they can't index that content for visitors to find.

Browser Viewing Size

Page size is going to become a factor in ranking. Otherwise Google would not have added the browser size tool to GoogleLabs.com shown in figure 6.9. This can be found at:

http://browsersize.googlelabs.com

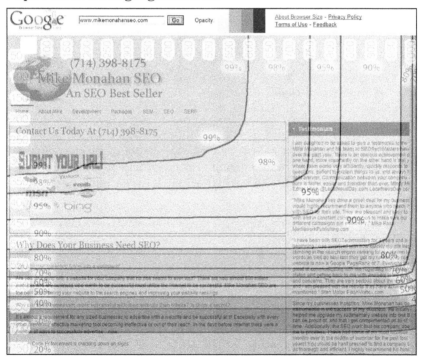

Figure 6.9

When I say "optimize" I mean that your page should look and work the best at the most common size. It should still look good and work well at other sizes, which is why I recommend a liquid layout. But it should be its best at 1024×768. The only exception to this rule is if your primary audience is senior citizens such as if you sell medical alert devices or Mediagap insurance. Senior citizens typically use larger fonts and screens at 800x600.

Let's look at some criteria that you should meet utilizing your screen size:

Initial visibility: This is how well your website looks above the fold without scrolling. There is a tradeoff between how many items are shown on the top fold vs. how much detail is displayed for each individual item.

Readability: This is how easy is it to read the text in each column of your website.

Aesthetics: This is how good your website page looks when the elements are at the proper size and location for this screen size.

All three criteria should be met at the full range of sizes, continuously resizing the browser window from 800×600 to 1280×1024. Each of your website pages should score high on each of the three criteria throughout the entire resolution range.

Your page should also work and look good at even smaller and bigger sizes, though such extremes are less important. Fewer than half a percent of users still have 640×480.

Links

You should have an area of your landing page dedicated to links. The links should be related to the content of the page and be active links to real websites. *Broken links* will lower your search engine rankings on major search engines.

Links have always been an important factor in how websites rank on the different major search engines. Most important are not only links from your site but to your site as well.

Alternative (ALT) Tags

Alternative tags for pictures and links are also important to have on your pages and help those who are visually impaired. These tags should contain a a brief description of the picture or graphic on a website.

One of the good things about ALT Tags are also a good place to include a keyword or two to help increase your keyword density. Human users rarely ever see your ALT Tags unless they intentionally turn off images to enable web pages to load faster or hover over the picture with a mouse.

Using ALT Tags To Improve Search Rankings

To improve rankings of your images using ALT tags, follow these rules:

File Name

Keywords used in image file names provide very specific information to people and search engines on the topic of the image. Img48455.jpg isn't a very good file name but orlando-golf-balls.jpg is if your keyword for the page is "Orlando golf balls".

Text Surrounding Image

A caption can help search engines associate the image with keywords used in the surrounding text.

Image Linking

Links from other pages to your image or the page your image is embedded on can help search engines find the image for crawling and also pass PageRank.

Image Sitemaps

You need to learn about Image sitemaps if you are having difficulty getting your images into a search engine like Google. You can add image specific tags to a sitemap and provide that information to Google

Alt Text

Adding descriptive text to the image ALT Tag attribute is helpful for search engines as well as a usability. You should not stuff a long string of keywords in the alt text though. In Figure 6.10 below, look at the coding added to an image to add an ALT Tag.

```
<table width="939" border="0">
<tr>
  <td width="450" height="413"><img src="OrlandoGolfBackDrop.gif" alt="Orlando Golf Logo" width="450" height="414" /></td>
  <td width="479"><div align="center"><img src="OrlandoGolfMap.gif" alt="Orlando Golf Map" width="469" height="336" />
```

Figure 6.10

To add and ALT Tag to a WordPress website let's look at an example on the next page in Figure 6.11.

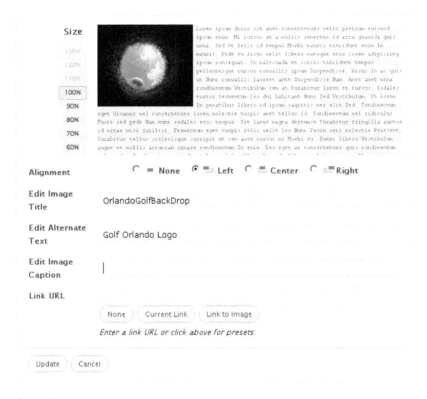

Figure 6.11

Other Items You Should Make Space For

Your website should have some of the items below on its main landing pages. The more of these the better. Each one of these increases your site's value on different major search engines.

- A little flash
- Conversion page (submission page)
- RSS Feed
- Video (YouTube if possible. It is owned by Google.)
- Blog (BlogSpot if possible. It is operated by Google.)
- Facebook, MySpace, or Twitter Feed or Widget
- Links to other pages in your body text
- Text links to other pages in your website if you use pictures, maps, or Flash for buttons.
- Text that can change frequently.

Adding RSS Feeds

Really Simple Syndication(RSS) or it's sometimes referred to as Rich Site Summary is an XML-based content format for distributing news, headlines, content, and more about a website. It is almost a requirement now for higher rankings to have an RSS feed on your website or blog to rank well.

RSS Feed readers come in all shapes and sizes these days. The Firefox browser has one built right into the Bookmarks feature. I personally use Google Reader. (http://www.google.com/reader)

You can also create feeds for your own website so your audience can subscribe to them. If you update your content frequently and promote the feed effectively, it can help drive more steady traffic to your website.

Advantages of Creating RSS Feeds

This is an excellent way to bring repeat traffic to your site. Think about it, every time a web surfer opens their RSS reader to get the headlines for all the sites they monitor, they'll also see your site's updates.

Instead of relying on them to bookmark your site and return at a later date, their RSS reader keeps your site fresh in their minds.

Many entities are now pushing out their newsletters and switching to this method of content distribution because you don't have to worry about dodging the spam filters.

When you send an email newsletter more than half of those people won't even receive it due to spam filters or junk mail algorithms. With RSS feeds, you don't have to worry about that because you're not sending an email, your simply sending out a news feed for all the readers to pick up.

How to Create an RSS Feed for a Static Website

If you are novice in creating XML code, I recommend using www.feedforall.com for static websites. They have an easy-to-use feed builder that lets you create and manage all your feeds in one place.

Once you have created your feed you have to upload the XML file to your web server. FeedForAll.com will automatically convert your feed into the XML format so you don't need to worry about additional formatting or coding and make your RSS Feed URL something like:

http://www.yoursite.com/yourfeed.xml

Anytime you add a new article to your feed, that XML file is updated.

FeedForAll also has a built-in upload feature so you can upload the XML file right to your web server with their software, as long as your web host has FTP access.

Creating An RSS Feed From a Blog

Google allows you to create an RSS feed using their blog website Blogger.com. WordPress is another website type that offers a free blog equipped with RSS feeds.

Other Valuable Content

Other Items that can be considered great content:

- A free whitepaper
- A how-to or manual
- A series of articles
- A YouTube video
- A podcast
- A badge or image
- A proprietary study
- A quiz, poll, or test
- A joke or cartoon
- A calculator or free software
- A blog or forum
- A wiki or knowledge base

Other Considerations for Your Website

For a website to rank well, the search engines must retrieve information from the website – not so much from the human side but from the coding side. The retrieval of data is a combination of the activity from the crawler, spider, bots, the database, and the search algorithm used by each search engine. These three elements work together to retrieve web pages that are related to the word or phrase that a user enters into the search engine's user interface.

The algorithms change frequently, which is one reason this book is updated every year. In SEO, ranking is what you'll spend the most time and effort trying to change. Your ranking in a search engine determines how often people see your page.

How search engines rank a page or pages is a difficult science to figure out and changes frequently. Search engines don't want everyone to know the exact science. If it were known to everyone it would be tough to get on the first or second page of a search.

Ranking is such a large part in search engine optimization and appears frequently throughout book. There are some things that can give your website an advantage right from the beginning. Let us take a look at two: hosting location and frequency of keyword use.

Hosting Location

There are a lot of locations that we talk about in this book. In this section of the book, I will specifically refer to the location where you host your website. I have a customer who is in good straights now but had tried to handle his own optimization. No matter what he did he couldn't get his website off of page 68 on a Google search. For every new SEO client I bring on I do a complete SEO Report to find issues with the website. What we found was that the website was being hosted on the same server as several porn-related websites. In SEO terms we call this being in a "Bad Neighborhood." That is where porn or blacklisted websites are using the same IP or IP Range as your website.

In this case, the website owner had bought his hosting on eBay for $42.00 per year. If you have a respectable business website, you have to be hosted on a respectable hosting provider. The Major search engines do not like to rank websites that contain pornography, racial comments, or other such content.

Frequency of Keyword Use

Websites must be relevant to the keywords you choose. So the frequency with which the keywords appear on a web page may also affect how a page is ranked in search results for that keyword. For example, on a page about office furniture, one that uses the words "office furniture" five times might be ranked higher than one that uses the words only two or three times.

When word frequency became a well-known factor, some website designers began using hidden words hundreds of times on pages, trying to artificially boost their rankings. Almost every search engine recognizes this as *keyword spamming* and ignore or even blacklist pages that use this technique.

Tips

- Don't repeat keywords in your title tags. Repetition can occasionally come across as spam when a crawler is examining your site, so avoid that in your title if possible, and never duplicate words just to gain a spider, bot, or crawler's attention.
- Include a call to action in your title. There is an adage that goes something like, "You'll never sell a thing if you don't ask for the

sale." That's true on the Web as well. If you want your users to do something, you have to ask them. The title is never a bad place to ask. But include your trophy keywords there, too.

- Create a website that contains Meta tags, content, graphics, and keywords that help improve your site ranking.
- Use keywords liberally on your site, so they are used in the correct context of your site topic and content. Keep them relevant and search engines will keep you relevant.
- Include reciprocal links to your site from others as long as those links are legitimate and relevant to the topic of your website.
- Continuously encourage website traffic through many venues, including keyword advertising, reciprocal links, and marketing campaigns.
- Submit your website to search engines manually, rather than wait for them to pick up your site in the natural course of cataloging websites.

Keyword Density

One of the biggest design rules to keep is the number of times you use your keywords (known as *keyword density*). Most search engines allow a relatively low keyword density. Google is by far one of the less lenient in this regard when ranking websites. Google likes to see a keyword density of 5 to 7 percent – much lower and you risk one of your competitors outdoing you in the optimization area or much higher than that and you risk your website bring penalized. Bing, Yahoo!, MSN, and other search engines seem to be stricter and want keyword densities of about 5 percent.

> **NOTE:** From the end of 2010 to around October of 2011 the results on Bing mimicked those on Yahoo!. It appears that Yahoo! is now using previous or similar algorithms to those used before the infamous Microsoft deal.

Use a word processing program to find out your total word count. Paste the HTML source code of the page into a blank document, then choose File, Properties, Statistics, Word Count. In Microsoft Office 2007/2010 it is found at File, Prepare, Properties, Statistics.

There is also a great tool to use to see the number of words and the keyword density on a page. http://www.gorank.com/analyzer.php. This tool is the most accurate.

Let's move on. If you are optimizing that page for a single keyword, you need to figure out how many times that particular word is repeated within that 250 word total.

Manually scan the page and count every repetition of your keyword. If you have Microsoft Word 2007/2010, you should also have an Replace function under the Home tab all the way to the right. Paste in the code and then type in the keywords in both the edit box and the replace box. The program will replace each occurrence of the word with itself...and produce a total count for the number of repeats.

Let us assume for this exercise that you have used a keyword 10 times on your page. To calculate the keyword density - take that figure and divide it by the total number of words on your page. So in this case 10 divided by 250 = .04

Keyword density is always referred to as a percentage of the total word count for the page. So now you need to multiply .04 by 100 to get the percentage figure.

Your calculation would look like this;

$$.04 \times 100 = 4\%$$

The page has a keyword density of 4%.

For effective optimizing that will boost your pages into the Top 20 spots on the major search engines you are aiming for a keyword density of between 5-7%.

What you have just been shown is about as simple as it gets for working out the keyword density of a web page. To recap, the formula looks like this:

10 divided by 250 = .04 x 100 = 4% -or- keyword count divided by total word count x 100 = keyword density in percent. So you can add your keyword another few times without penalty on most major search engines.

Algorithms fluctuate constantly at the major search engines so it is much simpler to optimize a few pages for different weighting or densities. A few pages at 5%, 6%, and 7% keyword density will mean at least one of your pages should rank well on each major search engine.

In Review

Heading Tags (H1-H6)

Syntax: *<h1>Keyword1 in the Heading</h1>, <h2>Keyword2 in the Heading </h2>, etc.*

The "Header tag" is nothing more than a headline of the page, so it should be kept short. 45 characters, including spaces, is a good target.

Each page should have a clearly defined <h1> header tag, to identify the primary subject of the page to both the user and the search engine. Be sure to use the primary search phrase you are targeting within this tag.

Note: It is important that the primary keyword is located in the first heading tag on the page, regardless of its type. Placing the keyword early in the header tag will increase its prominence.

Standard rules apply for the structure of HTML pages. Written in a document-like fashion, they should include:

- Title

- Major heading, describing the main purpose of the section.

- Subheadings, highlighting the key points of each subsection.

Many search engines rank the words found in headings higher than the words found in the body text of the document. Some search engines will also incorporate keywords by looking at all the heading tags on a page.

Don't try to stuff your heading tag with too many keywords, or words that are not relevant to the content in the body. Having multiple *<h1>* tags on the same page may cause you to be subjected to a penalty by the search engines, as it may be seen in the same light as *"keyword stuffing"*.

It is certainly appropriate to have multiple headlines appearing on a page, like *<h2>*,*<h3>*, etc., provided they follow a hierarchical order. The *<h1>* should be the first heading tag, followed by the *<h2>*, then the *<h3>*, and so on.

Phrase Elements

Use the **semantical tags** *<STRONG>* and *<EM>* tags for targeted keywords within the visible content of your pages, but sparingly. Those tags are alternatives to the <B> and <I> tags, which can also be used, but are for visual presentation purposes only.

ALT Attributes

Resist the temptation to stuff your alt. attributes with keywords. Keyword density is no longer as important as it once was, and doing so could subject you to penalties.

Keyword Density

Keep text on your website pages relevant to one keyword and write with that keyword in mind keeping the keyword count to about 4-5% in the actual text on the page.   Add the keyword elsewhere on the page in the Meta data, ALT tags, Titles, anchor text, and other places on the page to try and maintain a 6-7% keyword density.

Blog text, news articles, and press releases should maintain a 4-5% keyword density.

Chapter 7 – SEO Off-Page

If you are on page 1 of a Google search for the keyword or keywords that relate to your website you get all the business. If you are on page 3 or later, you get no business.

As your ranking improves, so does your website traffic. The difference between even first and fourth page in the SERP rankings can make or break a business.

So how do the search engines decide the order in which sites appear in the results? Well there are a lot of sciences that go in to that. First is the science of on-page optimization which includes great keyword density, outgoing links, social media, the H1 tag, and more. Basically what the user sees.

Another is the Meta data science we talked about in Chapter 3. Then there is the off-page SEO. The better your one-page work, the better effect your off-page SEO efforts will help you. With off-page SEO there are a lot of items that are included in the metrics that decides the placement of your website and this metric is ever changing. It doesn't include your domain name but what is included is everything from the age of your domain name, the quantity of incoming links, the quality of incoming links, your blog (so long as it is not hosted at your own URL) the text on incoming links, forum postings, news articles, and social media mentions.

That seems like a lot, but let me break it down for you in the next few sections:

Keywords In Incoming Links

The anchor text used to link to the web page should contain important keywords or keyword phrases. The linking text is viewed as "contextual" by search engines especially Google.

The Google PageRank is based on Larry Page's, a co-founder of Google, idea that a website that has good content and is more important will be linked to by many others. This is one reason that incoming and reciprocal links to your site are given a very high importance to its search engine rank.

Incoming links are links on other websites to your website. This metric is more reliable in search engines' eyes, because it is much harder to manipulate another person's website. If a link appears on the CNN home page, linking to your website with the term 'great travel website' in the anchor text, search engines can see that a highly respected site believes your website is worth linking to for the topic "Travel Websites". When it sees this it acts as if there is an imaginary voting system on the Internet and the link from CNN counted as a vote.

Numbers of Incoming Links

Link building is one of the biggest SEO tasks. You can get your website to a Google PageRank of 2 without a single link, but after that your site needs to become relevant to the search engine with as many links as possible from sites that are in the same industry, related to your websites topic or are news organizations.

Search Engines will often monitor the quantity of incoming links to a website. A large quantity of incoming links is an indicator of popularity or importance, and the search engines will favor sites with a larger number of backlinks. Search engines use the volume of incoming links to give better ranking to the more popular sites.

However, there is room to get in trouble. If you go and create 10,000 links in a week and then no other links are ever made, you are likely to get blacklisted from Google. Link building needs to have an appearance that it was made naturally and gradually.

If you are in marketing there is something I hate to tell you. Most consumer don't like you. In fact consumers are tired of your advertising on TV ads, billboards, and full page newspaper ads. They literally complain and rebel against pop-ups and pop-under ads, CPM, CPA, and CPC ads. They see ads now in bathrooms, on their phones, and especially the internet. I have seen a growing movement of people deliberately going out of their way to avoid advertising.

As an SEO person, I am in the marketing business, in virtually every aspect of social media. I consider myself an expert at creating links, building content, making links, and creating a web presence for my clients without them realizing they are being advertised to or it is in the interest of SEO. Because as soon as an online visitor gets a whiff that what you're doing serves a marketing purpose, it doesn't matter what the quality of the content is they will duck for cover, and go away.

It is time to educate you on not only what is SPAM but how to avoid becoming a spammer yourself. First I will tell you how to get the best type of links. The ones that come from official news sources.

Incoming Links Quality

Not all links are created equal; therefore some link builders will spend months trying to get one strong link from a big, important, or relevant website. A sometimes good link-building tactic is to try to get thousands of links from smaller sites, which are presumably easier to get than a link on a highly prestigious site. Many of those websites will not stay low ranking and build up a ranking of their own. When they do you reap an even greater benefit.

Once you realize the importance of relevant incoming links to the success of your website, you will understand the need to engage in link building and how a professional ongoing link building campaign is paramount to the success of your website.

There is a reason that search engines care about links to and from your website. Remember our imaginary point system from the early chapters? The search engines treat your incoming links from other relevant websites as a "point" for your site. The more you have the better. Some sites give you more points. News outlets such as LocalNewsDay.com, TheKnowVegas.com, ChicagolandNewspaper.com and CNN.com help your rankings increase faster because Google sees them as an official news source. A single link from a positive news story can be the equivalent of getting 300 PageRank 3 links from websites. That is from a single link. That is how important Google feels the links from official news sources is. Other site types that seem to give more points are .EDU and .Gov websites that provide links to your website.

Examples Of Bad Links

The number of pitfalls to link building are limitless. You have to be very exact when it comes to following the Google Webmaster Guidelines. If you see advertisements for the following type of links….Think twice.

- **10,000 links for $29.95 –** Very dubious offers from spam emails offering you 5000 links for $19 are too good to be true. They lead almost directly to a penalty.
- **Paid links on high PR sites –** It's actually quite easy to get noticed when you buy links on so-called high PR sites where the toolbar PageRank is 6 and above. When one website gets in trouble for buying links from the same sources, everyone listed gets the same penalty by default.

- **Hidden links in WordPress themes or counters –** Some Word Press themes sites are just SEO scams which rely on hidden links in the themes to be spread around. If you rely on such links for "link building". You will eventually be penalized. Some visitor counters have done that in the past as well.
- **Artificial link profile -** with always matching anchor text – when every single link to your site is well optimized saying something like "SEO company" this might look too artificial to stay unnoticed by Google.
- **Wrong language links –** Its obvious to search engines that an English site having thousands of links from Russia, India, Pakistan, or China makes the website standout and open to penalizing or blacklisting. Google engineers are smart enough to compare the language of your site and the sites that link to you.
- **Gaining too many links too fast –** it's not always the more links the better. Even good links gained too fast can result in a penalty. Link building must be natural. If you get 10,000 links in a week, you better be prepared to do that every week forever or Google will see it as unnatural.

Getting Links From Official News Sources

I am going to give away one of my best kept secrets. For years I have had access to over 50 official news sources that have been able to give me the best links to my clients websites and deliver a marketing message to my clients they could not get anywhere else. Not only does the news articles deliver the marketing message you want to deliver, it doesn't appear to be an advertisement, you create trust in your product or service, and you get a link back to your website that is the equivalent of hundreds of medium quality links.

So how do you do get the best link in the world for less than $50.00? Take a look at Figure 7.1 below. You will notice that the main article is about why you need Medicare Medigap Insurance. Notice that there is also an advertisement to the right of the logo for LowCostMedigap.com. Starting to see some coincidences here?

Figure 7.1

There are many local news papers nationwide. They have online newspapers as well as small paper newspapers you can get at supermarkets and local businesses. They like educational articles and they love to help those that are advertisers. It is a perfect example of, "You scratch my back and I scratch yours."

There are some rules though. First you need to pay for a banner ad for the website. Usually less than $50 per month. It is about $30 per month for LocalNewsDay.com which has about 15,000 visitors per week to their inline news site. TheKnow franchise has local newspapers in major cities all over the country and an add run about $40 per month on each website. The most expensive is Chicagoland Newspaper which runs about $75.00 per month but they have almost 20,000 unique visitors per day.

After you purchase advertising you need to submit a news article that is of journalistic quality where it doesn't seem like an advertisement. One that interests people but doesn't mention your company name until late in the article where your company and website are mentioned as an expert in your field and a quote from someone in your company. Hence you educate the consumer, give trust in your company, get a link to your website and deliver your message without appearing to be an advertisement. This is one of the best ways to subtly advertise and get your message to the consumer and your help SEO at the same time and at a very low cost.

So who do you talk to do this? Here are my personal list of contacts.

Contact	Online News Source	Email Address
Mindy Morgan	LocalNewsDay.com	Mindy@LocalNewsDay.com
Mike Smith	TheKnow Franchise	MikeSmith@TheKnowLA.com
Ty Nguyen	Chicagoland Newspaper	Ty@ChicagolandNewspaper.com
Chris Sales	NYC News Desk	Chris@NYCNewsDesk.com

Press Releases

Depending on how the algorithms are working with Google, press releases can often be one of the secret weapons of SEO companies. The thinking with search engines regarding press releases is that some companies release hundreds of press releases a year and lowers the value of the information each provides. If there is a link back to your website in the press release it does get some link credit. This is not the only things a business should rely on though. A business should never rely on press releases alone and always help raise the profile of their website. Either way, press releases remain a great way of increasing the exposure of company and its reputation.

Producing press releases for the Internet and is different than writing for traditional outlets such as newspapers and magazines. You need to write each press release based on a single keyword in mind. You then need to include that keyword as many times in your press release as possible with a link back to the page on your website that matches the article that matches the keyword you are focused on for maximum exposure.

There are some pros and cons associated with press release writing and distribution. These points will help you decide whether this service will suit your business.

Press Release Pros

Writing and distributing press releases boosts the number of links to your website. This is always a benefit to SEO as many press release websites are authoritative and have a high PageRank. Remember that making use of anchor text links in the articles is especially beneficial for your campaign so long as they link back to your website and the page on your website that focuses on the keyword used in your press release.

Press articles are easily distributed quickly to the most relevant parts of the Internet focused on your product or service. This can get high quality traffic to your website. Many people consider atypical press release format to be a more of a traditional form of marketing, this template remains an age-old favorite with the media. This means that news editors are more likely to take a look at what you have to offer as all the information they need is easily identifiable and in one place.

If you write your press release well, your press releases can help with the corporate branding of your company and aid in promoting the products or services you provide.

One last thing is that press releases help your online reputation strategy as well. A well distributed press release will often appear high in the search engine results if you use good keyword density, pushing down unflattering entries and making your company gain complete control of its image.

Link Spamming

To the all knowing eye, spammy links are easily found. A good SEO company provides links that have the appearance of being an organic and customer or vendor provided link.

Even before social media links had been part of the major search engine's algorithms, they were there, usually from SEO wannabes that didn't know any better. Let me warn you now, if you are involved in social media solely for the SEO value of the links from your favorite social media sites – you're doing it wrong and you are going to eventually meet with a less than favorable outcome.

You are treading in an area where far too many people have already abused this area. So much so that now increasingly savvy community members are *over*-sensitive to it. I have seen legitimate content called SEO spam simply because the user couldn't find another marketing purpose to apply a name to it.

How can you avoid being called a spammer? Provide GREAT, not just good, content that doesn't look like your directly advertising the service or product wherever possible. In general, the better your content = the less likely it will be considered spam. Let's take a look at different types of spammy content:

- Comment Spam
- Blog Spam
- Viral Marketing
- Being The Self Promoter
- Money Making Spam

Comment Spam

This type of spam needs no description. Comment spam is a major annoyance and usually a sub-category of SEO Link spam. Blogs, Forums, WordPress websites, Facebook pages, social media bookmarking sites, and the like all have to deal with this kind of spam.

When you go to a website, drop a comment with a link back to your website either by hand, use software, or use a bot that drops a link back to you website you are an offender.

You should never comment unless you have something to add to the conversation. Use links only if it is relevant to the conversation.

Blog Spamming

Blog spam is essentially when an unknown blog takes high quality content, like a viral video or images, from elsewhere and hosts it on their blog to attract traffic and attention with content they didn't create.

A secondary term called LinkJacking is essentially the same thing, only this time, it is well known/high traffic blogs doing it in order to get traffic specifically from social media sites such as Digg or Reddit.

Another difference between blog spamming and Linkjacking is that blog spamming takes multiple pieces of content from various sources to attempt to hide the fact that it is copied and it really spam. Linkjacking usually takes content from a single source and simply adds a unique description so as not to be "duplicate" content.

Blog spamming serves little purpose but to rob the original content producers of credit for their time and effort in creating the content.

Viral Marketing

Viral marketing is like hitting a "home run" in social media marketing. Having a piece of content go viral gives a number of obvious marketing benefits, especially everyone's favorite marketing buzz word: branding. That's why many big brands try to go this route. The problem? It's becoming harder and harder to achieve. Why? Because it has been done...a LOT. Not only are users becoming more cautious of this type of marketing, but the content's becoming redundant.

How to avoid this label: Your content must be or look completely genuine, stir up *real* emotions, and strive for originality. It's easier said than done, but not impossible.

Self Promoter

There's nothing wrong with the occasional self promotion here and there. The problem is when your website content is only self promotion with little other content or educational purpose. Consumers know when you are being self promoting and not offering to their conversations and it becomes a reason to exit from your online content. When sharing links from your site or blog exclusively and from nowhere else, people consider this spamming. Even if it's super fantastic, neat-o content, you're spamming people. Even if your blog has no advertising, marketing or business model: you're still a spammer.

When you share more than your own product or service, URL, etc., Not only are you better received, but others will be more willing to share your content again because they trust what comes from you. Sharing nothing but your own content, is the easiest way to end up in a place like **http://www.reddit.com/r/reportthespammers**.

Reddit.com is a place people can go to report the good and bad about websites. Now, we have all heard the phrase, "the squeaky wheel gets the grease," well the same concept applies right here. More people come to reddit.com to report spammers then they come to remark on how well someone is doing.

Money Making Spam

Most social media users feel if you get paid to submit links to Digg or Reddit, you are a spammer, even if the site(s) you've submitted make no money from it. If a site has too many ads, too large a call-to-action, or even too prominent a brand message, it might be considered spam. Even well known publications have been known to fall victim to this label. The fact is, if someone has something to gain by content being spread then it probably smells of marketing. And if it smells of marketing, than it probably is marketing.

You should limit your call-to-action advertising or comments. If you can, you should always hide your main business objective and first focus on making sure your content is being spread and educational if possible.

Varied Linking Text

Just to give a little history, once webmasters figured out that links helped your rankings, all sorts of abuse started to occur. People started creating ways to beat the system including link farms, massive reciprocal link networks, automatically generated content with automatic links, and automated software that automatically posted to thousands of links on the Internet. Most of these links were never meant for a human visitor to see.

This is where the major search engines began to fight back. They didn't want junk in their results any more than searchers wanted to see it. Search engines started counting some links more than others, and discounting some links and types of links entirely. Then they started to ban websites for using these practices.

Now, link building is no longer a simple "more equals better" formula and the mathematics behind search results has gotten much more complicated. Meanwhile, the ability to use "right link building" has actually gotten a lot easier.

Vary the anchor text slightly for your links allows your linking to appear natural to the search engines. The text used to link to a webpage should be varied and if possible contain a positive word. So if your keyword is "Dentist", you might put "Great Los Angeles dentist" or "Best Los Angeles Dentist" as the anchor text for your keywords.

Sidebar: Getting Good Links

Anchor text is the visible, clickable text of a hyperlink (also known as link text). For example, if this were a website, then in this sentence, this would be the anchor text. You don't always have control over your anchor text. If someone links to you from their blog, or someone writes an article about you, the writer may not give you "keyword friendly" anchor text. In those cases, just be happy they linked to you. But, in other cases, you may be able to choose your anchor text.

Search engines pay particular attention to the anchor text that they are following. So, for your anchor text, use descriptive keywords and anchor text variants under which you would like to rank and make sure the keyword you are using in your anchor text is linked to a page on your website focused on the same keyword. Many people make the mistake of making every link to their homepage. This gives your homepage a good ranking but all the other pages on the website suffer.

TIP: *Pick up the phone and make a call to the administrators/editors for the website you want a link from. Such a simple concept, and one that's adopted by virtually every sales organization in the world, and yet the vast majority of link builders out there fail to utilize the phone, instead opting for mountains of emails or heaps of social network messaging.*

WordPress Blog Commenting

When commenting on blogs, particularly WordPress blogs, use a keyword phrase in the "name" box and use a 4 to 5% keyword density when commenting on the blogs. That will often result in a backlink to your website for which you have control of the anchor text.

Forum Posting

When posting in forums, include your keywords or phrases as part of your forum signature as well as writing with your keyword in mind at a 4-5% keyword density is another way of encouraging backlinks.

Getting Good Website Links

There are an infinite number of places you can get good links to your website that are relevant and will increase your rankings. These are:

1. Websites in your industry (Experts, your suppliers, wholesalers, industry regulators, Industry training and certification sites.)
2. AngelasAndPaulsBacklinks.com is a monthly inexpensive newsletter with hundreds of easily obtainable links, articles on how to obtain links, and places that offer free homepage and deep links.
3. Charity websites, educational institutions, places you sponsor
4. Chambers of commerce, BBB, Industry associations
5. Customer reviews
6. Old sites with established domains
7. News organizations
8. Press release sites
9. Blogs and forums
10. Quality news articles
11. Websites from .gov and .edu sites
12. Social media and bookmarking sites
13. Customer review websites
14. Anyplace that you feel will bring you positive and relevant branding to enhance your company's credibility.

Sidebar: Getting Good Links From Customer Reviews

Google's acquisition of Zagat and its use of Yelp's customer reviews brings a great way of creating links back to your website and at the same time increase social mentions of your website on the web.

If you break it down, there are four types of businesses on the web:

- Businesses that get most of their business from referrals could care less about reviews.

- Businesses that get most of their business from referrals, get online reviews and think that nobody reads them or even cares about them.

- Businesses that think reviews are important and work hard to get a s many as possible.

- Businesses that try to get reviews and don't get very many.

The types that rely heavily on referrals and ignore reviews don't realize that some time in the next year or two someone is going to write something about them online and there is a very good chance it's going to be negative. Your website can avoid some of these by providing a way for people to give comments on your website. Whether public or not and always make sure you follow up on comments that are negative.

If negative comments get around on the Internet, which it usually does thanks to Google, their referrals are at risk of drying up. If the first thing that shows up in Google for your brand name or the your websites domain name is a negative comment or review, you are potentially in a very bad spot and risk losing business. In some extreme cases I have seen a company go out of business.

Positive reviews are great, the real power is in the reviewer. A customer willing to spend the time to review you is a brand ambassador is always a powerful ally. Instead of just asking them for reviews, you should be thinking about how you can harness your relationship with these valuable people to help spread the word, both online and off.

For those of you that try but can't seem to get any traction with reviews, you should consider the following, on how to build review generation into their business processes.

Customer Review Acquisition Strategies

When you get right down to it, there are basically four ways to get an online customer review:

1. Via phone
2. Via email
3. Via a Website
4. Via transcription from a hand-written reviews

Which method is right for you depends on how you conduct your business.

One of the biggest mistakes I see is businesses that don't collect email addresses for advertising. Most of the businesses I work with know they should but rarely do. Even when they do, they don't keep their list up to date and one clients list we worked on recently had less than 10% with current addresses.

If email doesn't work for your company, then you'll need to consider how you typically interact with your customers. If most of your business is done in person then give them a comment card to complete and then put those comments online. If it's over the phone, you may have to do it via mail. Try stapling a comment card with return postage to your invoice. Especially for those clients you have gone out of your way for.

When figuring out your customer review acquisition strategy, ask yourself what your staff can realistically do every day.

Some tips for asking customer reviews:

1. Offer Incentives? A large percentage of your customers will do it for free. If you offer to pay your top clients, it's possible it will backfire and they will get turned off, which could hurt your business by dampening the enthusiasm of these clients.

2. Make it easy for customers, but don't send them a link to review you on Google unless they have a Gmail address.

3. Do not ask people for Yelp reviews. This almost always backfires. You may get a few positive reviews in the short term, but if your customers are not active Yelpers, Yelp's SPAM filters remove them. You'll end up with no reviews and potentially some angry customers who wonder why their hard work reviewing your company went away.

4. Send a request to review your company promptly. Don't wait. People are most likely to give you feedback right away when they are happy with your service or product. The longer you go from the time of service to the time of your request, the higher the likelihood your customer will not give you a review.

5. If you have the customer's email address, follow up your initial request three days later with a reminder email containing links of where to go for review submissions. Reminder emails can account for a huge percentage of review conversions.

6. Don't setup a kiosk in your business. Funny thing is that some companies allow people to login to their Gmail and leave a comment right there in the business. The problem is, that all the reviews come from the same IP address. Even though they are valid, most SPAM filters and Google will see that they came from the same IP address and think they are being spammed.

> **Tip:** I have often heard from business owners they feel embarrassed when asking customers for reviews. If that sounds like you, my advice is to be totally candid with your customers. In other words, under promise and over deliver and hope for good reviews. One good way is to tell your clients that you are working on improving your business and online reviews are a good way to do this. I have found that this kind of candidness makes the asker feel better about asking for reviews, which improves the chances of actually getting them.

If you still can't figure out the review thing there are several companies out there that would be glad to help you such as the following:

1. CustomerLobby

2. CustomerRating

3. DemandForce

4. Ratepoint

Link Juice

The term "link juice," refers to the voting power that a link passes to a page in which it links. The fact is only Google knows exactly how much link juice is getting passed on from each link on a page. However, there are some basic factors we can use to determine how valuable a given link will be. Look for links with these qualities for better results:

- The page is relevant to your content.

- The link from the page to your page has a good anchor text.

- The other outgoing links on the page look relevant and appear to be to quality sites.

- The text around the link that you will receive is relevant. The page has been recently cached by Google, within the month. To check the cached date please see the instructions in Chapter 3.

- The page is a respected or authority page such as a charity, news, educational or government website.

Sidebar: The Orphan Page Link Test

An orphan page is a page that has no links from any other page and hence cannot be found by search engines. If you want to test if Google learns links. Place a link to the orphan page.

The next time Google indexes your page with the link to the orphan page, check to see if the orphan page was indexed by the search engines. If your orphan page gets indexed by Google, then there is a good chance the page you are testing is passing on link juice.

In site Linking

It's easy to focus only on inbound links, but there are important best practices for linking within your site as well:

Sitemaps – Have one. If not for your visitors, for search engines. It's rough for search engines to have to drill down and find all that content. Make it easy for them. Oh, and keep it updated! Secondly you need to make sure that you have a site map for the search engines. Preferably an XML site map which you list the location in your Robots.txt file as well as upload it to Google Webmaster Tools.

Anchor text within content – This may be even more important for onsite links than for offsite links. You have full control of your anchor text, so use it. Plus your site theme is already in place, so each link will have complete, natural relevance to the page it points to.

Breadcrumbs – Are a little piece of search engine love. Breadcrumbs are not only helpful for navigation, but search engines can pick up great anchor text from them. Breadcrumbs are the navigation elements that large sites use to help categorize content, and allow you to find your way back to core categories if you lose your way.

Featured products, news, etc. – Links from your homepage are, in general, considered more important than links from other parts of your site. So if you've got something you really want to show off, it makes sense to put it on your homepage, not only for usability, but for search engines as well.

Links to yourself – Link to your product or service pages from your own blogs, articles, resource sections, news releases, or any other relevant pages. Use the anchor text within each of these resources to send a little link love to your core pages. So, for example, if you sell toothbrushes, and you write a blog post about correct brushing practices, link the word tooth brushes from your blog post to your main toothbrush product page.

Directories

A directory is not a search engine, although the two types of sites are sometimes confused. A search engine finds its content by "crawling the web" via little roving programs called search engine spiders or robots.

A directory works completely differently than a search engine. A directory does not find content. It waits for you to bring the content to it. You submit your site, a human editor reviews and approves the site, and the directory includes your site URL under a category link (real estate sites, writing sites, baseball sites, whatever). Users can find sites by drilling down through categories and viewing lists of related sites. Many directories are *search*able, but that does not make them *search* engines.

Directories have been around for a long time, and submitting your site to directories used to be all the rage in search engine optimization. You'll still find plenty of services out there advertising that they will submit you to 1000's of directories. But like all SEO practices that have been overdone, mass directory submission doesn't work like it used to. That does not mean, however, that directory submission is dead. It just means that you have to do your due diligence before submitting to directories. Some of the directories I suggest are:

- Best of the Web – botw.org
- Librarians Internet Index - www.lii.org
- Yahoo Directory – directory.yahoo.com
- Business.com
- Jayde.com
- Open Directory — dmoz.org
- Joe Ant — joeant.com
- Starting Point – stpt.com/directory

Social Bookmarking Sites

To get your links on social bookmarking sites, all you have to do is create a profile and post them. That part is pretty easy. Getting people to bookmark or vote for your links can be the tricky part.

To get people to bookmark or vote for your links, you need to be patient, and you need to be active on your chosen bookmarking site(s). Find other people with similar interests and colleagues that you already know. Share their links. They will be more likely to pay attention to and vote for your links in turn.

Popular bookmarking sites include:

- del.icio.us - The oldest social bookmarking website and most popular. Users can also add people to their networks and share bookmarks.

- StumbleUpon.com – Has a browser add-on for saving and sharing websites. Works with IE, and Mozilla.

- Mister-wong.com - One of my personal favorites. The layout is nice looking and user friendly. Allows you to import/export.

- Digg.com - Digg allows you to submit stories, then digg users can "Digg" the stories, and make comments. Users can also upload videos, images and podcasts.

- Propeller.com - A social news and bookmarking portal that's part of the AOL network. Stories are submitted to specific channels, and then voted on by members.

- Simpy.com - Allows users to save, tag and search bookmarks, attach notes, and browse other user's links. Links can be public or private.

- Diigo.com - Allows users to bookmark, highlight parts of web pages, tag, add notes, create and join groups. Diigo is also a collaborative research tool.

- Sphinn.com - Social bookmarking site for marketers. Allows you to share news, articles, etc., and participate in discussions

Directory Links

Search engines have not abolished directories. Google has simply gotten much stricter when it comes to acknowledging specific directories. Despite that, they are still beneficial for building page ranking and increasing traffic.

There are many different types of directories that can be of great value to your website or blog. You can search for directories on Google for good ones or for a small fee you can get your website submitted to thousands of directories by having services such as SubmissionComplete.com or WebsiteSubmitter.org do the work for you. These sites charge between $15 and $69 to perform the submissions. But it sure saves a lot of time.

Buying Text Links

This is definitely an example of what not to do. The major search engines do what they can to make sure a website's popularity is not increased by the use of paid links or link farm.

Buying links from sites that are very relevant to your website though will help you. If you've developed a reputable brand, a few paid or sponsored links could help drive traffic, and they are highly unlikely to hurt your rankings. When buying links, here are few things NOT to do:

- **DON'T** buy links from unrelated or poor quality sites.
- **DON'T** buy too many links at once. Make sure your link building looks natural (plan it out over time).
- **DON'T** purchase links from someplace that you wouldn't want to be associated with.
- **DON'T** purchase links from a page with a ton of other links on the page – try to keep the number of links on the page under 10.

Buying Links

Now, if you are not link spamming, you probably don't have to worry about this one. But, if you are purchasing large amounts of links from questionable sources, and they say they will put your links on 100's of unique domains, chances are they own all these domains. If they own all of these domains, then the domains are probably clustered on the same static IP address (The IP address of the server they host all their websites on.) Having a large number of links from the same IP address can be a warning sign to the search engines

Outgoing links

Outgoing linking is critical for blogs and websites. Many webmasters stopped linking out in order to hoard their PageRank from others in their industry but now it backfires. Having too many outgoing links can be as bad a having none. Somewhere between 15-70 outgoing links on your homepage can be healthy for a website. But this invites a lot of challenges. You need to make sure that your links going out to other websites remain valid (Not broken), they don't link to those in a bad neighborhood (porn, spammy, hate, or political sites, etc.), there are no hidden links and they generally are in the same or a related industry, local, association, or a link to a website Google might consider a possible vendor.

How Many Links Does My Site Have?

There are several tools that can let you see what links are targeting your website. I was saddened to learn Yahoo Site Explorer is going away in 2012. (https://siteexplorer.search.yahoo.com/mysites). There is only one other I highly recommend and that is Majestic SEO (http://www.majesticseo.com). Google also has a limited link report now included in their Webmaster Tools console but it only gives output on what they find relevant and I have seen their relevant links reporting to be less than 1% on some websites.

Chapter 8-Pay-Per-Click (PPC)

This chapter will focus on the top two Pay-Per-Click companies. Why? Because there were three – Google AdWords, Yahoo! Search Marketing, and Microsoft adCenter. Now however, Bing which is owned by Microsoft and is now doing advertising for Yahoo!

There are others, including MySpace and Facebook, but these are the two with the greatest reach for your money. Between the two they represent both a majority of the directories and search engines on the internet.

Pay-per-click marketing is an advertising method that enables you to buy search engine placement by bidding on keywords or phrases. When people search using your chosen keywords, and you have bid an amount that will place you on a page a user is looking at, your ad will appear in the sponsored listings to the right or above the organically-placed websites, regardless of how your site ranks on any search engine.

Now before we start, PPC management is an exact science and I don't recommend that you do this yourself. There is a reason why there are companies that do PPC management for a fee.

If you aren't organically at the top of the search engines and you are a business that relies on your website for business, then you have to use PPC to draw in visitors to your website. PPC ads are paid ads which show up at the top or the sides of search engine listings and are sometimes called "Sponsored Listings." They also are placed on websites and other search engines associated with the search engine you are doing your marketing on.

Should I continue PPC after I have good organic placement?

The answer is yes! There are many reasons. Number one is you cannot guarantee that your organic placement will stay at the top. There are always other competing companies who will inevitably do their own SEO work to get ahead of your company. Sometimes a competitor will wind up in the news and all those news stories will show up before your company's listing. You could wind up on the second or third page for a month or two. Not only that, sometimes you drop down the organic list for no apparent reason at all.

This can really hurt sales and is sometimes not noticeable right away, unless you are checking Google and Bing every day for your keywords. However, if you are always running a PPC campaign to supplement your organic listings, you'll see your company name more than once on the screen. It also guarantees that no matter what happens with your organic placement, the keywords used on your PPC campaign will always be there.

If you are looking for a company to do your PPC campaign, there are some qualifying questions you should ask:

- How long has this company been around? You don't want a company that is new to the industry. Find out how much experience the owners have.
- What features and feature combinations does the company provide? Are there packages that include SEO, SEM, as well as PPC? Your company requirements might differ from other companies. Look at the different features and feature combinations that are offered.
- Do they have all inclusive packages or is this a service that has no fixed costs? If they don't have a fixed cost, you may be getting a bill for far more than you could ever imagine.
- How many campaigns can you run simultaneously? Some PPC management companies restrict the number of PPC campaigns you can run at any one time. Others have restrictions on the types of campaigns you can run as they only do local campaigns and not national or international ones.
- Does the company have client referrals? Client referrals are an often overlooked aspect of PPC company research. There should be a plethora of clients that are satisfied by the company. I know that with my company I have a list of 25 clients or so I like to give as referrals. Each one will tell you that our services are unbelievable.

Some companies have dozens or even hundreds of pay-per-click campaigns running at any given time. Keeping up with all those ads and campaigns can be a real challenge; if it's not your core capability, it could take you away from activities that would be more profitable for your company.

In fact, I have two companies I manage which have two project managers to keep track of the campaigns. There are daily tasks that require companies to hire PPC management firms to take care of the daily tasks involved in running all those PPC campaigns.

It's not as easy as signing on to Google and giving them your credit card. You can do that but you will be wasting thousands of dollars for very little results. Just like SEO, PPC is almost an exact science and it changes frequently as well.

For instance, there is keyword research, writing ad copies, tracking analytics, determining the return on investment (ROI) for each campaign, and any of the other tasks that attend pay-per-click campaigns.

Return on Investment (ROI) Formula

Return on investment (ROI) is a term that you will hear frequently throughout this chapter. It is associated with keyword advertising. PPC advertising is becoming increasingly expensive – you need a way to justify your keyword investments with solid returns and a way to measure the PPC campaign's effectiveness.

There are a number of formulas for determining the ROI. For my customers, I use a straight forward formula:

ROI = [Contribution] / [Cost]

To calculate Contribution for a PPC campaign:

([Your average profit per sale] x [Estimated number of Conversions]) – [PPC Cost]

To demonstrate, let's take the following example:

Monthly PPC Cost:	**$1,500**
Average Profit per Sale:	**50**
Number of Conversions (Sales) per Month:	**75**

This would make the break down the following:

($50 x 75) – $1500 = $2,250

So your ROI would be:

$2,250 / $1500 = 150%

The services provided by PPC management firms can cost you anywhere from about $500 per month for basic services to as much as a $250,000 flat fee for a complete campaign-management package over a specified amount of time. The question is whether it's worth it for you to pay this fee to free up your time and get the right expertise involved.

For a successful campaign, the answer is most likely "yes." A PPC management firm might be just what you need to help reduce the burden of managing single or multiple PPC campaigns and doing the job right. Just make sure you know what you're getting into before you sign a contract.

Since there is no contract yet, let's look at how to start your own campaign with Google AdWords and the Microsoft adCenter in the next few sections.

The funny thing about this section is that it went through major changes in 2009 and virtually every new SEO book I picked up, even the ones for 2011 have the old AdWords screens in their books and giving all the wrong information.

Oh, and another thing that people sometimes get confused about. Many people mistakenly believe that PPC and paid-inclusion (PI) services are the same type of marketing, but there are major differences. For starters, paid-inclusion services are used by some search engines to enable website owners to pay a one-year subscription fee to ensure that their site is indexed with that search engine at all times.

This fee doesn't guarantee any specific rank in search engine results; it only guarantees that the site is indexed by the search engine. PPC costs money when a searching user clicks on a link advertised in the sponsored listings of a page. You pay each time a user clicks on the link to your site or landing page.

Google AdWords

Since Google still has a leading edge over all the other major search engines combined, it makes sense that AdWords is the PPC component you hear the most often. AdWords is a challenge even for the most informed and talented. I cannot tell you how many times an I.T. guru from a company came into my office to inquire about having us manage their ad campaigns. They tell of how they have spent thousands on AdWords campaigns and got a lot of clicks but never a sale or very few sales. Why? Because it is again almost an exact science from the keywords you choose, the wording of your ad, bidding for placement, all the way to the landing page that each ad goes to.

Most think they can learn it all from an eBook they bought online or bought at a store. It is very easy to give your credit card to Google and wind up with a $1,500.00 bill and not a single phone call if you don't know what you are doing.

One of the biggest stumbling blocks is when you choose too broad of a keyword. I will give you an example. One of my clients owns a private gym here in Tualatin, Oregon. He tried his own PPC campaign and chose every keyword he could think of remotely related to gyms, exercise, and equipment. Less than two weeks later he noticed his credit card had been billed $500 (Google bills the card every time the amount reaches $500) seven times for a total of $3,500 by the time he got his credit card statement, with not one call that he could think of. He had been expecting to spend around $250.00 per month.

You can imagine his frustration and disbelief. It didn't deter him, but he tried some other things and set limits. Month after month he increased those limits until it matched what he was spending on telephone book ads, which did nothing for him anymore. Month after month, no results but lots of clicks. To the tune of $2,000. Which was spent usually within the first 10-14 days of the month.

He sat down with us and we took a look at some of the things he was doing with his PPC campaign. He was using 44 keywords which we reduced down to only 12. Because he had no clue about researching keyword costs he chose keywords that were at a national level and not local, but also had so much competition that he spent up to $25.00 for a single click!

Keep this rule in mind. Placement costs for ads is based on how much competition there is for a keyword. You actually bid on placement for those keywords. If there is a lot of competition you can spend a fortune quick.

His next major problem was that he chose words such as "exercise equipment" and "gym membership." These are great keywords on a national level but you have people all over the nation clicking on his ads and they live in other states or nowhere close to Tualatin, Oregon. So he wasted his money on people clicking on his ads who would never become a customer or even bother to call.

Next issue is that "exercise equipment" is too broad and there is too much competition. Someone searching for "exercise equipment" might be looking to buy exercise equipment, to repair exercise equipment, or to donate exercise equipment. They might be looking for new exercise equipment or used exercise equipment. The list goes on. The point I am trying to make: very few of those clicking were looking to get a gym membership.

Keep in mind that he had 30 more words that had similar or less critical flaws. I didn't mean to make this sound like a sales pitch but the fact is, if you are not expert, don't try to make yourself one overnight.

I now handle all of SEO and PPC campaigns for Mark Romine, the owner of the gym I mentioned above. Mark spent virtually every hour of his workday for an entire two months to try and get his campaign done right and failed. He graciously allowed me to use his name in this book on the condition that I printed this statement:

> *"If you use my name, make sure your readers know that as a business owner, they should spend their time doing other things selling and growing their business. I wasted more than $7,500 trying to do an AdWords [campaign] before one of my customers recommended Mike Monahan at MikeMonahanSEO.com.*
>
> *You guys get the results I wanted and more for about $500.00 per month. I get 500 times the business from my website then I do from the *** telephone book which I spend $2,100 per month on by the way."*

He went on to state why he still had to keep an ad but basically it was because he has a senior demographic which is about the only demographic besides the telephone ad sales people that crack open a telephone book.

Now being the biggest doesn't always mean being the best. When you're evaluating the different PPC companies you might use, be sure to check not only the traffic rate, but also the conversion rate, if possible. It's great if your ads receive a lot of impressions. If those impressions do not turn to clicks, you'll find that your PPC campaign is not at all effective.

> **NOTE:** *An impression is every time someone performs a search on one of your chosen keywords and your ad is displayed on the screen. Google tracks this information as well as the clicks. Also tracked are the numbers of times a particular keyword was clicked on, the ad that was used when it was clicked, and the cost.*
>
> *Another thing to note is that if you have more than one ad for the keywords you use, Google will alternate between them in the beginning. If, however, a particular ad is clicked on more often, Google will automatically show on the more popular ad a greater percentage of the time and will sometimes stop creating impressions of the non-performing ad altogether.*

One thing that many people don't know is that Google also offers TV, newspaper, and embedded-video advertising. Even the radio and phone models of AdWords are charged on a bid-per-keyword basis. To make things even more complicated, AdWords is linked to Google's AdSense program, which is an advertisement publishing program whereby website owners place ads on their websites with similar relevancy to your ads – sometimes competing sites. When users click through those ads and make purchases, the website owner is paid a small amount. Many website owners use this service to help offset the cost of having a site or to make money.

So if you place an ad with Google, your ad may show in the results of an AOL search, Ask.com, and Netscape as well. This helps give Google AdWords one of the largest markets available for keyword advertisements.

A larger market, however, does not necessarily mean better results or a guarantee of higher-quality leads. With Google AdWords, it is essential that you pay attention to the details that help place your ads, and use them to your advantage so they are the most effective. As an example, when doing research for a fire and safety company that I do the SEO and PPC for, we realized that there was so much competition and the cost was so great on Google that Microsoft's adCenter made more sense.

The competition for the fire- and safety-related keywords was primarily focused on Google and was quite low on Bing and its related search engines. Although there are less clicks, the ratio of competing websites to clicks gave my client an advantage. We still use the keywords on Google AdWords but we focus on Microsoft adCenter results and it is really paying off for the client, who now has a 5 to 1 ratio some months – at a much lower cost. Giving the customer a great ROI.

Signing up for Google AdWords

Signing up for Google AdWords is quick and easy. You can get there by going to http://www.google.com/services and choosing the link to AdWords or the "Get Started" button, as shown in Figure 8.1.

Figure 8.1

If you have a Google account you can enter it and sign it. Otherwise you need to choose "Start Now" and create an account, as shown in Figure 8.2 on the next page.

Figure 8.2

If you press "Start Now," you are given the option of using an existing Google account or creating a new account specifically for AdWords. After selecting, login as shown in Figure 8.3.

Google AdWords Express

Create an Account

Your Google Account gives you access to Google Places and other Google services. If you already have a Google Account, you can sign in here.

Required information for Google account

Your current email address:	
	e.g. myname@example.com. This will be used to sign-in to your account

Choose a password: _____ Password strength:
Minimum of 8 characters in length.

Re-enter password: _____

☑ Stay signed in

☑ Enable Web History Learn More

Get started with Google Places

Default Homepage ☑ Set Google as my default homepage.
Your default homepage in your browser is the first page that appears when you open your browser.

Location: United States

Birthday: _____
MM/DD/YYYY (e.g. "1/22/2012")

Word Verification: Type the characters you see in the picture below.

Figure 8.3

Your next screen allows you to set the country, time zone, and the type of currency you use, as shown in Figure 8.4. You have to remember that Google is a worldwide search engine and not just a U.S. search engine.

Set time zone and currency preferences

To set up your AdWords account, we need to know your time zone and currency (This is the currency you'll use to pay Google, not the currency you use in transactions with your customers).

Select a permanent time zone for your account.
This will be the time zone for all your account reporting and billing.

Time zone country or territory: United States   ▼

Time zone: (GMT-08:00) Pacific Time   ▼

Select a permanent currency for your account.
Review the available payment options for local currencies before you decide. Not all currencies are available in all areas.

US Dollar (USD $)   ▼

Your time zone and currency settings can't be changed after you setup your account.
Please review your choices carefully and then click 'Continue.'

Back | Continue

Figure 8.4

After you press "Continue," your AdWords account is created.

Figure 8.5

Press the link "Sign into your AdWords account." You are redirected to login, as shown in Figure 8.5.

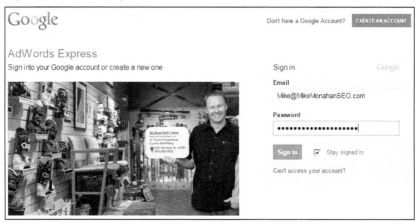

Figure 8.5

When you first login, it will give you the option to learn more about Google AdWords in Figure 8.6. Keep in mind that there is useful information on the links, but in my opinion, it gives you just enough information to be dangerous. The instructions teach you get the broadest range of clicks that makes Google the most amount of money.

Figure 8.6

If you look at the right of the screen, you have the option to create your first campaign. Click here and begin, as shown in Figure 8.7.

Figure 8.7

Keep in mind, this is one of Google's primary income sources and there are a lot of stockholders to pay.

Then you begin the registration process, which configures the basic edition of AdWords. The basic edition is great if you have never used a PPC program before. It includes one set of keywords, basic reporting capabilities, and basic targeting.

> **Note:** *At the bottom of the screen of Figure 8.8 there is an option to create Advanced Campaigns. This type of campaign is for very experienced users and creates multiple sets of keywords and more advanced targeting and reporting, in addition to a few other tools.*

You can begin with the basic starter edition, then you can graduate to the advanced campaign when you are ready. When you do, your starter campaign will be moved to your new AdWords account, so you don't lose any of your existing advertisements.

Next, Google wants to know about your business, as shown in Figure 8.9. This is to give you advice on the types of ads you should run.

Get advice for success

Step 1 of 2: Tell us about your business
Answer the questions below to get customized advice for setting up your account.

Do you offer more than one product or service?
Examples: televisions, cameras, computers
⊙ Yes ⊙ No

Do you offer different products or services to customers based on their location?
Examples: retailer that offers different products in North America and Europe, restaurant that only delivers in New York City
⊙ Yes ⊙ No

Do you want to advertise in more than one language?
Examples: bookstore with selections in both English and Spanish, translation service
⊙ Yes ⊙ No

See our advice   Skip this step and create your first campaign now

Figure 8.8

The questions in figure 8.8 are primarily for novice users. There is a link to disregard Google's advice and go straight to the campaign. I am going to move on and create a campaign for my spectacular, make-believe excavating company called "Los Angeles Excavating Contractors, Inc." as shown in figure 8.9.

Select campaign settings

General

Campaign name: Portland Furniture Stuff #1

Locations, Languages, and Demographics

Locations: In what geographical locations do you want your ads to appear?
- Bundle: All countries and territories
- Bundle: United States, Canada
- Country: United States
- State: Oregon, US
- ⦿ Metro area: Portland OR, US
- City: Portland, OR, US

Select one or more other locations

You can show additional location information with your ads. After you've created your campaign, return to the Settings tab to add location information to the campaign.

Languages: What languages do your customers speak?
English Edit

Demographic (advanced)

Figure 8.9

I can also choose an additional demographic such as ages, locations, occupation and much more by clicking on the "Demographic (advanced)" option.

Next you choose where you would like your ads to be seen, as shown in Figure 8.10. This screen can also protect you from click fraud. (We will discuss click fraud more in depth later in this chapter.) If you find yourself the victim of click fraud, you can change your "Network, devices, and extensions" setting based on where the fraud is occurring.

Networks, devices, and extensions

Networks:
- All available sites (Recommended for new advertisers)
- ⦿ Let me choose...
  - Search ☑ Google search
    ☑ Search partners (requires Google search)
  - Content ☑ Content network
    - ⦿ Relevant pages across the entire network
    - Relevant pages only on the placements I manage

Devices:
- All available devices (Recommended for new advertisers)
- ⦿ Let me choose...
  - ☑ Desktop and laptop computers
  - ☑ iPhones and other mobile devices with full Internet browsers

Bidding and budget

Bidding option: Basic options | Advanced options
- ⦿ Manual bidding for clicks
  - You'll set your maximum CPC bids in the next step
- Automatic bidding to try to maximize clicks for your target budget

Budget: $ 200.00 per day
Daily budget represents your average spend over the month, actual spend on a given day may vary.

Figure 8.10

In Figure 8.11, there are some optional advanced settings. For instance, you can choose where you want your ad to show and the delivery method. The defaults are shown.

Next, you can change the dates your ad run, set the rotation frequency, and place a limit on the number of times your ad can be shown in a given time period. Why would you want this? Let's say that you have a strong ROI and too many impressions send you too much business. You can set a cap so you don't get 100 calls to your one-man business within 20 minutes after the ad begins.

Figure 8.11

Next is the hard part – trying to decide what you want your AdWords ad to say (Figure 8.12). If you don't have experience with this, you should get professional help. It is another absolute science to determine the words that draw people to click on one ad versus another. It is industry specific.

Figure 8.12

Next is the keywords. Now you may want to just use the ones you decided in Chapter 3, but you can supplement them with other keywords, even if they have a lot of competition. Keep in mind, though, that some of these keywords can be pricey and you might want to do some research using the Google's Keyword Tool we also talked about in Chapter 3. In Figure 8.13, you can see where to enter your keywords. Be sure to add them one per line.

Figure 8.13

The importance of negative keywords

Not all keywords are created equal. Therefore there are many keywords you don't want used in your PPC campaigns or you will be wasting money on people clicking on your ad and driving 'bad' traffic to your website.

In order to raise your overall quality score and prevent this 'bad' traffic, you're going to add some negative keywords at some point. Let me give you an example. Let's say you own a golfing store and you want to focus on the keyword 'golf'. When someone searches for 'golf tee time', do you want your ad to get seen or clicked on? I don't think so. If your negative keywords were '-tee' and '-time' your ad would never be displayed since you identified them as negative keywords.

You need to constantly review your keywords and think of any other words that could be associated with your words that don't apply to your business or service and add them as negative keywords or you will be losing money.

Google AdWords provides a search query report that lets you see the keywords a searcher used before clicking on your add. The good thing about the search query report is that you can add negative keywords right from the report. Just by selecting the queries that you don't want people to find your website with and hit the 'add negative keyword' button. I'd recommend doing this every few days in the beginning of any campaign and then periodically as one of your AdWords management routine depending on how much traffic you're getting. It will save you a lot of money in the long run.

Choosing Your PPC Campaign Costs

In Figure 8.14, you see where you enter in the maximum amount you wish to bid for first page placement of Google search results. Keep in mind that if you leave the spaces blank you are writing a blank check. You will automatically outbid your competition. It will add up quickly, trust me – especially for those competitive keywords.

Figure 8.14

158

Next you have to fund your account by clicking "Save and continue to billing" (Figure 8.14). Billing simply means that you provide Google with a credit card number that they can use to charge your monthly advertising costs.

I would like to say that once you fund the account, your ads will begin showing immediately. But that is not true. Typically it takes Google about 2-3 days to approve or reject your add based on the content of your add. Google wants the ad to contain no foul language or email addresses, as well as many other published and unpublished rules.

Once your ad is approved, it will start immediately. However, in my experience, you only get a few hundred impressions the first week or so before it really kicks in and starts working. So don't expect to start AdWords today and get calls tomorrow.

Monitoring Your Campaign

The Campaign Management tab is where you'll perform most of the tasks to manage your account and see the results of your money and control the costs of your ads, as shown in Figure 8.15. This tab contains an overview of the campaigns that you have running, as well as links to an account snapshot, tools for managing your accounts, conversion tracking tools, and a website optimizer.

Figure 8.15

The Ad groups tab allows you to create groups for ad campaigns and see a more detailed look at the monetary settings, as shown in Figure 8.16.

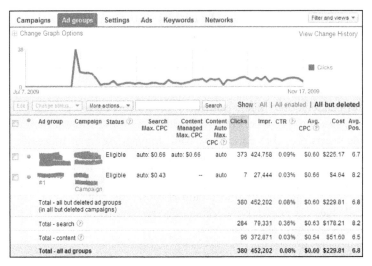

Figure 8.16

The Settings tab shown in Figure 8.17 allows you to change all the settings that were displayed in Figure 8.16. Simply click on any of the Budget options and it will allow you to change them.

The Ads tab shows the ads you have and how many clicks each ad received.

The Keywords tab allows you to see what keywords were clicked on and how many times they were shown. You can also change the keywords you are using by adding or removing them.

The Networks tab (as shown in Figure 8.17) shows information on where your ad was click on and whether it was on Google.com or another one of their partner sites.

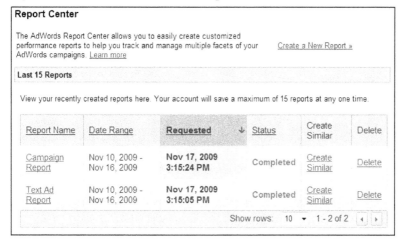

All online campaigns							
Messages Q Alerts (1)				Jul 7, 2009 - Nov 17, 2009			
	Clicks	Impr.	CTR ⑦	Avg. CPC ⑦	Cost	Avg. Pos.	
Search	284	79,347	0.36%	$0.63	$178.21	8.2	
Google search	222	40,942	0.54%	$0.62	$137.77	8.1	
Search partners ⑦	62	38,405	0.16%	$0.65	$40.44	8.3	
Content	96	374,140	0.03%	$0.54	$51.60	6.5	
Managed placements ⑦ show details	0	0	0.00%	$0.00	$0.00	0	
Automatic placements ⑦ show details	96	374,140	0.03%	$0.54	$51.60	6.5	
Total - All networks	380	453,487	0.08%	$0.60	$229.81	6.8	

Figure 8.17

At the top of the Google AdWords screen there are a few more options. In the next few sections, let's take a look at the Reporting tab, the Billing tab, and the My account tab.

Reporting Tab

Click on the Reporting tab, and then choose Reports. You'll arrive at the Report Center screen, as shown in Figure 8.18. You can see existing reports and the links to create new reports.

Report Center

The AdWords Report Center allows you to easily create customized performance reports to help you track and manage multiple facets of your AdWords campaigns. Learn more   Create a New Report »

Last 15 Reports

View your recently created reports here. Your account will save a maximum of 15 reports at any one time.

Report Name	Date Range	Requested ↓	Status	Create Similar	Delete
Campaign Report	Nov 10, 2009 - Nov 16, 2009	**Nov 17, 2009** 3:15:24 PM	Completed	Create Similar	Delete
Text Ad Report	Nov 10, 2009 - Nov 16, 2009	**Nov 17, 2009** 3:15:05 PM	Completed	Create Similar	Delete

Show rows: 10 ▾   1 - 2 of 2   ◂ ▸

Figure 8.18

There used to be only three reports you could run: the Statistical, Financial, and Conversion reports. Google has come a long way, as you can see in

Figure 8.19, which shows all the reports that are currently available. Each report is also customizable with many options.

1. Report Type
Choose a report from the following options: Learn more about report types

◉ Placement / Keyword Performance	View performance data for keywords or placements you've specifically targeted.
○ Ad Performance	View performance data for each of your ads.
○ URL Performance	View performance data for each of your Destination URLs.
○ Ad Group Performance	View ad group performance data for one or more of your campaigns.
○ Campaign Performance	View performance data for your campaigns.
○ Account Performance	View performance data for your entire account.
○ Demographic Performance	View performance data for sites by demographic.
○ Geographic Performance	View performance data by geographic origin.
○ Search Query Performance	View performance data for search queries which triggered your ad and received clicks.
○ Placement Performance ⑦	View performance data for content network sites where your ad has been shown.
○ Reach and Frequency Performance ⑦	View reach and frequency performance data for your campaigns.

Figure 8.19

Billing Tab

This tab allows you to keeping track of your invoices, billing information, account access, and account preferences.

This tab provides you with two options. Select either Billing Summary (which shows your payment type, the amount of the last payment, your current balance, and the current charges for each campaign), or Billing Preferences (which allows you to change the way you are billed or the credit card information on file).

My Account Tab

This tab allows you to change those Google accounts that can access your AdWords account and reports, as shown in figure 8.20. It also allows you to change your time zone, language, PhamacyChecker ID, or tracking options; get the Google AdWords terms and conditions; manage your business hosted page at Google Sites; or cancel your AdWords account altogether.

Account Access
If you manage this AdWords account with others, see who has access to sign in. Invite others to create their own login email and password to access this account by clicking 'Invite other users.' Learn more
[+ Invite other users]

Users with account access

Adwords user	Last logged in ⑦	Access level ⑦	Actions
▓▓▓▓▓▓▓▓▓	Nov 16, 2009	Administrative access	Actions ▾

Figure 8.20

Figure 8.21

Common AdWords Issues

No one really likes to be told they are doing something wrong. Over and over again however, I see our clients making the same mistakes over and over when they set up their accounts for AdWords, Here is a list of the most common mistakes.

1. **Using geo-modified keywords in your geo-targeted campaigns**

    What does this mean? If you have a pizza restaurant in Los Angeles California and you are using geo-targeted campaigns leave the word "Los Angeles" out of the "pizza restaurant" key term.
    This can result in a lot less traffic, since there is a strong chance the ads will not display due to a "geo-targeting mismatch." One solution for this: use geo-modified keywords only in campaigns *not* using geo-targeting.

2. **Duplicating keywords across ad campaigns**

   What does this mean? When you run more than one campaign selling something don't target the same keywords. If you have two ads competing for the same keyword you are bidding against yourself and bringing the cost up for that keyword for both ads.

   When you have a good keyword, it may seem like a smart move to spread the goodness around to all of your ad groups and campaigns. However, duplicating keywords won't help your performance.

3. **Jumping the gun**

   What does this mean? Give your bids a chance. Many times, we have seen advertisers make bid adjustments, or pause or delete keywords well before enough data has been collected to make an educated decision. For example, your cost-per-acquisition (CPA) target might be $30, and because you think your keyword isn't giving you enough impressions or clicks, you pause it or increase your bidding amount. Our experience has shown that many advertisers do this too quickly. A good rule of thumb is that if you haven't reached your $30 or the amount that you set for your target wait and judge.

4. **Putting your phone number in your ad**

   What does this mean? Why wouldn't you want to give your prospects another way to contact you and save money on a click? At first it sounds like bad logic, however a phone number in your ad can decrease your click-through rate and quality index score, which in turn drives up your cost-per-click and pushes the ad further down in Google results.

   The basic rule is that Google displays ads that get clicked on more often and charges them less.

This book isn't really about PPC campaigns and we just barely touched on Google AdWords. There is so much to learn. Now let's take a look at the Microsoft AdCenter .

Microsoft adCenter

Microsoft adCenter, formerly MSN AdCenter, is Microsoft's advertising program. PPC ads through Microsoft adCenter are distributed on Bing, MSN, Live, Yahoo and many other smaller search engines.

Go to **http://advertising.microsoft.com/home** to setup an account, as shown in Figure 8.22.

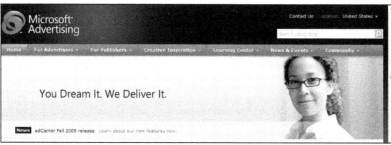

Figure 8.22

If you already have an account, go to **https://adcenter.microsoft.com**

Default.aspx, as shown in figure 8.23.

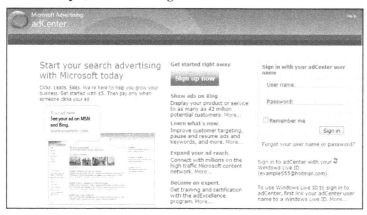

Figure 8.23

There is a new guide which explains all the new features of the Microsoft adCenter:

http://advertising.microsoft.com/wwdocs/user/en-us/learningcenter/adCenter_2009_Fall_Upgrade_Feature_Guide_US.pdf

In Figure 8.24, you see a list from Microsoft.com which explains the new features of the Microsoft adCenter.

Top 5 Features

- **Search Query Performance Report**

  The Search Query Performance Report will pull reports that contain the actual queries that users perform that resulted in your ad being clicked. This report will provide you with information to help you manage your keyword lists by adding keywords that are aligned with actual user queries, in addition to identifying potential negative keywords to add.

- **Default Time Zone**

  The Default Time Zone feature will allow you to set a default or preferred time zone at the account level. Additionally, this feature will require a campaign level time zone to be selected in order to proceed with campaign creation if a default time zone has not been entered at the account level. This allows you to have the appropriate time zone aligned with every campaign.

- **Ad Preview Tool**

  The Ad Preview tool was added in advance of the Fall 2009 Upgrade, but it is being moved from the Campaigns tab to the new Tools tab with the fall upgrade. The Ad Preview tool assists you in confirming that your ads are showing on Bing without incurring unnecessary impressions or accidental clicks.

- **Agency Invitation and Termination**

  adCenter advertisers will be able to invite an agency to manage their adCenter account. When an advertiser invites an agency to manage their account, they will be inviting the agency to manage all of their accounts; there will be no capability to invite an agency to manage only specific accounts or campaigns.

- **Managing Multiple Accounts**

  The Customer Selection page included in the Fall 2009 Upgrade will ease the pain of agencies, SEMs and large organizations, and help them efficiently manage all of their accounts in adCenter.

Figure 8.24

Setting up your Microsoft adCenter account is slightly different from setting up a Google AdWords account. One of the first differences is that Microsoft wants $5.00 and your billing information up front, even before you create a first campaign ad. The setup fee of $5.00 is charged to the credit card you provide for payment and charged immediately to your account.

Once you have provided billing information, you can begin to set up your first Microsoft adCenter campaign ad. When you sign into adCenter, you're taken to a general page that includes five tabs, which you can use to manage your adCenter ads. These tabs are Home, Campaign, Accounts & Billing, Tools, and Reports as seen in Figure 8.25.

Figure 8.25

Home Tab

In Figure 8.25, you see the Home tab which shows your campaigns, account information, Alerts, What's New and FAQ's. This is the screen you see when you immediately go into your Microsoft adCenter account.

Campaign

The Campaign tab in the Microsoft adCenter (as shown in Figure 8.26) is similar to the Google AdWords Campaign tab. When you click the Campaign tab, you are given an overview page, where you can create or import PPC campaigns. To create a campaign, click the Create Campaign button to start the creation process.

Figure 8.26

To keep you from getting bored, I am not going to walk you through the creation process because you are asked to provide all the same information that we just went through for creating a Google AdWords campaign.

One thing is a little different in the adCenter campaign creation process, however: the importing capability is unique to the Microsoft adCenter. Using this capability, you can import PPC ads that you've created in Microsoft Excel or another spreadsheet program. If the ads were not created in Excel, you need to save the file as a .csv file for importing.

Accounts & Billing Tab

The Accounts & Billing tab is where you will find the financial information for your PPC accounts. From this page you have access to access and configure your company information, create a Business Page, configure users, change payment methods, get your billing statements and identify a client-agency relationship to identify a company that is handling your PPC campaign.

Tools Tab

The Tools tab is used for maintaining your PPC campaigns with research and other tools. The Tools tab in adCenter gives you tools to help generate a keyword list, an ad Preview Tool to see what your ad will look like, and a Microsoft Excel 2007 Add-in tool to create campaigns.

Reports Tab

The final tab in the adCenter console is the Reports tab. When you click the Reports tab, you are taken to the Create New Report page, where you can do just that. Once you've created a first report, it will appear on the Recent Reports tab with any other reports that you may have created.

You don't need to create a new report type each time you need to generate one. Simply save the report as a template; and then the next time you want to run a report, select the template during the report creation process. The list of reports you can create is shown in Figure 8.27.

Figure 8.27

There are certain instances where Microsoft adCenter can outperform Google AdWords, particularly since so many people formulate their marketing efforts toward Google and have not taken advantage of Microsoft's adCenter.

Many organizations use more than one PPC campaign provider. Using multiple PPC vendors means better coverage with your PPC ad, which can lead to better conversion rates and a better ROI.

Before You Begin Using PPC

There are several things to consider before you being a PPC campaign. Because you're paying for placement or advertising space for your keywords, you're not necessarily going to get the best results with all the keywords or phrases that you choose.

In some cases you must continuously test and evaluate to see which keywords draw in the demographic that will buy your product or service. I recommend that you begin small, with a minimal number of keywords, to see how the search engine you've selected performs. You can also see the results and determine what it costs for first page placement of your sponsored ads.

You should also be able to gauge what it costs to run a campaign in terms of the amount of traffic it delivers and how well that traffic converts into paying customers as well. Even if you make two sales you can gauge and average how many clicks it took to make a sale and the cost.

Having a method in place that enables you to track your return on investment is imperative. If your goal is to bring new subscribers to your website, you'll want to track the conversions, perhaps by directing the visitors funneled to your site by your PPC link to a landing page set up just for them.

 You can then monitor how many clicks came to that page in Google Analytics. This is easy to track if you have a special phone number or sales page setup for users coming from your PPC campaign. All this together will allow you to quickly track your ROI and to determine how much you're paying for each new conversion or sale.

Questions to Ask Before You Begin a Campaign

Before investing a lot of time and money into a PPC service, you may want to review a few different PPC Management services to determine which is the best one for you. If you choose to do it yourself you can gauge your readiness by seeing if you can answer these basic question:

1. How many searches are conducted each month through the search engine for which you're considering a PPC program for the keywords you have chosen?
2. What is the competition versus the number of searches for each keyword you have selected?
3. Does the search engine have major partners or affiliates that could contribute to the volume of traffic you're hoping to get?
4. How does the search engine or PPC program prevent fraudulent activity?
5. Is there recourse to get a refund or help with the investigation if click fraud occurs?
6. Do you know what to look for to determine if click fraud is occurring?
7. How difficult is it to file a report about fraudulent activity and how quickly is the issue addressed?
8. Do you have control over where your listing appears on the search engine?
9. Can you choose to have your listing withheld from affiliate searches or websites?
10. Can you limit the amount you spend by day or by a particular search?
11. Do you know what your PPC campaign budget will allow?

12. Do you have time to learn PPC in depth?
13. Do you have the time to monitor your PPC campaign daily?

Some search engines and websites have strict guidelines about how sites appear in their searches, on their website, how partners and affiliates calculate visits, and how fraud is handled.

You need to think of these before you start. If you cannot answer the questionnaire with reasonable certainty that you can handle the task, it is more cost effective to have a professional run your PPC campaign.

If you are not up to the task, you could be stuck paying for clicks that didn't actually happen or are of no use and cost more than you can afford.

PPC Advertisement Text

The text of your PPC advertisement is the single most important element in determining the success or failure of your PPC campaign. Don't get confused. The optimization of your site for SEO and PPC advertising are two *separate* activities.

In fact the closest thing that ties them together are that they both use the same keywords. Choosing those keywords for both your SEO and PPC campaign does determine your success or failure in both.

Those chosen keywords should lead your targeted demographic (also known as qualified visitors) to your site through direct links. A successfully researched and implemented SEO strategy defines and optimizes your site for keywords relevant to the site topic that help visitors to find you by using search engines.

The combination of SEO and PPC ensures that your site is drawing *qualified visitors*. Once you understand the relationship between PPC and SEO, you can begin to consider what it takes to make PPC ads successful. It all starts with the right advertisement text.

In PPC you should never use category words which are broad. Category words are those that can relate to many things that your website doesn't provide. Let us consider the example we used earlier where one of the keywords for the local gym was "exercise equipment." Well, that broad category keyword could get people to see your ad and click if they are trying to buy equipment or sell equipment or repair equipment. Want to pay for the useless click from those people?

Product words are more specific (think long-tail), and these are the words that people search for when they're ready to make a purchase. For example, keywords that make up a better long-tail word for a Los Angeles Gym are "la gym", "la racquetball," or "la fitness center":

Sidebar: Avoiding negative keywords

Negative keywords are words that cause a PPC ad *not* to be shown. These are words that can be associated with the topic that you're targeting, but not with the specific product or service that you are trying to advertise.

For example, if your website sells classical music, you should never use keywords such as country, heavy metal, or "rap." Most of the search engines are now smart enough to flag those words as negative keywords and reduce the number of times that your ad is shown.

It's important to keep your keywords grouped together if you are using different landing pages of your website. It's these words that you will be working with as you create your keyword advertisement text for each set of keywords.

Note: *Using your keywords in your advertisement text can increase your advertisement click-through rates by as much as 50 percent.*

It always helps if you write down several clear sentences that express the message you want visitors to see. Just brainstorm and get the ideas written down. Make sure you include the benefits of your product or service as well. You should also write down several benefits that might draw in your searching demographic.

There is a way to cheat. See what words and phrases your competition are using by researching your keywords on Google or Bing and looking at the ads your competition is using.

Writing Your Ad

Now that we have your list, we need to set the tone for the demographic we are looking for. For example, there is a big difference between the teenage generation and the senior generation. If you're trying to reach teens for video game sales, you'll want to write your advertisement in a language that attracts them. On the other hand, if you are trying to reach seniors, your slogan might be something more old-fashioned.

You shouldn't try to reach everyone with one ad. If you do, you'll probably be reaching no one at all. Each demographic should have its own unique guidelines for ad text, and you should take the time to learn the requirements for the PPC campaign you need to create.

You should write and create your ad to be relevant and compelling. Here are some tips to help you:

- Include keywords in your ad text.

- Tell your potential visitors exactly what you offer and why they want it.

- Don't exaggerate claims regarding the benefits of your products or services.

- Instruct your potential visitors to action saying things like "Click now!"

- Create a sense of urgency if possible. Such as "Discount today only," "limited availability," or "offer expires soon."

- Draw valid demographics, not views. The purpose in PPC advertisement is to draw potential visitors to your site, not just get clicks.

- Use long full sentences and abbreviate when possible. Try to cut only non-keywords.

- Use strong, motivating words – you'll have a very limited amount of space in which to write your ad.

- Experiment endlessly. If your PPC ad is perfect right out of the gate, it will truly be an anomaly. Trust me.

You'll likely find yourself readjusting the ad you create frequently because of changes in your products or services. Set aside at least an hour or two a day to put into your PPC ad campaign, especially in the beginning. Only through experimentation and testing can you achieve PPC success and not break the bank..

Getting the Most out of PPC

As a website owner you are always trying to get new and old customers back to our site. We want those human visitors to come to our websites and to buy what we are selling. To entice new customers to your website you cannot rely on your site being on the top of the search engines with no competition all the time.

Having a consistent PPC campaign is essential. Not only that but you can target your PPC campaign toward many more keywords than you can optimize your site for and make changes quickly and effectively.

We have learned in this chapter the effectiveness of the PPC Model, which is the most popular advertising model. Pay-Per-Click is exactly what it sounds like. The advertiser bids on keywords and tells the advertising company that they will pay a certain number of cents or dollars for every click on the ad that you place on the search engine or its partner websites.

There are more places for PPC advertising than you might think. All these websites have advantages in one way or another and might be effective for your websites advertising. Here are some websites you might consider for your PPC budget:

> http://adwords.google.com/
> https://adcenter.microsoft.com/default.aspx
> http://advertising.yahoo.com/
> http://www.411web.com/
> http://www.7search.com/
> http://www.abcsearch.com/
> http://www.adbrite.com/
> http://www.ask.com/
> http://www.enhance.com/
> http://www.kanoodle.com/
> http://search.looksmart.com/
> http://www.lycos.com/
> http://www.miva.com/
> http://www.search123.com/
> http://www.searchfeed.com/

> **NOTE:** *Yahoo no longer makes the list because they are now operated by Microsoft adCenter.*

There are some disadvantages to PPC as opposed to organic SEO listings, including the high cost of bids for certain keywords, poor conversion rates on purchased clicks, and click fraud which we discussed earlier.

Impressions in Cost Per Thousands (CPM)

The Cost Per Thousand Impressions Model (CPM) is often associated with banner advertising, but can now be purchased for text ads as well. This type of advertising is available from these sources:

> **http://adwords.google.com**
>
> **http://www.realtechnetwork.com/**
>
> **http://www.joetec.net/**

Generally, per click, CPM advertising is much cheaper than PPC. It's cheaper because its effectiveness is usually less. As with any other type of advertising, you need to track click-through and conversion rates to determine if the advertising is effective for your business.

How much cheaper is it? Well, using Google AdWords, you can sometimes buy CPM advertising for as little as $2 per 1000 impressions. The major appeal of CPM advertising is its perceived low-cost, with rates ranging between $2 – $3 per 1000 impressions. Watch out though. Google could have 10,000 impressions for popular keywords in two days.

Just make sure to keep an eye on your advertising budget. From firsthand experience, I can vouch that it may appear inexpensive, but in a short time it can add up quickly.

Pay-for-Inclusion Services

Another tool that you can use to get paid results on a search engine is a service known as *paid inclusion*. Sometimes this is also called *pay for inclusion (PFI.)* Similarly there is another term called *pay per inclusion (PPI)*. It is similar although there is a small difference between the two. PFI is a strategy whereby you pay a fee, small fee to be included in a search index. This fee doesn't guarantee your ranking on the search engine. It's a simple flat fee that is usually paid annually.

PPI is a strategy in which you pay a small fee to have your websites URL included on a search engine. There is a twist however. The fee that you pay for PPI is based on the number of clicks you receive as a result of that inclusion on the search engine. Again, PPI does not guarantee your ranking on the search engine. Your only guarantee is that you will be listed on a search. Moreover, that per-click fee can often be comparatively high, in the range of $.25 to $.50 per click to your website.

Click Fraud

Say you own a website that allows Google AdWords to appear on the site. Knowing you make a profit the ads are clicked on, you go to the site whenever possible and click on the ads. Cha-ching! Money in your pocket. This would be what is known as click fraud.

Sometimes click fraud happens when a person, group of people, or automated script clicks on PPC advertisements. Because the concept of PPC is that advertisers pay each time someone clicks on their ads, this drives the cost of ads higher and higher without resulting in any conversions.

Sometimes there is no immediate monetary benefit. For example, your competition might do it just to make your costs higher. Some advertisers also believe that PPC providers commit and even encourage click fraud to drive profits. This might not be so far from the truth. Several court cases have resulted in settlements when PPC providers such as Google and Yahoo! were sued for contributing to or allowing click fraud.

Unless all the clicks come from the same IP address, it's hard to prove that click fraud is actually happening. There are many software programs, called clickbots, that can create clicks from what appear to be spoofed or different IP addresses.

In many cases, there are indicators of click fraud such as an inflated number of clicks without conversions, clicks that all occur from the same IP, the same city, or if the time of clicks is unusual. These can all be signs of click fraud.

Another good indicator for me is when the level of clicks from Google partner websites are more than half the number of clicks on the actual Google search engine website. That is a big red flag for me and when that starts happening I know to turnoff the ads on affiliate websites.

If you suspect that you are being targeted by click fraud, immediately contact the fraud department of your PPC provider. If you don't receive satisfactory results from reporting the activity, then you should consider pursuing some type of legal action or discontinue the ads that are suspect.

Click fraud in the end can cost your company thousands, even tens of thousands, of dollars and ultimately destroy your PPC advertising campaign altogether. Only close monitoring of your stats for any signs of click fraud will help prevent it.

Look at this chart in Figure 8.28. Because of constant monitoring we picked up on what appears to be an automated click fraud on day two of the fraud. Look at the figure. Can you tell the day?

Figure 8.28

We noticed the day this happened right away. We went to Google to see where they were all coming from and it was several affiliate websites. It was easy to see the huge increase in clicks. Halfway through the next day we eliminated the problem. It hurt initially but at least we didn't go bankrupt not knowing the problem was there.

Click Fraud Is a Crime

Click fraud is a crime, whether you are falsely inflating the number of click-throughs on PPC ads either for personal gain or simply as a way to harm the competition.

In an effort to insulate themselves from criminal charges and to create as many problems as possible, some advertisers will employ what are called "clickbots." These are software programs that search for and click on PPC links to drive up prices. These "clickbots" are usually automated and very often almost impossible to trace back to their owners.

Another form of click fraud are called "Paid-to-Read" searchers, also known as PTR's. Businesses actually hire readers to read and click through PPC ads online. It's much harder to track multiple individuals than to track a single individual at one location using repetitive activity or "clickbots" to commit click fraud.

Search engines are being made to answer for click fraud, and the associated costs that PPC users are having to pay because of it, causing search engines to crack down on the problem. If you get caught conducting a click-fraud scheme, you could face stout fines and possibly even a criminal prosecution that could result in jail time.

Now that your head is about to explode with all this information on PPC campaigns, let's switch gears and look at how social media can help rankings in the next chapter.

Chapter 9-Social Media

It is important to embrace Social Media and marry it with your business. Fact is, the more exposure you get, the better chance you will get an increase in profit.

The New Math:

Social Media Phobia + delay = Lost Revenue

Let's go back to my analogy in the early chapters where everything you do adds to the imaginary points value that Google and other major search engines use to assess your rankings. The more you make your website interactive, the longer people will stay. The general thinking is, the more *social media elements* you add, the more often visitors will visit and find your website relevant to its subject matter.

Search engines believe those rules mentioned in the last paragraph, so you should make social media play a big role in your website's optimization. If you are a novice you might be asking right now, "what are social media elements?" When you understand what social media elements are, it's not a long leap from there to *social-media optimization*.

Social media is content created by people using highly accessible and scalable publishing technologies. A better definition might be that social media elements are works of user-created video, audio, text or other multimedia that are published and shared in a social environment, such as a blog, wiki, or video hosting website. Well known sites that engage in social media are Google+, BlogSpot, Blogger, Twitter, YouTube, Flickr, LinkedIn, and Facebook.

Creating your own social media elements such as blogs on your website or participating in other social media websites is what brings traffic to your website and adds to your websites content. One of the best things about social media is that in general most elements are free in terms of monetary investment. There is, for the most part, no cost to participate in these networks except for your investment of time, which depending on how involved you get could become substantial.

When correctly tapped into social media, marketing spreads like a virus. This is why it is sometimes called viral marketing Viral marketing is a not a bad thing. When you participate in social-media, you can almost guarantee that your marketing will soon have that viral quality you're seeking.

Unfortunately, social-media optimization is not as simple as going to a website and signing up or starting a one paragraph blog and waiting for people to come to your website. For the most part, they won't.

Approaching social media in that manner will waste your time, and by the time you figure it out the bad reputation you may leave behind may haunt your website or domain name. Managing your reputation on the web is called *reputation management* in SEO circles and I could write another book just on this topic. I have hundreds of stories on what to look out for and stories of companies ruined on the web because of social media.

The basics to keep yourself from having a bad reputation in social networking is this: when you provide input using social media methods, make sure you do the following:

1. Provide only relative content and no exaggerated claims.
2. Add positive comments and don't make it appear as though you are trying to outdo someone else or are advertising your services. People don't forget when a faker tries to jump in their midst for purely marketing purposes. You are marketing but this is social networking. You are making friends.
3. If you are an expert, make sure your claims are accurate. There are real experts on every subject who will point out your flaws with actual data.
4. Don't ignore people's issues with your product or service. Address them immediately or you are inviting everyone who has ever had a small issue with your product or service to add their two cents.
5. Don't bad mouth a competitor – your only inviting a tidal wave of retribution from your competitor and others.

Seems easy enough, right? Social-media optimization is about first joining communities and creating relationships or friends. It's by going through the process of becoming part of the community and providing relevant and helpful information that your brand will begin to be recognized by other community members. That's when you can announce that your website has useful information, and your efforts will begin to pay off.

Social Media's Value

Some sites have obvious value in social media. Websites such as MySpace, Twitter, YouTube, and Facebook are all websites that no one thought would amount to anything when they began, but they each suddenly took off in their own way, becoming some of the most popular sites on the internet.

Internet users like something to do and to be a part of something bigger. They love to be a part of the community, and that includes online communities as well. The generation that has just entered the workforce and those growing up right now are very computer and internet savvy. For the most part, this generation has been a part of those social networking sites during their schooling. These sites have provided everything from evaluations of teachers, classes, entertainment events, self advertising, keeping up with the latest school rumors, and even schools providing their school event calendars.

When this generation is out of school they become involved in all kinds of activities online, from shopping and downloading music to participating in social networks. The kids are networking socially for different reasons than adults, but both have learned to participate.

Social-Media Strategies

So you have a website and you need to market it. Using social media is different than most marketing techniques you are taught in economics or marketing in college – At least until they stop using 15-year-old text books. Now there are thousands of sites and you can make your own social media components, but the goals are the same. In the end your goals are to:

- **Know how to target your audience and deliver the right message:** If you approach the wrong audience with the wrong message, you'll learn a quick lesson in reputation management when the court of opinion attempts to destroy your reputation.
- **Create valuable content:** Good content is key to social-media marketing. If you make it a point to create fresh, unique content regularly, visitors will come to you because they know they can find the current information they need. If you're afraid of giving away all your eggs except on a one on one sales call, you will get your message out very slowly.
- **Be a valuable resource, even if it doesn't help you monetarily:** If you try to help without expecting anything in return you gain points and you can gain a good reputation which will, in turn, draw users to your website. Always wearing your salesman hat works in the corporate world, but online it is a death sentence.
- **Be a user resource**: Internet users, and especially those users who participate in social media and social networking, expect you to provide information that is useful and relevant to them. If you're not providing accurate and helpful information, they'll go to someone who is and bad mouth you on the way.
- **Help your content spread:** One way of advertising your website's services or products discreetly is to use your trophy and long-tail keywords in your helpful tips and comments on social media sites. Search engines also index this information and when people use search engines to search on those keywords,

your blog or other social networking submissions show up. Another good tip is to collect or group your helpful information into other online content such as a PDF, an audio file, or video file which you can provide links for.

- **Increase your linkability:** You want useful information that other site owners find valuable enough to put a link on their website to yours. The linkability of your site is determined by the amount of content that you have available to users who might come from social networks. Old information that rarely changes will not help, so make sure your content is updated regularly.

- **Make bookmarking your site easy:** Don't make users try to figure out how to add your blog or site to their content feed. Post your URL or code for visitors to add you to their important links or their website. Use a tool called RSS Button Maker at **www.toprankblog.com/tools/rss-buttons** to create a button.

- **Reward helpful users:** If you have users that are helpful and/or send business your way, find a way to reward those users so they will continue to be helpful, especially if you made the sale.

- **Don't be afraid to try new things:** Use your creativity to do something different as often as possible. In social-media optimization, creativity is rewarded.

Social media marketing is a great tool if used wisely. It can also be a terrible one if you use it wrong. Using the wrong tactics or using them only half way will render your efforts worthless. You can also expect that it will be very hard to rebuild the trust that you destroy on the web.

There are some rules of etiquette to follow that will help you keep out of trouble. Let us take a look at those in the next section.

Social Media Etiquette

As an SEO expert, I find that companies come to me frequently because their web reputation has been injured, many times unintentionally by their own staff and sometimes through no fault of their own.

Let's take a look at a few rules of etiquette that you should follow to keep yourself from becoming a statistic in the bad category:

1. Spend some time listening to your audience before you join the conversation so you can gain an understanding of the language, the tone, and the expectations of the conversation participants.

2. After you begin to interact with social media elements, use the information that you gather watching and listening on a social

networks to ensure that your strategy is targeting the correct people and that the responses to your input are positive.

3. Track your site metrics to see if there are any sudden spikes or dips in your web traffic which could indicate that your involvement is effective or ineffective.

4. Provide only content that adds value to the conversation. If your content doesn't add anything or is inaccurate, the other participants will either ignore you or begin to destroy you.

5. Use RSS feeds. RSS feeds instantly update those who have chosen to watch your content. This means that your links will spread faster than you could ever imagine.

6. Keep in mind that social media is all about relationships. Both engage in and be willing to encourage participation.

7. Make an individual approach as an expert in your service or product. Approaching as the business or company will automatically create suspicion. They may think you are just there to sell something. If you don't have the time yourself, consider hiring bloggers or others to handle your company's social-media participation.

Social Media Outlets

There are many types of social media elements out there in the web world for you to tap into. It is sometimes referred to as Web 2.0 and is definitely the major shift in SEO right now. Web 2.0 is all about the social nature of the internet, and if you don't tap into that social aspect, the SEO on your site will quickly be out-of-date and ranked very low on every major search engine. Using social-media elements, however, you can get a jump-start on your social-media strategy.

So where do you start? Here are some suggestions on what sites you should visit and incorporate into your website:

- ✓ **Google Plus**: https://plus.google.com
- ✓ **Blogger:** www.blogger.com
- ✓ **Blogspot:** www.blogspot.com
- ✓ **CitySearch:** www.citysearch.com
- ✓ **Crunchbase:** www.crunchbase.com
- ✓ **Delicious Bookmarks**: www.delicious.com
- ✓ **Digg:** www.digg.com
- ✓ **Twitter:** www.twitter.com
- ✓ **MySpace:** www.myspace.com
- ✓ **Facebook:** www.facebook.com
- ✓ **LinkedIn:** www.linkedin.com

- ✓ **Merchant Circle:** www.merchantcircle.com
- ✓ **StumbleUpon:** www.stumbleupon.com
- ✓ **Reddit:** www.reddit.com
- ✓ **Newsvine:** www.newsvine.com
- ✓ **Fark:** www.fark.com
- ✓ **Clipmarks:** www.clipmarks.com
- ✓ **Smogger Social Media Blog:** smogger.wordpress.com
- ✓ **Yelp:** www.yelp.com
- ✓ **YouTube:** www.youtube.com

These sites each have a different social media element which can be incorporated into your website.   But here is a little tip! In SEO circles the saying goes, "The more you do with Google, the more Google will do for you." It couldn't be more true in social media either. Why am I telling you this?   Well from that list above, Google owns and runs Google+, Blogger.com, Blogspot.com and YouTube.com. It also heavily barrows information from Yelp. So if you're just starting with social media elements, which do you think will give you the greatest rankings on Google? You're right, brain scientist, the ones owned by Google.

Chapter 10-Setting SEO Goals and Making a Plan

For most people the goal is simple, outdo what your competition does for the same keywords and beat their rankings. So I guess the chapter is done. Well, maybe it's not that simple. Maybe I should break it down just a little.

Before we begin, you should have a search engine optimization plan in place. This will help you create your SEO goals. This will help your focus as the purpose of making critical changes to your website for optimization.

Your SEO plan should be updated every 3 months based on what your competition is doing versus what your previous changes have accomplished. In the next chapter, we will look at website analytics which will help you understand where your needs are. It will also help you see where you need to concentrate your efforts at any given time.

Before reading this chapter, however, you should have a good understanding of your trophy keywords and the other keywords you want to focus on. If you don't, you should visit Chapter 3 and make sure you know the keywords your company needs to use and the competition that is competing for those keywords.

In the beginning, you are most likely going to be focusing your SEO on getting your site listed on all the search engines. For this part, Chapter 3 should be your first stop. If you haven't done all the steps outlined in Chapter 3, then you should stop now and jump back there and make sure that your website's URL is listed on all the hand submissions and you have your website being submitted through automation to all the other smaller search engines and directories.

By now you should be familiar with the focus of the other chapters. We have already talked about adding your keywords into the content of each page and making each page focused on one subject, getting relevant links to your website, adding keywords to the content of each page, adding Meta tags, adding correct titles with keywords, adding multimedia, adding social media, and providing the correct word density on each page for a focused search engine.

Each one of these components is a must on your website and is all a part of your SEO strategy. These are all a part of your SEO plan and all of these components are an "add it once and forget about it" type of deal. You need to continuously monitor what is working, what is not, what your competition is doing, and make adjustments as necessary to maintain and update the elements of SEO that help you rank well.

The basic rule here is that your efforts will change, but they will never end. You need to plan to continue using, modifying, and updating your website to help your SEO rankings, and changing your strategies based on search engine changes, new internet components, etc.

For instance, last year having Twitter and RSS feeds on your website did virtually nothing for rankings. The year before having a YouTube video on your website did almost nothing for rankings. This year they are an absolute must-have to increase rankings.

This year a major change took place. Bing didn't even exist last year and our recommendation was to focus your SEO strategies only on Google with Yahoo! as an afterthought. Now because of all the changes, you might actually get more business by optimizing for Bing than your ever realized. Bing has a major market share now. With a majority of the website optimized for Google and not Bing, there is market share to gain by optimizing for Bing, especially in the very competitive keyword arena where the competition is higher than most for a keyword.

Today, every major search engine focuses on many components of a website in ranking a website. Only a few of the smaller search engines focus on a single aspect of a website their rankings. This means that over time, if you are focused only on a single keyword or links for your website, you will find that your SEO efforts will begin to fail quickly.

You have to keep your efforts up and not let down your guard. You can spend a year getting your website's rankings high and be on the first page for any search with your keywords only to lose everything in a week. The fact is you can spend months getting your rankings up and they can be lost in a fleeting moment if you are not careful.

Let me give you an example. There is a very large software company that I do the SEO for. I spent a year and a half getting them to a Google ranking of 8 out of 10. It was one of my most prized accomplishments and I jumped for joy and bragged to everyone I worked with the day I looked and their website ranking was an 8/10 on Google. Only a month later they were a 2. So what happened?

Someone took over their website development who didn't have a clue about SEO. The new designer worked with the owner of the company to create a flashy new website without any consultation from me. In fact, my point of contact with the company didn't even know it was being done. The new website was all Flash and looked great.

The trouble is that when it was created, none of my SEO work was incorporated into the website. Even worse, the new web designer changed all the page file names for every page that was indexed with the search engines. So when users on the search engines searched on their keywords and clicked on a link to their website, there was no page. Rather, there was an error saying the page didn't exist. They were now invisible on the internet. Sales dropped to all time lows in a single month. It was two weeks before someone at my office noticed what was going on and contacted the company. By then it was too late.

When you went to their "About Us" page that used to be named "aboutus.html" it went to an error page because the new web developer named the file "about_us.php". This happened four months ago and they have reverted back to the old site as the SEO work I needed wouldn't incorporate into the new site. Search engines don't like websites that change their URL of their pages and ranking really is based on URL and not actually by website. Each page on your website has its own ranking from Google based on its relevance and all the other items we discuss in this book.

Today, the software company website that was once on the first page of every major search engine for their keywords is on page 3 of Google and has a ranking of 4/10. Their sales went from averaging 150-200 sales per month to only 63 last month. This was a catastrophe for them. They were on an uphill trend adding new employees and growing all because of the SEO work I was doing for them. Today they are four employees fewer and just barely staying in business.

A website needs constant growth and relevant material constantly to maintain its SEO status and keep the site from becoming what is known to search engines as a stale website. (A website where the material never changes.) Those changes, however, need to be looked at from an SEO optimization perspective from every angle. Most outsiders think that every web designer is familiar with SEO. From my experience, very few have any knowledge of it. It is a specialization that most web designers and developers know little or nothing about.

So what should your SEO Plan include? Let's look at this in the next section.

Time and Effort in an SEO Plan

The first thing your plan needs to include is lots of time. Then add more time to that. This is one of the main reasons that most companies sub out their SEO work. Not only because it takes someone who lives and breathes SEO to keep up on the latest trends and technology, but because of the amount of time involved.

Simply adding new content here and there on your website and changing a Meta tag or two won't help you increase your rankings on the major search engines.

> **NOTE:** *If you are doing the SEO yourself, to keep pace and save some time, you might consider designing your site similar to a blog where content is easily changeable.*

Your SEO plan should be considered a dynamic document that changes all the time based on your needs assessed from monitoring not only your website, but the search engines and your competition on the search engines. If you can't figure out what your competition is doing to one up your SEO work, then you need to call in a professional and you need to do it fast because what you do today has virtually no effect on search engines for months. In essence, you are planning today what you want to happen on the search engines 3-6 months from now. An SEO plan will help you stay on track.

Now that you understand how important it is to put time into your website's SEO, we need to create a clearly defined goal built around your business needs. Virtually every business has different needs and at different levels even when two different company websites are in the same industry.

A small local business would focus only on the local area long-tail keyword searches, whereas a large business selling nationally or in a large geographical area would need to invest time, money, and considerable effort into increasing the exposure of their website to potential customers outside its geographic region on a larger level using more generic shorter keywords.

For example, if you sold sports equipment in Los Angeles, you would target a local campaign using the keyword of "los angeles sports equipment." If your website sold sports equipment nationally you would target a much harder SEO keyword with more competition such as, "sports equipment". The fewer the words, the harder it is to get your site listed higher in the search engines. The broader the keyword, the more competition there is for that keyword.

In Los Angeles there are probably 80 websites competing for sports equipment and maybe ten percent do any professional website optimization. However, nationwide there are probably thousands vying for first place with those keywords and if only ten percent do website optimization, you have a lot of competition to beat.

Both the smaller company and the larger company need to implement an SEO plan. The larger company that needs to concentrate on a national level with lots of competition will require more than this book can offer (unless you are just starting your website).

If you are trying to do a national campaign with lots of competition, most likely your competition is employing powerhouse professional help. This is not the time to experiment. Your revenue (the money you make from your website) is an important factor. Your SEO plan and goals should not only focus on increasing your website visits, but also on increasing your revenues. You can track revenue by funneling your website visitors through individually targeted sales transaction pages while they are visiting your website.

You should make sure the goals you set are realistic. It's very easy to become unfocused with your SEO efforts and get discouraged when those efforts don't meet your goals or expectations. It's very easy to spend gobs of money on SEO and never accomplish anything.

Your SEO goals and the plan you create must be flexible and grow with your organization.

SEO Plan Details

Now that you have a set of goals in mind for your website, it's time to create an SEO plan. The SEO plan is the document that you'll use to help you stay focused as you try to implement your individual SEO strategies.

Keyword Research

Continuous keyword research should be your second line item after your time entry on your SEO plans details. Google Analytics (discussed in the next chapter) has a way of looking to see what keywords were used to find your site. Many times it becomes clear that there are a market of people who find your site that you didn't even know.

I will give you an example. My SEO website targets many keywords, but I noticed that several people searching for better website rankings searched using the keyword "search engine help" and found my website way down on the list of a search engine. After a few of these in one month, I added the keyword to my PPC campaign. After getting about 80 hits from that in one month, I optimized a landing page just for that keyword. I now get about 200 hits per month from that term which is business I never would have gotten had I not been analyzing the keywords people were using to access my site.

 It was a minor change in the bigger picture. I was already creating content for the site, but by focusing on some of the most logical and well known keywords. I didn't crawl in the mind of a prospective searcher but Google caught it for me. I just had to interpret the results.

You should never discount the little things. Even minor details, such as refocusing and changing your keyword efforts or modifying the tagging on your pages can have a major impact if it is done right. For every website that I do SEO, I find a little niche on a monthly basis that my clients' competition never catches and I capitalize on that. Using those little niches in the right places can make a major difference in the amount of traffic that your site receives.

Reputation Management

The next item you should have in your plan is reputation management, which is a critical part of any online business. If you Google anyone of my SEO client's URL's, you see nothing but good or neutral press. The top 10 results of a search are usually corporate sites, blogs, press releases and other landing pages I optimized or created for them. This is no accident. Many clients who do any volume of online sales will get a disgruntled customer or two and sometimes a negative news article or blog entry or other problem can affect their online reputation.

Sometimes this bad press is known when it comes out in a news article that everyone sees and talks about. Sometimes, however, a disgruntled person can place negative information on blogs, as comments, and many other places that can be indexed into the search engines and work to destroy your online presence little by little. If you do not take time to monitor you SERP (Search Engine Results Page), you may miss the reason you are dropping in sales or hits to your website because of the negative that is displayed. In one case I had a customer who owned a large mortgage company. Their company does about 8,000 loans per year and have to turn down some clients for a loan, often at the last minute because of some unforeseen issue such as the client used a credit card or bought a car and dropped their credit scores, disqualifying them for the loan product for which they had been approved. It was inevitable, like it or not, that those few disturbed clients who posted their comments on blogs managed to fill up four of the top ten spots on a Google search for many of their important keywords.

Then the inevitable happened. The web visits stopped and the phone calls stopped coming. This is a good example of what can happen if you don't have monitoring your online reputation a part of your SEO plan. You're probably saying, this is nice to tell me but where do I start if I find negative links or information about my company?

Before this ever happens, you should identify key editorial contacts at industry and business publications, ezines, and press release portals that can help to place positive press in its place. Make a separate page in your plan to log these contacts. You should always be looking for opportunities to post comments on relevant articles and place links to your company's URL.

Today, you can publish stories in minutes, versus days, weeks or months. So when you do post content, it not only appears on the Website, but on search engines, syndicated content sites, and news search engines as well.

Best Locations To Post Positive Commentary
Part of reputation management is making sure that there are more good things about your company or URL found around the Internet than bad things. Just one upset customer or a very jerky competitor can make your life on the Internet a living nightmare. There is a solution. A relatively simple solution, that will work a most of the time unless you're dealing with a more SEO knowledgeable individual where more advanced tactics are needed and then you should seek professional help. You need to bump the negative listing down in the search results to progressively to lower positions. This reduces the likelihood that the bad comment will ever be seen. Keep in mind, most people never go beyond the 1st page of search engine results.

First, if you are listed and there is a way of commenting back, comment back. But never include your URL or business name in the comments back and fill the text with as many words as possible. The idea is to dilute the keyword density and bring it as low as possible. Second, if you can comment back from multiple individual names, create accounts and leave comments throughout several weeks and from multiple IP addresses. When you have one unhappy customer but 5-6 happy customers, it doesn't get rid of the bad comment but it does create a more neutral situation.

The last thing to do is start writing your own positive high keyword density commentary, editorials, reviews, and articles, This can often be done by building a profile on various websites. The profile name should be the exact term/phrase that the negative comments are ranking for. Here's a list of 40 such sites you can use to build positive commentary:

1. Google+ (plus.google.com)

2. LinkedIn (LinkedIn.com)

3. Twitter (Twiiter.com)

4. Local News Day (LocalNewsDay.com)

5. Stumbleupon (StubleUpon.com)

6. Facebook (Facebook.com)

7. Digg (Digg.com)

8. Simpy (Simpy.com)

9. Technorati (Technorati.com)

10. YouTube (YouTube.com)

11. Blog Catalog (Blogcatalog.com)

12. Zimbio (Zimbio.com)

13. Reddit(Reddit.com)

14. TheKnow Los Angeles (TheKnowLA.com)

15. Blog Mad (BlogMad.net)

16. Chicagoland Newspaper (ChicagolandNewspaper.com)

17. Peek You (Peekyou.com)

18. Hugg (Hugg.com)

19. Blog Flux (BlogFlux.com)

20. Netvous (netvous.com)

21. Curbly (Curbly.com)

22. Bumpzee (BumpZee.com)

23. Pownce (Pownce.com)

24. ViewZoo (ViewZoo.com)

25. Plime (Plime.com)

26. MyBlogLog (MyBlogLog.com)

27. Giggg.com (Giggg.com)

28. DotNetKicks (DotNetKicks.com)

29. Diigo (Diigo.com)

30. CoComment (CoComment.com)

31. LiveJournal (LiveJournal.com)

32. Faves (Faves.com)

33. Mixx (Mixx.com)

34. Friend Feed (FriendFeed.com)

35. Meta Cafe (MetaCafe.com)

36. Quizilla (Quizilla.com)

37. Kirtsy (Kirtsy.com)

38. Photo Bucket (PhotoBucket.com)

39. Deals (Deals.com)

40. BlogSpot (BlogSpot.com)

Even before there are negative comments, you should always create targeted press releases that can be linked-to from a variety of sources. The press release should also be optimized for the best relevant keyword density so it appears as high as possible in related searches. If you skipped learning about keyword density, there is an index in the back of this book. I would recommend learning about how to use that to your advantage.

Launch your own blog and become friendly with other bloggers, because bloggers are the most publicized arm of social online media. Bloggers are increasing their credibility with the consumer, which means their opinions really do matter. This is somewhat like a "Third Party Endorsement." Having bloggers post negative comments about you or your brand can spell disaster. Be prepared to get into the conversation by posting comments on blogs with negative content about your product/services and link back to your own press release or blog.

Another very effective tool is the use of sub-domains. Google sees them as separate websites, but they do still carry the authority and trust of the root domain. When you create a sub-domain, you must not simply copy content from your main domain. The content must be different. The new sub-domain must have useful, unique content. It does not need 100 pages; just ten or so pages per sub-domain will do. All you need is two to three well-optimized sub-domains.

Sign up for a Twitter account and place the Twitter Wiki on your website, but keep updating it with relevant information about your site. You might also consider MySpace and Facebook, or other social bookmarking network entries. And of course, post links to your press releases using keywords in your text links.

Managing your reputation requires the creation of relative content on your own website, distribution of positive content, as well as strategic participation in online discussions. When you combine these strategies, an integrated search engine reputation management program is in place and ready for action in the event a negative piece of information is indexed about your company or URL.

Press Releases For Added Credibility

A business should never rely on press releases alone and always help raise the profile of their website. Either way, press releases remain a great way of increasing the exposure of company and its online reputation.

Producing press releases for the Internet and is different than writing for traditional outlets such as newspapers and magazines. You need to write each press release based on a single keyword in mind. You then need to include that keyword as many times in your press release as possible with a link back to the page on your website that matches the article that matches the keyword you are focused on for maximum exposure.

There are some pros and cons associated with press release writing and distribution. These points will help you decide whether this service will suit your business.

Writing and distributing press releases boosts the number of links to your website. This is always a benefit to SEO as many press release websites are authoritative and have a high PageRank. Remember that making use of anchor text links in the articles is especially beneficial for your campaign so long as they link back to your website and the page on your website that focuses on the keyword used in your press release.

Press articles are easily distributed quickly to the most relevant parts of the Internet focused on your product or service. This can get high quality traffic to your website. Many people consider atypical press release format to be a more of a traditional form of marketing, this template remains an age-old favorite with the media. This means that news editors are more likely to take a look at what you have to offer as all the information they need is easily identifiable and in one place.

If you write your press release well, your press releases can help with the corporate branding of your company and aid in promoting the products or services you provide.

One last thing is that press releases help your online reputation strategy as well. A well distributed press release will often appear high in the search engine results if you use good keyword density, pushing down unflattering entries and making your company gain complete control of its image.

PPC

Monitoring your PPC account is, of course, important. Whether you use Google AdWords or Bing's AdCenter or related pay-per-click programs

keywords are working for you and which ones get a lot of clicks but don't turn into sales. Too broad of a keyword, as we learned in previous chapters, can cost you a lot of money with very little results.

In terms of reputation management, a PPC campaign can help as well. While optimized press releases and related content may take days or weeks to appear high in relevant search results on search engines, paid text ads are virtually instantaneous and provide total control over placement (by keyword) of your message.

Reprioritizing Pages

In the beginning, prioritizing your web pages is easy. Give priority to the pages that focus on each of your keywords, and in the same order that your keywords are in. You should prioritize your efforts on the pages that support those trophy words and draw the most amount of traffic and sales.

These are top-priority pages and visitors should naturally gravitate to those pages. These should be focused landing pages that utilize all the optimization techniques, including social media and keyword density optimization. The content should remain relevant and constantly be updated so it never gets stale.

Pages such as your home landing page or those that will generate the most traffic or revenue should be a road map and included in your SEO plan and goals should be set for your marketing efforts. If four of the web pages on your site are your top priority, those should encompass a majority of your time and efforts in your SEO plan.

Additional Plan Items

After you have prioritized your sites web pages, you should assess where you stand and where you need to be with your current SEO efforts. Make a checklist and dedicate time to assess all the pages in your website. Those that should be checked more frequently are the following:

- Keywords
- Keyword density
- Title tags
- Social media elements
- Site/page tagging
- Page content relevancy
- Replacement of stale content
- Frequently changed content
- Blogs
- Social media optimization
- Social bookmarking
- Site linking
- Press release writing
- Article submissions
- Video optimization
- RSS Feeds
- Search engine placement
- PPC

Items that can be checked less frequently:

- Site map accuracy
- Longevity of domain registration
- Robots.txt optimization
- Site map
- HTML source code and errors
- Alt tags
- Link development
- Manual link requests to related sites
- Directory listings
- One-way links/two-way links
- HTML design
- ASP. and other coding such as Java and Flash
- Linked URLs

Completing the Plan

At this point you should have collected all the information you need to put into your SEO plan. You should also have a good idea of the priority of each item and what needs to be done frequently and which ones can be done on a less frequent basis to increase or maintain your website's search engine rankings.

Now it's time to put all of the information that you've gathered into a comprehensive plan comparing your available time and determining the SEO efforts you should be making to best utilize that time. Your SEO plan is more than just a simple picture of what's included in your website and what's not. This is the document you should use to help determine your website's current search engine rankings, reputation management, your needed marketing efforts, capital expenditures, time frames, and how you're going to keep your website from becoming stale.

The plan should look much like a business plan when you are done. It includes your goals, a work plan, marketing information, how you will grow your business, plans for managing problems, and much more.

Those strategies can include efforts such as manually submitting your site or pages from your site to directories and planning the content you'll use to draw search engine bots, spiders, and crawlers. It should also outline which pay-per-click programs you plan to use and a time line for the testing and implementation of those efforts, as well as regular follow-ups.

I always recommend that you supplement your SEO with a well-managed PPC campaign. But the goal is to maintain your URL on the first page of a search engine's search using organic SEO to maximize those naturally occurring elements. When you build on each internal and external element on your website to create a site that will naturally fall near the top of the search engine results pages (SERPs), you achieve high SERPs rankings free — other than the time it takes to implement your SEO plan.

Achieving each ranking point for organic SEO can take anywhere from three to eight months if you implement the right SEO plan. Don't get upset if you don't see immediate results from your SEO efforts. Stick to your SEO plan. If you don't see changes within 3-6 months or your rankings get worse, you should reevaluate your SEO plan or seek professional help.

Chapter 11-SEO Tools

If you search the internet you can find a plethora of SEO tools for sale. However, from experience I can tell you there is a free tool for just about everything. Not only that, but ninety percent of the tools that you have to pay for may also do the following:

1. Separate your money from your bank account.

2. Get information from you on how to contact you so someone from India or Pakistan or some other offshore entity can hard sell you on their SEO services, tools, or whatever you're searching for at ridiculous amounts. I might add that there are some legitimate SEO services in Middle Eastern countries but you will find the fraudulent ones much easier. They usually contact you.

3. Con you into paying for SEO tools that many times are free.

4. Con you into paying for a tool that works worse than the free tool.

Lucky for you, you are reading a book by two authors who have pretty much been there and done that for all of the above. Be very skeptical of any SEO option not included in this book or on one of our blogs. In this book, we outline free alternatives that work just as well for every type of tool. Many of the times these free tools work better than the paid alternative.

This is the section in many other SEO books where I am very disappointed because endorsements for software galore are given and the free alternatives are left out. In fact while we were writing this book, we had a company offer to pay us $5,000 for an endorsement in our book for their analytics software and another offered us $2,500 for endorsing their SEO website full of different SEO tools which are pay-per-use.

Both wanted us to leave out different free products, especially Google Analytics and Google Keyword Tools. Unfortunately for those websites and software companies, we have our own reputation management to maintain and we decided early on to make this a true SEO reference guide and not endorse any paid product unless there wasn't a better free alternative. You can be assured that we have accepted no paid endorsement fees for this book and contracted that with the publisher. This means you can trust what we write.

In the next few sections I will be looking at many different toolbars, free plug-ins, extra buttons, and software and website tools to help you with your SEO efforts.

Toolbars and Plug-Ins

In site optimization and monitoring, browser toolbars are especially useful. Best of all, the ones you really need are free. In this section, I will talk about the Alexa Toolbar and go more in depth on what you can do with the Google Toolbar using plug-ins. If you did not read how to install the Google Toolbar, you should go to the back of the book and read the Appendix D and install it.

Since the Google Toolbar will encompass most of this section and has plug-ins to learn about, let's take a look at this first. Now I am assuming that you read and followed the instructions to install the Google Toolbar and installed the PageRank icon in the bar. Now, my Google Toolbar looks like the one in Figure 11.1.

Figure 11.1

I bet your wondering what all these little icons in Figure 11.2 are and how they got there. You're probably also asking yourself, "What do they do and how can they help me?"

Figure 11.2

Google has many plug-ins that can be accessed by pressing the "Adjust Toolbar Options" (the icon that looks like a wrench) on the Google Toolbar and selecting the Custom Tools option. When you do this you will see a screen similar to the one in Figure 11.3.

Custom buttons and search types

Select which buttons appear in the toolbar. Drag and drop to reorder.   Add more buttons...

☑	Page Size Lookup - SEO Tools - Page Size Lookup	⊞ Edit	Remove
☑	SEOLens - Searches from various SEO related sites / foru...	⊞ Edit	Remove
☑	seomanagement - SEO Tools	⊞ Edit	Remove
☑	Page Rank check monitor - Smart PageRank enables web...	⊞ Edit	Remove
☑	Multiple Datacenter Link Popular - SEO Tools - Multiple Dat...	⊞ Edit	Remove
☑	SEO Newswatch - News of the SEO world all in one place.	⊞ Edit	Remove
☑	SEOBook Link Research Gadget - Free SEO research tool ...	⊞ Edit	Remove
☑	Keyword Suggestions for Google - SEO Tools - Keyword Su...	⊞ Edit	Remove
☐	Craigslist Seeker - Search the 'for sale' section of craigslist	⊞ Edit	Remove
☐	I'm Feeling Lucky - Search and navigate to the best result	⊞ Edit	
☐	Search Site - Search only on the current Web site	⊞ Edit	
☐	USA - Find pages in a country	⊞ Edit	
☐	Google Images - Search the Web for images	⊞ Edit	
☐	Google Video - Browse or search for video	⊞ Edit	

Figure 11.3

To add SEO plug-ins and search Google for additional SEO tools, select the "Add more buttons…" link at the top right of the screen. You must first download and install the plug-ins which are accessible by clicking on their associate buttons on the Google Toolbar. They will install into your web browser without any coding from you. Most SEO plug-ins are designed to work with the Internet Explorer, Google Chrome, and the Firefox browsers. You will find that you get the most functionality using the Firefox browser; it usually becomes the browser of choice for most people in charge of SEO.

> **NOTE:** If you use Chrome, you'll find that many of the plug-ins available are not compatible. You can go to a website called ChromePlugIns.org to find many of the SEO tools that are compatible with the Google Chrome browser.

Choosing Plug-Ins Wisely

There are hundreds of SEO plug-ins that are available. Few plug-ins monitor more than one element of optimization, so in order to have multiple facets of your SEO strategy measured, you need multiple plug-ins. The key is determining what you need.

200

This is where I will put a big warning!

DO NOT BUY ANYTHING OR SIGN UP TO GET A FUNCTIONAL GOOGLE TOOLBAR PLUG-IN. DON'T GIVE A CREDIT CARD OR BANK ACCOUNT INFORMATION TO ANYONE EITHER!

In texting, when you use capital letters you are yelling. And in a sense I was. Many of the plug-ins on Google are placed by people wanting to sell you their version of a plug-in. Most of the times it is just a modified version of a free one already available.

For websites, you can choose among several different plug-ins, each usually monitoring something different. Some monitor links, while others monitor PageRank or keyword density, and still others monitor several elements. The selection process, then, begins with understanding what's available and what you can do with it.

So we have now hit the "Add more buttons…" link under Custom Tools on the "Adjust Toolbar Options" on the Google Toolbar. "So what do I do now?" you may be asking. Well, that's easy. In the search box, simply type "SEO" or "SEM" and press enter. You will see a list such as those in Figure 11.4.

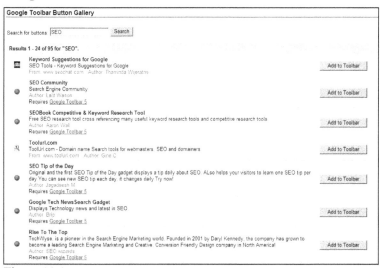

Figure 11.4

That search turns over 90 different SEO related buttons that you can add to the Google Toolbar. I recommend the following for good SEO Analysis:

1. Keyword Suggestions for Google

2. SEOBook Competitive and Keyword Research Tool
3. Google AdWords Campaign
4. SEO News
5. SEO Search Engine
6. Toolurl.com
7. Multiple Datacenter Link Popularity Check
8. SEO Tip of the Day
9. SEOBook Link Research Tool
10. SEOLens
11. Page Rank Check Monitor
12. Website Traffic
13. Code to Text Ratio
14. Page Size Lookup

As you can see from this list, there are a variety of different tools that you can plug into the Google toolbar. Everything from keyword research tools to SEO news and blogs is available. All you have to do is decide which ones are most useful for you and your SEO needs.

Each one has its own set of instructions but for the most part they ask you just to enter very little information such as a URL, IP Address, or keyword to get results.

Now let's take a look at the Alexa Toolbar and how that can help us in our quest to get better rankings.

Alexa Toolbar

The Alexa Toolbar, shown in figure 11.5, is tied into Alexa's web-traffic statistics, so the numbers that you'll find when you use this toolbar are a little skewed.

Figure 11.5

However, Alexa provides enough information to make the toolbar useful. Also, Alexa's results are a major influence on rankings found on the major search engines.

As you can see, the Alexa Toolbar looks quite a bit different from the Google Toolbar, and offers some good information. Once installed it also tracks where you go on the internet which helps Alexa determine the average traffic to a site. So visiting your own websites frequently will help to improve the rankings on a Alexa.

Installing the Alexa Toolbar

To install the Alexa Toolbar, type http://www.alexa.com/toolbar into your browser, as shown in Figure 11.6 and 11.7.

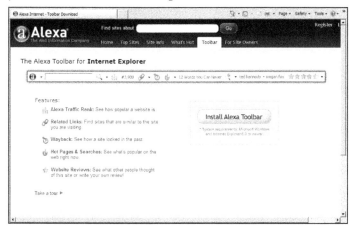

Figure 11.6

Figure 11.7

After you are done entering the demographic information and pressing "Submit," you will get a success message, as shown in Figure 11.8.

Figure 11.8a

You will now be given an option to take the tour that explains all the features of the Alexa Toolbar, as shown in Figure 11.9a and 11.9b.

Figure 11.9a

Features of the Alexa Toolbar

Web Search
The Alexa Web Search is a whole new way to search the web. Begin by typing your search term into the box then press enter. You will be transported to a world of behind-the-scenes information about each site on the web. Don't waste time sifting through lousy sites. Use the Alexa Web Search and know before you go.

Site Info
Alexa's exclusive Site Information allows you to peer behind the scenes of each site on the web. Get access to contact information, site stats and user reviews of web sites. Plus you can even write your own reviews.

Related Links
Alexa's Related Links are a great way to discover new sites. As you surf the web, the toolbar is constantly updating with information about where other users visit.

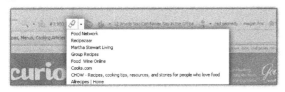

The Wayback Machine
Having trouble getting access to your favorite site, or want to see what it looked like in the past? The Wayback Machine can transport you back in time to see archived copies of your favorite sites. Click the Wayback button, select a date, and go!

Figure 11.9b

Analytics

Analytics are used to determine all kinds of things about the traffic to your website. There are many packages that can cost stacks of money, but most do not track or report half as well as Google. Their sales techniques to sell their inferior software are interesting and usually pretty much the same when they compare their web analytics programs to Google Analytics.

I recommend using Google Analytics. You can always look for better products but watch out if these are their only claims:

A. "Install on your own server"

B. "Restore historical data from files"

C. "Can track behind a firewall"

D. "Track robots, crawlers, and spiders"

Google Analytics is a free website statistics application that you can use to track your website traffic. You can begin using Google Analytics by going to www.google.com/analytics. You must have a Google user name to access the program.

If you do not have a Google user name, you can create one when you sign in the first time by provide an e-mail address and a password. Type the verification word from the graphic provided, and then agree to the Terms of Service by clicking "I accept. Create my account."

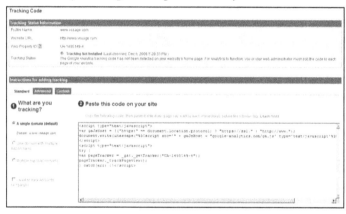

Figure 11.10

Once you've created your user name and password, accessing the tracking capabilities of Google is easy. You'll need to copy a small piece of code that Google gives you onto your website pages just before the closing Body tag: "<\Body>". Let's take a look at the text that Google provides for the coding of your website (Figure 11.10).

After you've added the code to your website, it will take a few days for Google to gather enough information to provide reports about it. More useful information will come after a full month of analytics.

Google Analytics is a service provided by Google that allows you to view and interact with detailed statistical information about the visitors to your website. After you have given Google some time to collect information about the visitors to your website, you can formulate that into reports.

The information from Google Analytics allows you to see who is visiting your website, how they are getting there, how long they stayed, what browser the visitors used, what keywords were used, and most importantly, what the visitors did once they were on your website.

Figure 11.11

Being able to quickly access relevant information about your website visitors is important because it will allow you address a range of marketing issues, relating both to your website and your business as a whole. You will be able to track online and offline marketing campaigns, understand what your customers and prospective customers are looking for, and pinpoint areas of your website that need improvement.

When you first login to Google Analytics and select the domain you want to view, if you have more than one, you are presented with a Dashboard view of your domain, such as the one showing LocalNewsDay.com (Figure 11.11).

Most website owners could only wish for over 16,000 visits in a single month such as those pictured here from the monthly report for LocalNewsDay.com. However, there is a story here. When I took over their website's optimization two years ago, the monthly visits only averaged about 800-900. It is absolutely amazing what being at the top of Google and Bing for your keyword searches can do. This is why you need SEO for your website.

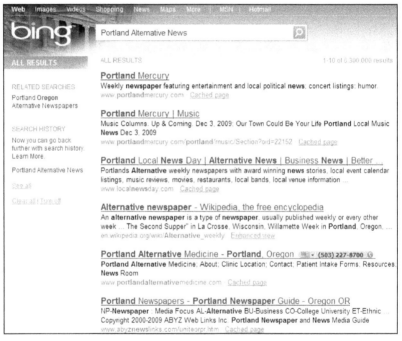

Figure 11.12

Notice a search on "portland alternative news" on Bing or Google places LocalNewsDay.com on the first page of every major search engine, as shown in figure 11.12. Understanding and utilizing relevant analytics about your website visitors will allow you to make your website work harder for you, increase your ROI, increase your search engine rankings, generate more sales leads and allow you to better allocate resources.

Now let's take a look at some of the reports and information you can obtain from Google Analytics to help you.

Analysis in Action

Access to visitors' statistics is one thing, but the true value of analytics comes in the form of analysis and action. Improvements to your website should come out of a defined process and a decision based on information and knowledge. Analytics allows you to make those decisions and then measure the results. Below is a list of some of the most informational analyses from Google Analytics:

- Visitors
- Traffic Sources
- Intelligence Reports
- Expanded Goals
- Site Engagement Goals
- Advanced Table Filtering
- Expanded Mobile Reporting
- Share Advanced Segments
- Share Custom Reports
- Multiple Custom Variables

Google Analytics gives you many technical graphs, but value is only gained when that data is used to drive action to improve your website. So how do we begin to analyze results in Google Analytics?

Firstly, you need to understand what your website is about and what it actually does for your business. This may seem like a obvious place to start, and hopefully you know this by now.

So what is the purpose of your website? Is it to generate leads? To sell products or services? To register subscribers? To provide support? Once you identify the purpose of your website you can begin to identify ways to improve your website. Generally your initial focus will either be content or a specific process you want to optimize.

The most important ways to improve your website content is by analyzing Google Analytics reports in the next section.

Analyzing the Keywords Report

The first report after viewing how many visitors you received should be the keywords information under Traffic Sources. Do the keywords align with the purpose of your site or business? Are there keywords that are not optimized but are drawing relevant visitors?

Figures 11.13a and 11.13b can both help you with this.

If you identify an organic keyword that is important to your business, but has a high bounce rate, then develop content that specifically targets visitors using that keyword.

Figure11.13a(Top)

Visits	Pages/Visit	Avg. Time on Site	% New Visits	Bounce Rate
459	**4.93**	**00:03:25**	**83.88%**	**41.18%**
% of Site Total: 53.87%	Site Avg 4.57 (7.72%)	Site Avg: 00:03:07 (9.81%)	Site Avg: 72.65% (15.45%)	Site Avg: 43.08% (-4.41%)

Search sent 459 total visits via 303 keywords

Show: total | paid | non-paid

Site Usage | Goal Set 1

	Keyword	None	Visits ↓	Pages/Visit	Avg. Time on Site	% New Visits	Bounce Rate
1.	weldsafe		23	4.91	00:02:20	60.87%	34.78%
2.	discount welding supplies		21	5.05	00:01:54	100.00%	9.52%
3.	weldsafe.com		21	4.19	00:01:19	80.95%	47.62%
4.	welding supplies portland oregon		12	4.50	00:02:28	66.67%	16.67%
5.	bsx welding jacket		11	27.82	00:48:37	0.00%	0.00%
6.	steel saw 2		9	4.22	00:02:34	11.11%	44.44%
7.	welding supplies		9	5.11	00:02:02	100.00%	11.11%
8.	weld safe		7	3.29	00:00:29	100.00%	42.86%
9.	welding supplies portland or		7	6.71	00:03:47	57.14%	14.29%
10.	blue demon welding products		5	8.20	00:02:06	100.00%	0.00%

Filter Keyword: [containing ▼] [ ] [Go] Advanced Filter   Go to: [1]   Show rows: [10 ▼] 1 - 10 of 303 [◄] [►]

Figure 11.13b (Bottom)

Analyzing the Site Search Report

Setup Site Search as shown in Figure 11.14 to identify gaps in content.
Are people searching for something that your site already answers? If so,
you should look at your navigation system. Can they get there easily?
If Site Search contains search terms that you know won't bring up
relevant content on your site, you need to ask yourself why. Do these
search terms identify opportunities to generate new content or fill the

desires of your website visitors?

Figure 11.14

Analyze the Top Content Report

When you look at top content report in Figure 11.15 are there any pages that have a low average time on page or a high bounce rate? This generally indicates that a page isn't giving visitors what they are seeking. Review the pages that have the lowest time on page and highest bounce rate.

			Views:
Time on Page ?	Bounce Rate ?	% Exit ?	$ Index ?
00:01:21	**53.42%**	**36.77%**	**$0.00**
Site Avg: 00:01:21 (0.00%)	Site Avg: 53.42% (0.00%)	Site Avg: 36.77% (0.00%)	Site Avg: $0.00 (0.00%)

Pageviews ↓	Unique Pageviews	Time on Page	Bounce Rate	% Exit	$ Index
75	67	00:00:31	46.67%	33.33%	$0.00
71	67	00:05:51	81.54%	80.28%	$0.00
68	53	00:00:29	31.58%	25.00%	$0.00

Figure 11.15

Sidebar: What is the bounce rate?

Google Analytics can tell you how many of your visitors are *bouncing* from your site. This is labeled as your "bounce rate," which is the percentage of visitors coming to your site and leaving immediately.

High percentages of bounces is an indication that your site is not optimized properly or relevant for what the visitor is looking for. If the bounces happen on landing pages that are designed to greet visitors, contain a lot of information, or are for marketing URLs. Visitors who bounce from your site are not finding what they thought they would find, based on the search engine results or advertisements they clicked through may lose ranking or get a bad quality score.

You can begin to see how to analyze results in Google Analytics based on the purpose of your website. Once you understand how your site works as a business tool, you can use Google Analytics to inform your process.

Google Analytics With Intelligence Reports

How would you like to have 24-hour a day access to a dedicated assistant who is focused exclusively on your site's analytics? Your assistant would be so diligent and detailed that they wouldn't miss a thing. Sound too good to be true? We're giving you one. Say "Hello" to Analytics Intelligence.

Your new hardworking assistant, Analytics Intelligence, can't replace you or a professional analyst. It can, however, find key information for you and your professional analysts so that your team can focus on making strategic decisions, instead of sifting through an endless sea of data.

Analytics Intelligence constantly monitors your website's traffic. Anytime something significant happens, it adds an automatic alert in your Intelligence reports. If your bounce rate suddenly jumps on one of your referrals, Analytics Intelligence creates an alert. Of course, it's up to you to go find out that the bounce rate jumped because someone inadvertently changed the landing page or for some other reason. But you might not have noticed that there was a problem that needed fixing if your trusty assistant hadn't alerted you. Figures 11.16 and 11.17 show the alerts screen in Analytics Intelligence.

Figure 11.16

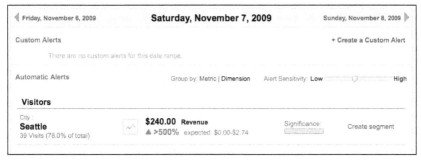

Figure 11.17

The automatic alerts will give a webmaster immediate information about traffic jumps or changes according to the configured thresholds you create. This can include major traffic changes to certain pages on the website, a change in a page's bounce rate, page views, or a higher or lower than usual visitor stream from a specific country, state or region as shown in the automatic alerts in figure 11.17.

Figure 11.17
This gives the webmaster a quick overview of traffic developments on a specific web project or website.

There are built in alerts that you can choose, but you can take Intelligence reports to the next level with Custom Alerts. These allow you to define your own alert triggers and receive an email alert. For example you can create a Custom Alert to notify you when your Google AdWords campaign traffic meets a revenue target or when your organic keyword terms from your SEO efforts has resulted in a certain number of visitors to your site.
There is almost a limitless number of alerts you can configure. Now it's time to set some goals in Google Analytics in the next section.

New Feature of Google Analytics Goals

A website goal is a high value action that you would like your website visitors to perform. On a content or lead generation site, this could include subscribing to an email newsletter or completing a contact form. On an e-commerce site this could be the completion of a checkout process. You can access goal data across numerous reports within Google Analytics, plus you will have access to goal specific reports under the 'Goals' tab.

If you have ever set up optimization or visitor goals in Google Analytics, one feature that you may have wanted is the ability to set more than four goals per profile. Now, Google Analytics profile can be setup with 20 goals. These are also now conveniently arranged in four groups containing five goals each.

Another new feature is the addition of site engagement goals. Standard goals are great for reporting on particular actions you want your visitors to take (buying online, filling out a contact form or registering for your email newsletter), but what if your primary objective is providing quality content and an engaging experience for your visitors?

Site engagement goals is your answer. Now you can set a goal conversion for time on site or pages per visit allowing you to access the power of goal reports within Google Analytics. If you are a SMB (Small to Medium Business), non-profit, government, or any organization with a content- or branding-focused site you should definitely begin using site engagement goals.

Mobile Reporting in Google Analytics

Google Analytics now allows for improved tracking of mobile devices, so you can now track interactions within your iPhone and Android apps to measure usage and engagement.

A new tracking code for mobile sites built using PHP, Perl, JSP and ASPX will also become available, allowing you to track all web-enabled mobile devices (not just mobile devices that run JavaScript).

Tips to Help You Utilize Google Analytics

1. Setup e-commerce tracking. If you have an e-commerce website make sure you enable e-commerce tracking within your Google Analytics website profile and add appropriate e-commerce tags to your website. If you don't have an e-commerce website you can still use e-commerce reports to associate a dollar value to particular website visitors.

2. Link your Google AdWords account to your Google Analytics account. Once your accounts are linked you will have access to AdWords visitor data within Google Analytics.

3. Track your marketing campaigns. Campaign tracking is a crucial element in understanding how your marketing campaigns are performing. By tagging online and offline campaigns you can begin to evaluate and compare the effectiveness of your marketing initiatives. Tag everything!

4. Manually tag your CPC (Cost Per Click) campaigns. If you use a CPC system other than Google AdWords, you will need to manually tag your campaign URLs. CPC campaigns that are not tagged will be logged as "organic" (or unpaid) searches within Google Analytics.

Chapter 12 – Don't Do It!

I have so many instances and references where I myself have made mistakes or where others have fallen before me and I have learned from their mistakes. In this chapter we will talk about:

As you go about working on your websites, optimizing things and managing your social media programs, it's easy to lose track of information, or overlook something. In this post we'll take a look at some things you want to avoid doing. It may also be worth taking a look through your site and your programs to make sure you're not doing any of these things moving forward.

Cloaking

Cloaking is the process where you determine who the visitor is coming to your website, then show content depending on who that visitor is. Typically, the system detects a search engine crawler, and swaps more search-friendly content in place for them. Human visitors would then see a different content page. Taken to the limit, the content is completely different. This is an obvious problem for the engines, as we expect to see the same content as anyone else would. Showing us one piece of content and other visitors a different piece of content is misleading. You want to avoid this.

Link buying

It's no secret that inbound links play a role in ranking. It's also no secret that we don't want you buying links. There are a lot of services out there pitching this service, and calling it anything but "link buying" these days. The bottom line is this: you are taking a big risk if you are buying links.

If we discover the link is purchased, at best we'll simply ignore it and not pass any value, which is what happens in most cases. This is still pretty bad for you, though, as you paid money for something that now gives you no value. At worst, if it gets to be problematic for us, we'll take action against the sites involved.

Link farms

Link farms are simply pages of links that are created just to artificially boost a linking strategy in an effort to speed the appearance of the website in the top search ranking positions. Typically you pay money to join them or buy software that allows you to mass send your links.

Links to your content should grow organically. Link farming essentially involves a network of sites which all link to your content. On paper this would seem to create the impression that a bunch of sites now link to your content. In reality, Google sees link farms and dismiss their value. You will pay money and will receive no value for it.

Three-way linking

Let say that Site A links to Site B. Then Site B links to Site C. Site C links to Site A. This may seem to be preferable to reciprocal linking, but it's not, really. Reciprocal linking can not only introduce us to your newest content or site, but can also deliver direct traffic to your website. True, it doesn't carry the same value as a straight one-way link, but you've got to start somewhere.

Three-way linking is often an attempt to avoid being seen building reciprocal links. Don't sweat reciprocal links and avoid three-way linking. You will most likely get caught up in one of Google's algorithms.

Duplicating Content

Duplicating content is a pretty simple concept. You're posting content which already appears somewhere online. Using articles from third-party sources, copying and pasting from another source and using standardized product descriptions for items you're selling all fall into this category. Your content should be unique and not appear anywhere else online. Building unique content takes work.

Another form of duplication can happen when you fail to manage permutations of your URLs. When you attach a tracking code to your URL, for example, you create two versions of a URL, both of which will return the same content. You can help guard against this by managing the issue through the use of the **rel=canonical** attribute.

Like Farms

Like farms are similar to link farms. In this instance, you're essentially trying to manipulate the "likes" you receive by agreeing with others to like each other's' content. These are now quite obvious to a search engine, and we simply ignore the data we see.

Auto-follows in Social Media

Using an auto-follow service to help grow the number of followers you have on Twitter is another dead end. You essentially end up following as many people as follow yourself. If you have 3,000 followers and follow only 100 people yourself, this reflects a situation that many people want to hear what you have to say; which is completely a sign of authority.

The thin content approach

Thin content can describe many approaches to producing content. To help you understand what it is, we'll explain how to produce content which is not "thin" in nature. When producing content, your goal should be to provide deep details. Enough information that anyone who arrives on your website would need no further sources to feel they have everything they need to understand what they were searching for.

We covered how to build quality content in a previous article, so check that out for more information. Just remember to avoid trying to take short cuts when you produce content. The search engines need good quality content to return worthwhile results for searchers. If you fail the quality content test, you simply won't rank and drive traffic.

Flash

When used correctly, it can enhance a visitor's experience, unless you're trying to get mobile devices to be compatible. The non-mobile side of your website shouldn't be built entirely in Flash, nor should your site navigation be done only in Flash. Search engines have claimed for a couple years now that they're better at crawling Flash, but it's still not a substitute for good, crawlable site menus and content.

AJAX

The same issues mentioned regarding Flash apply here to AJAX. Google has now claimed it can read AJAX and index what it has found but I have not been able to find any examples of this. AJAX can add to your site's user experience, but AJAX has historically not been visible to search engine crawlers. In order to let Google to index your AJAX website content, Google offers guidelines to help make AJAX-based content crawlable, but it's complicated and the SEO "best practice" recommendations remain the same. Don't put important or unique content in AJAX.

Complex Java Script menus

Javascript is another technology that search engines are getting better at crawling, but is still best avoided as the primary method of presenting site navigation. Google has explained:

While we are working to better understand JavaScript, your best bet for creating a site that's crawlable by Google and other search engines is to provide HTML links to your content.

That's still the best practice today: Make sure your site navigation is presented in simple, easy-to-crawl HTML links.

Dynamic URL's

A "dynamic URL" is most simply defined as one that has a "?" in it, like

http://www.yourdomain.com/page.src?ID=3456

That's a very simple dynamic URL and today's search engines have no trouble crawling something like that. But when dynamic URLs get longer and more complicated, search engines may be less likely to crawl them (for a variety of reasons, one of which is that studies show searchers prefer short URLs). So, if your URLs look anything like this, you may have crawlability problems:

http://www.yourdomain.com/page.src?ID=3456&XID=9765487&CID=3333 94445&VID=34521456&SESSION=875694875

Google's webmaster help page says it well: "…be aware that not every search engine spider crawls dynamic pages as well as static pages. It helps to keep the parameters short and the number of them few."

Dynamic Code On Pages

Code that is held in a database and pages that display the output dynamically and on pages that deliver unique output will have issues being indexed by the search engines. Some pages also have what is termed as "code bloat."

Code bloat is situations where the code required to render your page is dramatically more substantial than the actual content of the page. In many cases, this is not something you'll need to worry about—search engines have gotten better at dealing with pages that have heavy code and little content.

Robots.txt Blocking

First, you are not required to have a robots.txt file on your website; millions of websites are doing just fine without one. But if you use one (perhaps because you want to make sure your Admin or Members-only pages aren't crawled), be careful not to completely block spiders from your entire website. It's easy to do with just a simple line of code.

In no circumstances should your robots.txt file have something like this:

User-agent: *
Disallow: /

That code will block all bots, crawlers, and spiders from accessing your website. If you ever have questions about using a robots.txt file, visit robotstxt.org.

Bad XML Site Map

An XML sitemap lets you give a list of URLs to search engines for possible crawling and indexing. They're not a replacement for correct on-site navigation and not a cure-all for situations where your website is difficult to crawl.

If implemented properly, an XML sitemap can help search engines become aware of content on your site that they may have missed. But, if implemented incorrectly, the XML sitemap might actually deter bots, crawlers, and spiders from crawling.

If you're curious, I've only once recommended that a client use XML sitemaps, and that was a website with upwards of 15 million pages. If you need to get a professionally created XML sitemap, you can have one created at **www.smcreator.com**.

Abnormal Keyword Delivery

The reason I am discussing this first is because it is the most common occurrence. I read all the time on SEO blogs that a person got his website on the first page of Google by placing his keywords a hundred times at the bottom of his website landing page in text that was the same color as the background of his website. The person is so excited that he discounts and ignores all the professionals who comment that he shouldn't do this. Sometime the blog creator or commenter who has his site on the first page of Google even bad mouths the SEO professionals trying to help him.

I come back and read all the time how just a few short months later, the same guy that was so excited that his website was on the first page of Google has written, "You guys were right. Google banned my URL for doing this." It is easy to temporarily be the most relevant site on Google the wrong way. But Google and the other major search engines have ways of figuring it out quite quickly. And once you are banned, you better call in the pros to help you. There is a section dedicated to this as the end of this chapter.

SEO Spam

SEO spam is the SEO version of email spam. Email spam pops up in your inbox where it's least wanted and those who are sending it believe that the law of averages is on their side. They think if you send out enough messages, eventually someone will respond.

SEO spam uses the same principle, except SEO spam fills the search engine results pages on search engines with results that have little or no value to the searcher. This can get you quickly banned. Imagine if you went to Google and every time you did a search you got results that were for something totally different than you searched for, or if the top 10 spaces of the search results were filled with the same company. If that happened you would switch to Bing in a heartbeat to get better results. Right?

Google and the other major search engines don't want this to happen. So if you do something that a search engine sees as spamming, your search rankings will be penalized. It's now even more likely that you will be removed from search rankings entirely. If Google bans your URL it's as if you website has been removed from the internet. It is almost invisible.

A term for some SEO spam is called *black hat SEO*. Black hat SEO refers to the use of aggressive SEO strategies, techniques and tactics that focus only on search engines and not a human audience. Some examples of black hat SEO techniques include keyword stuffing, link farms, invisible website text and doorway pages, which we will learn about later in this chapter.

Black Hat SEO is more frequently used by those who are looking for a quick financial return rather than a long-term investment on their website.

> **NOTE:** *Black Hat SEO will most likely result in your URL being banned from major search engines. However, since the focus is usually on quick high return business models, most experts who use Black Hat SEO tactics consider being banned from search engines a somewhat irrelevant risk. Black Hat SEO may also be referred to as Unethical SEO or just spamdexing.*

To make things a little more perplexing, search engines change their definitions of spam regularly. What works and is acceptable today may well be classified as spam tomorrow. This can have a profound effect on your rankings. One day you may be ranked high and on page one of a search and the next you may find that you're on page 8 of the results all because of the links you maintain.

The easiest way to monitor search engine changes is to keep up with what's happening in SEO on the Google Webmaster Central Blog (**http://googlewebmastercentral.blogspot.com**). You can also learn about what's changing on ISEdb–Internet Search Engine Database (www.isedb.com), High Rankings Advisor (www.highrankings.com), and SEONews.com.

The general rule is, if you're doing something on your website that you have to worry might get you banned from major search engines, you probably shouldn't be doing it.

If you read anywhere that SEO spam techniques are okay, or that you won't get caught because search engines don't pay attention, ignore this advice at all costs. The penalties differ according to the search engine, but if you are caught spamming even once, most search engines will delist you from search results immediately. I have seen it a hundred times and have had it happen to me on accident when I went overboard experimenting. Yes, even the experts make a mistake or two. But we learn from them.

Here's what is definitely considered spam:

- Trying to make your site appear more relevant to the search engines by embedding hidden keywords in your website.
- Artificially generating links to your website from unrelated sites for the purpose of increasing your ranking based on link analysis.
- Artificially generating traffic to your website so that it appears more popular than it really is.
- Submitting your website repeatedly for inclusion in the rankings.

NOTE: *You should submit your site once and then wait at least six weeks before submitting it again.*

Doorway Pages

Doorway pages are created to do well for particular phrases. They are also known as portal pages, jump pages, bridges, gateway pages, entry pages, and by other names as well. Search engines have developed ways to easily identify these pages. They are primarily to make a page seem more relevant for search engines, and not for human beings.

You should always have your pages designed for human eyes and not just for a search engine. There are various ways to deliver doorway pages. The low-tech way is to create and submit a web page that is targeted toward a particular phrase or keyword.

These pages tend to be very generic. It's easy for people to copy them, make minor changes, and submit the revised page. Sometimes these are so similar that the search consider these duplicates and automatically exclude them from their listings.

Another problem is that users sometimes arrive at the doorway page. Say a real person searched for "welding supplies" and the doorway page appears. They click through, but that page probably lacks any detail about the welding supplies that you sell. To get them to that content, webmasters usually propel visitors forward with a prominent "Click Here" link or with an automatic page redirect.

Some search engines no longer accept pages using any redirects (sometimes referred to as fast Meta refresh). This has led to some black hatters doing a bait-and-switch, or "code-swapping," on the search engines. Some black hat webmasters submit a real web page, wait for it to be indexed and then swap it with a doorway page.

The trouble is that a search engine may revisit at any time figure out what you have done.

Meta Jacking

Meta jacking is the taking of the Meta tagging from one page and placing them on another page hoping to obtain good rankings and relevance. However, simply taking Meta tags from a page will not guarantee a page will do well. In fact, sometimes resubmitting the exact page from another location does not gain the same position as the original page.

Agent Delivery

When you target a single doorway page to a single search engine this is called "agent delivery." Each search engine reports an "agent" name, just as each browser reports a name.

Agent delivery pages are tailored pages that direct users to the actual content you want them to see. It also has the added benefit of "cloaking" your code from only the search engine you are targeting. The major search engines have gotten wise to this, though. They change the name they report specifically to help keep people honest.

IP Delivery / Page Cloaking

To avoid the agent name changing, you can also deliver pages to the search engines by allowing only the search engines IP address. If a bot, crawler, or spider visits your doorway page and reports an IP address that matches the search engine's or the IP resolves to a certain host name, it can see the code of the website.

Spamblogs

These are software or machine-generated blogs which have only one purpose – increase search engine rankings.

Page Highjacking

Page hijacking occurs when very popular webpage coding is stolen and used to represent your website to the search engines. When users perform a search and see your webpage in the search results, they click through the link only to be taken to your actual page.

Sybil Attacks

Sybil attacks are when a spammer creates multiple websites that are all interlinked for the purpose of creating a false link structure. These are sometimes called incestuous links.

Link Bombing

One anchor text tactic to avoid is link bombing . Link bombing refers to the methods used by black hat SEOs to artificially inflate their website ranking by connecting an unrelated keyword to a specific website. For link bombing to work, more than one website designer must be willing to participate in a link exchange.

What to Do If You Have Been Banned

If you have been banned from the major search engines, you may find it the worst experience of your life, especially since the internet is now the official yellow pages for most and being banned from the major search engines is like locking your business doors and taking the phone off the hook.

Most of the time you will know what was done that got you banned. In this case, it may require explaining to the search engine the tactic you employed, why you employed it, and how you fixed it. Google, for instance, allows you to send in an explanation by going to the

Google Webmaster Tools

(**https://www.google.com/webmasters/tools**) and clicking on the "Site Reconsideration" link on the left-hand side. This will take you to the web page which outlines written and video instructions to resubmit your website.

It could take a couple of months to a year to be reindexed into the search engine. In some cases it is quicker and easier to ditch the old URL and start a brand new one. Then you have to work your way back to the top of the rankings again. Just make sure that you have fixed or stopped doing whatever was done to get your URL banned in the first place.

Outgoing Link Issues

Linking out is crucial for blogs and even static websites. Many webmasters stopped linking out in order to hoard PageRank and not allow others in their industry to get a better rank. Google engineers absolutely discourage this practice. In fact, so much so that Google has started to really want to see industry related links that are two-way links on not only the homepage but the deep pages as well. Linking out can be risky though. Here are some things to look out for.

Broken links

Too many broken links on a page raise a red flag in the Google algorithm, so you need to make sure your links going out, are always good. This might not be a penalty in the strictest sense, but you drop suddenly in rankings once more than one or two links are broken on the same page.

Links To Bad Neighborhoods

Bad neighborhoods are server IP addresses that host websites Google finds bad. Such as porn sites, hate sites, some political sites, spammersm etc. Most of these links happen more naturally as part of link decay. Sites disappear and domain grabbers buy them to display ad loaded "domain parking" pages. These pages can be bad as well.

Too Many Outbound Links Can Be Bad, As Well As None At All

This figure changes, but currently our testing shows, Google is fine with up to 76 outbound links on a page but degrades the pages ranking after this number. A website that has more outgoing links than content itself can lose its search visibility. This might not happen overnight like the typical penalty you'd expect, but it can amount to one in its effects. Also, pages without a single outbound link are now being termed "dead-ends". In this case there are no outbound links and Google has been placing a severe penalty on these pages.

Hidden Links

This may sound crazy. How do you hide a link? Well in add-ons, in CSS coding, etc. I am adding this section because of a counter added to a WordPress website that contained a links in it to other websites. The link was not only hidden; but was absolutely spammy. We couldn't figure ot the source of the problem until an AccuQuality.com report we ran on the website revealed the over 180 outbound links and the reason Google was penalizing the website.

Content

Google consistently stresses that "content is king", but it also can mean trouble. If there is no king in your kingdom, or the king is dressed in rags, or you borrowed you king from somewhere else you look bad to Google. Here are some content issues you should look out for:

Duplicate content – duplicate content on your own site or even elsewhere can result in a significant ranking drop. While Google does not consider this a penalty, most webmasters who experience the problem do.

Low quality content – Google's high quality update dubbed Panda and it later updates, focuses on low quality content. Shallow, keyword-rich content on some pages can make your whole site drop in Google.

Scraped content – Scraped content is text taken from other sites and displayed on yours, is a surefire way to get deranked very quickly. Especially since Google has introduced the "Panda Updates".

Unlegible content – Content that is written in broken English or misspelled can hurt you badly. So much so that AccuQuality.com now spells checks your entire website in their report. As a general rule, your content needs sound good to the human visitor as much as to the search engines crawler who is visiting.

Ads

Google is not really a search engine but an advertising company as almost all revenue of the Google corporation stem from ads displayed in the search results themselves and on third party sites. Nonetheless, the pressure on Google has grown over the years to tackle the problem of so called MFA (Made for Adsense) sites that pollute the Google index. With Google "Panda" the search giant finally did tackle this issue. So this means there are some new rules to follow:

Too many ads (low content to ads ratio) – ever since Google "Panda" has been the talk of the town, most pundits have pointed out that a too high number of ads, especially Google AdSense ads, may lead to a penalty.

Affiliate sites with no value – Google always explained that affiliates are not an issue, but only as long as they offer some good content and additional value beyond the actual affiliate offer. Be sure to add different content, products, or services or you will face a penalty sooner or later.

Bad Press Or A Bad Online Reputation

The issue of so-called "SEO outing" has been a hot one in 2011, as numerous high profile websites have been ousted and along with them their SEO teams or companies. Many SEO practitioners argue on moral grounds that outing is a despicable practice. They might be right, but as long as there is nothing to out you, fare best. So you'd better manage your reputation online and from time to time check what the SEO team does.

NYT and WSJ

High profile old media outlets like the NYT (New York Times) and the WSJ (Wall Street Journal) like to scandalize SEO, so if you get a call from a journalist you'd better not brag about your great SEO tactics. Google, in most cases, reacts to high profile outings aka bad press.

Third party trust metrics like Blekko, WOT, McAfee Siteadvisor

If you don't show up in Blekko, because you are banned there, and when sites like WOT and SiteAdvisor lists your site as deceptive or dangerous, this might mean you are heading towards a Google penalty. Google does not use these sites' data but has other means to screen the Web for the same issues.

Making Google look stupid

You do not need an NYT article, a SEO blogger or Google employee to get penalized for a bad rep. Publicly showing off your black hat SEO successes makes you vulnerable to the "making Google look stupid" penalty. Leading SEO specialists agree that from a certain point on,

Google can't keep quiet about it and will penalize you in order to keep its face.

Technical issues

Not every sudden drop in rankings and traffic is a penalty; some are stupidity or gross negligence. You can shoot yourself in the foot by messing with some technical aspects of web development.

Robots.txt

The robots.txt is not really needed to improve SEO. It can break a lot of things though. Just recently I blocked one of my blogs from being indexed by Google. Of course I suspected a penalty at first but then checked Google Webmaster Tools to find out I made the mistake.

No follow

I've seen leading blogs barred from the Google index because they activated the WordPress privacy mode. It simply meant that all of the blog was set to noindex, nofollow which equals blocking it in the robots.txt.

Duplicate titles and descriptions

When your site uses the same or a very similar page title and description for every single page, it's no wonder most of them won't show up in search results. This isn't a penalty either. It's just logical.

Non-crawlable links in JavaScript

There are still JavaScript site menus out there that can't get crawled by Google. Always check whether your menu uses real HTML links with "<a href="">" in it. Or at least the whole URL must show up.

Neither a penalty Or Your Fault

In some cases a loss of rankings or search traffic has nothing to do with you or your site. Something else changed instead, and that's why you get outranked all of a sudden.

Algorithm changes

Google changes and refines its algorithm all the time. Major changes are called updates, and sometimes mean dramatic shifts in search results. Just search for "Google Panda". The only thing you can do then is to find out what changed and why your site does not match the new ranking factors.

Competition got better

A common "problem" is also that your competition does more SEO work than you do and one day they outrank you. A ranking change from #1 to #2 on Google can mean a traffic loss of 60 to 80%.

Current events

Sometimes breaking news may push your site down. Google News results get displayed on top, and for less competitive phrases news media start to rank in regular results as well. Most of these ranking changes will vanish after a few days.

SERP display change

Google experiments all the time with its search results' display. Most notably, local results from Google Places take away large parts of the screen real estate. You might rank at #1 in organic results and still get displayed at the bottom of the search results page.

There are numerous reasons to see a search traffic slump one day out of the blue. It doesn't have to be a penalty, but if you engage in some of the high risk SEO tactics mentioned above it can be one. Make sure you have at least two web analytics tools to check what happened. Google Analytics is not perfect and sometimes the ways it measures traffic get changed overnight without notification.

How to sabotage your SEO Campaign

There are a number of ways you can really sabotage your SEO campaign with a professional SEO company. I have been making a list of issue with my clients for quite some time.

Changing the website without telling your SEO company first

Whether it's launching a new product or service or rebuilding an old version of your website, or a full redesign, it's really important to get the SEO advice **BEFORE** any changes are made. Most professional SEO's can instruct you how to properly change page URLs and not damage or lose your SEO positioning. There's nothing worse than finding that your rankings have plummeted because the site has been changed and not properly optimized or redirected during without notice.

CMS that doesn't allow SEO optimization

It is usually not your fault. CMS system that do not allow the implementation of important elements such as Title Tags or ALT Tags is clearly a major issue. It is really upsetting to a website owner when he gets a website created and only to find the CMS can't actually implement SEO items. One of the worst is when the title is taken automatically from the H1 field and can't be edited separately or that there is no way to add ALT Tags to a picture without special coding.

Not approving social media, articles, or website changes quickly

SEO is continually evolving, and dramatic changes can happen overnight, without warning as with an example of the Panda updates or Google Real World Search. You need to allow your SEO professional the leeway to quickly react, and give your SEO the flexibility to be able to adjust both strategies and actual on-site optimization quickly and decisively if necessary. Their ability to do this can be severely hampered by the need to go through lengthy sign-off procedures.

Just gonna 'help out' with my link building

Don't get me wrong, it's great when clients take an interest in link building. But not when the client thinks he is doing us a favor by paying $50 for 10,000 profile links (this has happened many times). This doesn't work and in the long run, ruins our ability to grow links that look natural to Google.

Changing your FTP Password

I love clients who ask us to do optimization. We have the FTP password long enough to download their super large website, then the password is changed. During the time the password is changed, we make changes, optimize the pages, clean up the website, and are ready to upload their nice optimized website only to find the website owner has changed the FTP password and invited another web developer without notice to make changes to the live site. When we are ready to upload the website, not only do we have to wait for the new password, once we have it, if we upload our changes to the root folder it will overwrite the changes approved by the customer and made by the developer in between our changes. This has happened twice with the same client. It is very frustrating.

Another problem with changing the FTP password without telling your SEO professional is it makes it very difficult to make quick changes to your website in response to search engine algorithm changes.

Listening to your website designer or hosting company.

The last most frustrating thing is when a client decides to go against your recommendations as an SEO professional when the trusted hosting or website designer speaks against it. The fact is, most website designers and website hosting companies do not keep up daily on SEO. They really believe they are giving good advice but in all reality it is old information they have previously learned but has changed.

A case in point was when I argued with a client that the Meta Tags can be removed from the website because they are not used anymore. The client was adamant about removing them. The client did it because the website designer told him they weren't needed. Less than 4 days later all his keywords dropped 3 to 20 places and he called me to ask us what we did to his website thinking I sabotaged his website. Of course the FTP logs clearly showed he was the only one who made changes.

It still took us two more weeks to convince him that the Meta data needed to go back on.

Chapter 13 – Basic Marketing Principles

Throughout my career I have been thought of by many as being one of the best sales persons both online and in real life. There are many things that help me make sales. In this chapter, I will outline the little things that add up one by one to help you make sales. Although the focus here is on online sales, these are sales principles that you should use every day both online and in real life to help you sell.

Sales Principles

These are my top 12 direct marketing principles you can use to make sure your internet marketing really works for you:

Stability

People want to know you are not going to disappear overnight so if you have been in business for any length of time, this will add credibility to you and your offers.

Statistics

Use genuine statistics to give you more credibility when listing the number of customers served, money saved, profits made, true results, and so on.

Testimonials

I can't overestimate the importance of getting relevant and credible reviews from your customers and clients, saying how you and your products or services have helped them.

Self Credibility

If you can, establish yourself as an expert in your field. Not everyone can write numerous books or be on TV. However, you can write articles and have them published on your product, service, or industry. You can run workshops that are designed to demonstrate or train how to use your products or how effective your services are.

Reprints of articles about you in the press or having your articles published in the media lend weight to your credibility as the expert or authority in your market and are highly valuable to you. Show your market that you are in demand, and have status as an expert.

You can also show you're an expert with industry certifications, awards, memberships, and accomplishments that are relevant to your market.

Demonstrations

It is a lot cheaper to sell online with the use of online videos or 'how to' DVDs to sell your product. If you hire a sales person he can only be one place at a time. The internet can be the equivalent of hundreds of sales people. A website that is properly designed can make it very easy to show a demonstration of your product or services, both on and offline.

You can also create and distribute a demonstration eBook by printing it out and talking through what it contains live on screen. Camtasia is free software that lets you make a screen capture video where you can demonstrate your website talking though the sales letter or giving a demo of how easy it is to download your eBook.

> **NOTE:** *You can also print eBooks cost effectively at Lulu.com and CreateSpace.com.*

Guarantee

If you can't guarantee the product or service you're selling, then find something else to sell that you can guarantee. To really make your potential customers feel safe buying from you, have an ironclad guarantee.

Accessibility

On your website, having your full contact detail information is a big boost to your potential customer confidence. Using just an email contact or a form shows you are hiding. Put your email, phone, and address that shows that you are in the U.S. and are credible.

> **NOTE:** *Never give a P.O. Box as your address as it immediately makes people suspicious.*

The Personal Touch

Be visible in the business you're in and make sure you have a live voice answer your phone if possible. In my SEO business, if I let voicemail pickup for one day I never get a sale. If I answer the phone, I usually always make a sale. Also, tell your customers about yourself. Make it personal to them and show them you are a real individual.

Admit Imperfections Upfront

No matter how good your product or service is, it will most likely have a disadvantage somewhere. Admit it up front and honestly comment on this fact.

Answer questions and objections in a timely manner when a potential customer asks them via email or the phone. Buyers buy more often when they can call an office throughout the week and email at any time with questions and get a human response.

People Will Buy to Save Money

People who are interested in your product or service will usually do nothing unless you ask for the sale and give them incentive. People are just bombarded by too many sales pitches and try to choose the best one.

The best pitch is to create urgency to buy now, such as informing them that the price is going up next week. But you have plenty of options here: you can offer a reduced price, a bundled special deal on your products or services, or a smaller free item for buying an larger item now.

Special Tactic for Creating Urgency

A special tactic to create urgency is to put an end date on your promotions and discounts – buy it now before the price goes up next week, next month, tomorrow. Even if your regular price is your promotional price, do a monthly campaign. When they look online they see a higher price if you don't buy by the end of the month.

If your business looks like it is always in permanent sale mode, there's no urgency for the customer to buy. Customers are not stupid; they see the advertising and know that this company ALWAYS has a sale on.

That is why it's important you create a deadline for your promotion. By having a defined end date showing in bold letters, it creates urgency and a reason for your potential customer to act now or lose out on saving money.

Tell People the Value They Are Getting

The discounts and value to the customer are not always obvious. So make it clear. If you put a value next to the items you are selling, don't assume your prospect or customer has worked it out for themselves. If the total value is $250, tell them it is $250 because if you leave them to add it up for themselves they generally won't do it.

Research

Research is an essential aspect of marketing. Inadequate research of your products and target market is one of the biggest pitfalls that can affect a marketing strategy. Research provides a wealth of information that is vital to your sales.

Determine what market is going to most likely benefit from the product or service you provide. This is the group of individuals you will want to target – in some areas, there may be multiple groups. While it may be possible to market to all these groups, in most situations it is better to market to a single group which contain a large percentage of similar traits. This makes it easier to consolidate a marketing plan as well as eliminate a significant amount of research, time, and effort.

The second aspect which needs to be researched for a marketing plan to be successful is your competition. It is also one of the reasons why marketing fails to produce appropriate results. Researching your competition is not just about researching the prices of a competitor. It includes noting things such as their sales techniques, finding out what marketing tools and resources they use, and how often those tools.

Many business owners and beginning internet marketers fail to note anything more than price and perhaps general layout of their competitors website and end their research there. They miss vital information that can save time, money, and effort when it comes to setting up their own marketing strategy. If you are not the most successfully-marketed business on the internet promoting your product or service, find out who is. Find out how they market and what makes them successful.

Collect information on the types of deals, offers, discounts and promotions that your competition uses and offer something different to help your business stand out. Many people simply do what their competition does. In doing so, they often lower their marketability and their marketing plan can ultimately fail in this area. You might pick up more market share by doing what the completion doesn't.

Marketing Tools

Having enough research to create your marketing plan is only the first step in solving the problems that often cause marketing plans to fail. The next step is to take the time to pick out the right tools. Having the right tools for the job is essential to ensuring you get the most out of your marketing strategies.

Marketing tools have diversified over the years. Tools are not limited strictly to email and promotional options. Video, social networking, SMS texting, Blogs, Twitter, Facebook, PPC, and many more are available to you. You just have to pick the tools that are going to be easy for you to learn, use, and require minimal maintenance with maximum potential results.

Don't Just Dream It, Do It!

One of the biggest reasons I am so successful is that if I get an idea, I do it. Nothing stands in my way. Hence you are reading this book because I came up with an idea for it while taking a shower. Don't picture that, by the way. In John Pinette's words, "You'll have nightmares!"

One of the biggest reasons why marketing strategies and businesses end up failing is lack of action and giving up. Marketing is an active part of your business, it is not a "set it in motion and let it run on its own" component of a website. In order to ensure that a marketing strategy succeeds you must be actively engaged in working that plan and revisit it and make the strategy better based on experience. This means that email marketing messages should be updated and redesigned regularly.

SMS, Facebook, and Twitter messages should be rewritten after every send. These messages should be short, contain only the minimum necessary information, and focus on one item at a time. It is important to remember that this type of marketing is relatively new and involves sending messages to Wiki's, blogs, members, and mobile devices that often indicate repeat messages.

Videos should be produced, edited, and updated to as high a level as possible. Computers and technology can turn just about any computer into a production studio with the right software. Keep videos interesting, engaging, and relevant. The videos should be related to the company, the products, or the services offered.

It is important to set up a marketing schedule and find out how much time, generally through trial and error, that you need each day, week or month to handle all your marketing tasks and keep everything up to date.

The reasons why a marketing plan might fail are numerous. I hate to outline some of them here, but you need to know so you can take steps avoid them. Some of these reasons include the following: failing to do the proper research into the market, not doing proper SEO, not having the right tools available, not researching cheaper delivery methods, having too many tools or not using the tools you have effectively, and not having inventory on hand that you are selling.

Taking the time to make sure that you have the information you need as well as putting in the effort to ensure your success can go a long way to eliminating these reasons.

When you develop a marketing message, you have to hit many levels of desire. Good marketing happens when you give logical reasons for your prospect's emotional-buying decisions. Some good marketing messages include:

- Save time
- Save money
- Make money
- Try for free
- Avoid effort
- Increase happiness
- Find success
- Be pain-free
- Get better health
- Have fun
- Enjoy your life
- Gain praise
- Feel safe and secure
- Feel liked or loved
- Be popular

Your task is to find a message which matches to your product or service and start promoting your marketing message in your marketing strategy.

See What Your Potential Clients Desire and Play on That

You should develop the ability to see what others want, need, and desire through your own research. You will be successful if you are always satisfying your customer's needs. Sometimes you have to look for the gap and create a new product or service or develop an improvement of an existing product or service.

You should always focus on service and deliver what you promise on time. My general rule is to always under promise and over deliver. Tell a customer that he/she will not have it until Friday even though it arrives on Wednesday. If something is delayed, the customer is not upset and when you deliver it early you look like the hero.

The internet allows you to start small and grow to any size business that you want to. Following the advice and principles I have laid out in this chapter will help your customer numbers grow and your profits grow with them.

Dealing With Adversity

My last words of advice are always maintain honesty and integrity in your dealings and stay true to your values even when dealing with stressful situations. Every business owner is going to have to deal with anxiety, frustration and problems, so cope with them by developing tenacity and perseverance.

If sales don't happen the first time you talk to a potential client, look at these statistics from the National Sales Executive Association:

- 2% of sales are made on the 1st contact;
- 3% of sales are made on the 2nd contact;
- 5% of sales are made on the 3rd contact;
- 10% of sales are made on the 4th contact (and)
- 80% of sales are made on the 5th – 12th contact.

For most businesses, if you don't offer an opt-in contact, like a regular email newsletter or blog postings, you're missing out on most of your potential sales.

When setting up an opt-in internet marketing campaign, you should offer incentives to subscribe. To entice people to opt-in, you can offer:

- Special pricing for email list members
- A first look at new products
- Ability for customer to select subjects and emails they receive
- Promise not to share email or other personal info with other companies

Using opt-in contact allows you to significantly increase conversions by introducing yourself over time to your potential customers, in a soft-sell manner

Website optimization is important; the goal is increased internet traffic, sales and sales leads. But whether you've hired an online SEO consultant or you're doing the process yourself, affordable search engine optimization by itself does not accomplish those last points which increase sales and sales leads. It just drives the potential customers to your website. You still have to close the deal.

Chapter 14- Optimizing for Major Search Engines

Optimization for Major Search Engines

- Optimization for Google

- Optimization for Bing, Yahoo!, MSN, and Microsoft Live

- Optimizing for Yahoo!

In general, search engine optimization basics are all the same. Each major search engine differs slightly in what it's looking for, however, so what makes you rank well with Google does not make you rank well with Bing (which, incidentally, provides the search results for MSN, Microsoft Live, and now Yahoo!).

It is still up in the air what will happen with smaller search engines that chose Yahoo! to do their search results but it looks like most will be allowing Yahoo! to forward Bing's results. These include:

- AllTheWeb
- AltaVista
- Go
- HotBot
- Lycos

So Bing is really a challenge to Google now.

In the next two sections, we will tell you how to optimize your website for better rankings with Google. Then we will explain how to optimize your website for better rankings with Bing. Included is a special report by Jason McCormick an SEO Expert. He has done a one and a half month study testing every aspect of Yahoo!'s search results using test websites which we have optimized and engineered specifically for testing search engine algorithms.

We will also include technical and content suggestions to help you rank higher with both Google and Bing.

Optimization for Google

This book has been focused heavily on Google, as it still maintains the lead in search engine searches. They have lost a lot of ground because of Bing and the millions Microsoft poured into an advertising campaign, but are still well above the fifty percent mark in internet searches.

Knowing this, how do you get Google to take notice of your website? What weights make your site rank higher? We are going to answer this question in these sections.

Google is traditionally, from my experience, the slowest of the major search engines to rank a new website – especially if you have a new domain name. Even if you manually register your site with Google using the steps in Chapter 4, it may take months before you can actually type in your domain name and see a result. That doesn't mean it is ranked either. Even with expert SEO it has taken me up to 8 months to get a new ranking on a site. Lately this has been around 3 months from notifying Google to actually getting the website indexed. I do this by putting plain text links on a few highly ranked websites.

Google Sandbox Period

The period between when Google is notified and it finally gets indexed is known as the "sandbox period".

How can you avoid the sandbox period when you need a new domain? My recommendation is to buy a domain name from GoDaddy Auctions(www.GoDaddy.com). Every domain you buy from a GoDaddy Auction is at least a year old and some have already had some pretty good SEO work done and there is already links to the domain. Domains are also available on just about any subject or industry.

One of the best things about buying a GoDaddy domain from their auction is the original date that the domain was registered on GoDaddy is the date that is listed when you do a WHOIS check (domain registration information). Google usually continues to index these domains and rarely puts the new purchased domain in a sandbox period.

Google doesn't sell organic placement, either. There are ads above and to the right side of the search results, but sponsored ads are the only placement that is available for purchase. That means that where your websites placement is based on your SEO and search engine marketing efforts.

Another heavy weight that adds votes to your website is the traffic to your website. You need to install the Google Analytics on your site to enjoy these additional votes to help improve the rankings on your website.

> **NOTE:** *Recently a lot of weight has been added to the Title Tag if it matches the first three keywords in the Meta Tags, the description contains the first three words, and the keyword density is around 7%.*

Sidebar: Google Caffeine

Google Caffeine to improves how fast Google can index and deliver relevant new content. This update did not change the algorithm but what is indexed and given to the algorithm has. One of the biggest changes is putting more relevancy on the "above the fold" area of the viewable content on each website page.

My recommendations to you is to make your website 100% relevant in the 800x600 viewable area at the top of each webpage. Place perfect keyword density, a relevant <H1> tag, all the links to your social media, and limit the pictures. If you do, Google Caffeine will be your friend.

Google PageRank

Google has a proprietary ranking algorithm and although they trademarked some parts of it, it changes frequently. An element of that algorithm is called Google PageRank.

Google explains PageRank like this:

> *"PageRank relies on the uniquely democratic nature of the Web by using its vast link structure as an indicator of an individual page's value. In essence, Google interprets a link from page A to page B as a vote, by page A, for page B. But, Google looks at considerably more than the sheer volume of votes, or links a page receives; for example, it also analyzes the page that casts the vote. Votes cast by pages that are themselves "important" weigh more heavily and help to make other pages "important." Using these and other factors, Google provides its views on pages' relative importance.*

Google PageRank is based on a balloting system that compares your site to all the other pages on the web that are of the same topic or topics. Then their algorithms take all the indexed information on those sites to determine which pages are most relevant to a search query based on numerous elements of the page.

An inbound link to a page counts as a vote of support, so links as discussed in previous chapters are very important. A page that is linked to by many pages with high PageRank receives a high rank if all the other components of optimization are in place. If there are no links to a web page, there is no support for that page. You will rarely find a page ranked by Google without inbound links. Know what the keyword density is or how well the other components of optimization are performed.

Google Instant

Google recently announced "Google Instant" in September and showed a new feature of the Google interface designed with a new search engine algorithm to improve the user experience. Google Instant is really about showing you more search results. Google Instant turns a search into a real-time stream of results which flow onto your screen as you type your query as shown below in Figure 14.1 as I start typing in a search for pocket knives.

Figure 14.1

With each letter you type, a whole new set of results displays on the screen. This is important for several reasons. First, you will now see many more search results than you would have otherwise. Most people never click through to the second page of search results so this is a way for Google to display several more pages of results.

If it is not in the first ten blue links (or really the first five or six), it might as well not exist for most people. With a Google Instant search, instead of people seeing only ten results, they may now see 50 or 100 (depending on how many letters they type and how far they get through each search query).

After testing the changes brought on by the results of Google Instant, several configurations clearly have an advantage. Those websites who have the key search words in their domain name or as the very first word(s) in the title that the users are searching for are not really effected by the change. Also those websites who have changed their pages to be completely relevant for only one keyword or one long-tail keyword are reaping the rewards of Google Instant.

I had theorized for a long time that Google would find a way to change the search to allow a page to be relevant for only one search term for quite some time and they found the way to deliver it.

From here on out you need to look at your pages either modify your current pages or add pages so that your pages are optimized for only single search terms or the search term and the plural version. If the plural version of the word is longer you would place it first. As an example, if your search term is a Oklahoma real estate brokers, you would make your title:

Oklahoma Real Estate Brokers | Oklahoma Real Estate Broker

You should also have the keywords in your Meta Keywords tag and in the Meta Description tag as well. If you don't know what I am talking about, refer back to Chapter 3.

For many large websites creating new pages focusing on just one product, service, or keyword is a burden, but the sooner the changes are made, the sooner you will reap the rewards. Many companies are seeing their full keyword position not changing and do not realize they are losing visits because they are not optimized for Google Instant.

If you make changes right away, you will reap the immediate reward of being found in searches before others catch on to the changes they need.

According to Google, its classic search interface took nine seconds on average for each search results to be returned. The new interface utilizing Google Instant algorithm saves 2-5 seconds per search.

Optimizing Google Instant For Products

Research is important as well as the placement of the keywords in your Title and Meta tagging.

Use common sense when writing a post or optimizing for Google Instant. Always use keywords from the user perspective. What do I mean? Let's say you are selling a Motorola Droid 2 cell phone.

To research the users keyword or words, analyze the Google Instant search results about how users interacted previously with search terms by typing some related keywords for your product.

Figure 14.2

The above screenshot (Figure 14.2) is popping up some search results for the keyword "Droid By Motorola" which is based on previous search keywords used by the Google search engine users. You will notice that Google search suggestions are indicated as well and you can see that as you spell all the way to "Motorola Droid X". Every keyword that comes up in between would be an individual page I would recommend you optimize for that keyword.

If you are writing a review or a blog post it would also be better to include all those phrases or keywords as well in your post. If you include all the terms you researched in your post or page titles it will increase the probability of your website being listed under Google Instant search results.

Google Webmaster Tools

Google has some general guidelines if you want to rank successfully. These guidelines and recommendations are laid out on Google's Webmaster Central (www.google.com/webmasters) which we explained in Chapter 4. You will also find tools available at Webmaster Central that enable you to analyze your site to help make it more Google-friendly. Those tools include the following:

- **Site Status Wizard**: This tool helps you to determine whether your site is currently being indexed by Google.
- **Webmaster Tools:** A set of tools designed to help you improve the indexing and ranking of your site and adding a link to your website's site map.
- **Google Site Map Generator:** Under the Webmaster Tools you can find the Google Sitemap Generator to make a sitemap of your website.
- **Content Submission Tools:** This tools is used to submit your site to Google, or to add products to Google Base or content to Google Book Search.
- **Google's Webmaster Blog:** Here you can find tips and strategies for ranking well in Google. Also you will find information on how the Google algorithm has changed.
- Webmaster Help Center: If you don't understand something about Webmaster Central, here's where you will find an explanation.

Some of the things that you should pay close attention to and follow through with is:

- Submit a sitemap of your site so Google knows what pages they should index.
- Tell Google what is the canonical URL you want to use (site.com or www.site.com).
- Detect issues with duplicate title tags and meta descriptions.
- See a list of URLs restricted by robots.txt.

- Detect crawl ability issues.
- Find 404 error pages.
- See the most common keywords people find your site through.
- Get a list of links pointing to your site.
- Tell Google how they should index your images.

iGoogle

Other useful tools for improving your search engine rankings are the various Google APIs (Application Programming Interfaces) that are available at iGoogle.com, as shown in Figure 14.3. These programming interfaces enable you to use Google technology to do many things, but most are geared toward improving the optimization of your website.

Figure 14.3

There are many help tools on the site to help you optimize your website. Many of them are pay-to-use tools, but usually you can find a free tool to do the same thing as the paid ones.

The use of Google APIs should be limited to creating applications and gadgets that your site visitors find useful. When you fulfill a need, visitors to your site continuously return, and that builds momentum. This in turn improves your search rankings simply on the merits of traffic and usability. That's a great vote for your site and Google will notice.

246

Pushing Your Google Optimization Over The Top

Along with great keyword densities and good Meta tagging, there are some things that can really push your Google optimization over the top.

1. Submit a video sitemap through the Google Webmaster Tool

You should use the Google Webmaster tools provided by the major search engines. Among other wonderful things, they accept XML sitemap submission, which directly tell the search engine about every web page on your site you wish to be indexed. A video sitemap does exactly what you think, it helps search engines find all your videos. For more information follow the instructions here:
(http://www.google.com/support/webmasters/bin/answer.py?hl=en&answer=80472)

2. Make sure your video format is supported by Google.

Google sitemaps only accepts the .mpg, .mpeg, .mp4, .m4v, .mov, .wmv, .avi, .asf, .ra, .ram and .flv files.

3. Use the Robots.txt file properly

Google doesn't ignore the robots.txt files for your website. If you disallow User-agent "Googlebot" anywhere on your website, Google will not crawl or index those pages. So it is important to be triply to be sure that all the URLs included in your site map allow Googlebot access.

4. Use a Content Delivery Network (CDN) or other means to speed up your website performance.

Hosting your own videos can help you outrank other websites or it can cause you to die in the rankings. If your website doesn't have the bandwidth or logistics to quickly display video, it can slow your website down. Using a content delivery network such as YouTube.com will help your pages load super-fast, which is now a major search engine ranking factor for Google. Google doesn't want to send searchers to slow landing pages.

5. Create a mechanically sound website.

Your website must be mechanically sound in every way. Google ranks sites now based on how good the coding of your website is. If your website is not completely compatible with all the available browsers, has broken links, errors in the code, stale or outdated coding, lacks W3C compliance, or any one of 400 other coding violations you may find it hard to rank at all on Google.

How do you know if you have these mechanical issues? You need to use a service such as **SEOAudits.com** or **AccuQuality.com**. They are the only tools I recommend and use to run over 400 tests on every page of your website and deliver a comprehensive report. They even spell check every page of your website and give you links or instructions on how to fix most of the issues in their reports.

New Google Features To Watch or Try

I have been watching Google experiment with their Auto-suggest algorithms and add it to multiple search services they run (including Google News, image search, etc). Here are the main Google Search Auto-Suggest sources and how they are different from one another.

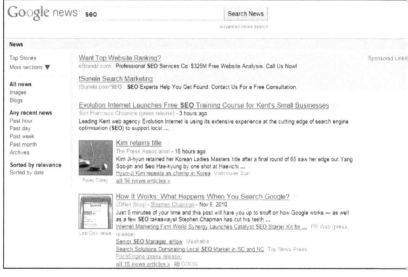

Figure 14.4

1. Google News Suggest

Google News Suggest was launched in late 2009. This is an invaluable tool for search marketers. The good thing about Google News Suggest is that it would suggest hot trends to you, so you may know what's hot without even searching the news (Google News Algorithm presents suggestions that are particularly relevant for **news-related queries**).

Here are the front page news and the suggestions that make it obvious as shown in Figure 14.4:

2. Google Image Suggest

One of the main reasons why website owners should keep an eye on Google Suggest is that Google Image Search is still the easiest way to get traffic, so be sure to target it carefully.

The Image Search suggestions include many specific words like "wallpaper", "cartoon", "photos", "landscape", "logo", "pictures":

3. Google Product Suggest

Google Product Suggest was launched in September 2009 and it is obviously an interesting tool for e-commerce focused projects. Type any search term and get up to 10 product suggestions.

4. Google Products/Google Shopping

Google Products and Google Shopping all start at **http://base.google.com**. This is a newer feature that allows for products to be sold on Google and have then appear near the top of search results. Google has placed a box which displays product suggestions in the SERPs as shown here in Figure 7.5 when I type in "hair dryer". (See the Google Shopping Recommendations section at the end of this section.)

Figure 14.5

Here are the current recommendation for Google Shopping for Google Products.

> 1. Product Title - Primary keywords should be in title, not more than twice.
> 2. Product Description – make sure the keyword is listed

once. Repeating keywords more than once may lead to penalties.

3. Freshness of feed - Products that are new and uploaded on a regular basis are listed above stale products. Upload product feed at least once a week, preferably 2x a week.

4. Place keywords in the URL of your products page.

5. Offering Google Checkout improves position and the frequency of the ad rotation.

6. Better Google Checkout reviews improves product showing frequency.

7. Also add the complete brand and model name in Alt tag your images on product pages.

8. Research your products at base.google.com.

9. If you are doing feeds to Google make sure the prices exactly match the prices on the product pages.

5. Google Video Suggest

In terms of video search, we are given two different options: Google Video search and YouTube Search. We have already described how with keyword research and brainstorming, Like YouTube Suggest, Google Video suggestions could work in certain niches for video optimization and keyword ideas (and inspiration):

6. Google Maps Suggest

Google "smarter" search suggestions were introduced in April of 2009 as well. They got smarter in two ways:

- Personalized suggestions (These are based on your search history and location). You should log out of Google before you check if your business pops up there.)

- Enhanced database (The search suggestions include additional information, such as the address of the business or the district that a place is in.

What To Check On Your Website If You Think Google Is Penalizing Your Website

Some Google penalties are just filters that are applied automatically. While many penalties can be both manual and automatic, some of the filters are obviously algorithmic.

Google Sandbox

Check to see if your domain is in the "New Domain Sandbox". This is the so-called sandbox filter has been around for years, but was never officially acknowledged as far as I know. It applies when you change domains or start out with a completely new domain and site. Without a proper "moved to" sign Google will apply this penalty to old established sites as well when they change domains. Use a 301 redirect for old sites and try to gain a significant number of authority links in the early days of a new domain to beat this filter.

Heading Tag Issues

If you have multiple H1 tags you will have problems because this is the title of your page. If you think of a page like a book, a book has just one title. Likewise a web page has only one H1 title tag. Google assumes that multiple h1 tags are a trick to spam its index, and penalizes sites using multiple h1 tags. Use H2, H3 and other headline tags instead but never skip. If you use a an H3 tag make sure there is an H2 tag in the coding before the H3 tag. Never use H Tags as a way of formatting your text.

Too Many Keywords

Keyword stuffing (high "keyword density") – one of the oldest spam techniques is so called keyword stuffing. Be sure to add your keywords to your website copy, but no more than a few times in each paragraph. Make sure that your total keyword content never goes over 7% on the page. It's more important to keep the text readable by the human visitor than any percentage of keywords.

Robots.txt File

The robots.txt is not really needed to improve SEO. It can break a lot of things though. Just this past month one of my clients had a web developer make some changes and with just a misplaced "/" caused the entire website deindexed by Google. At first I suspected a penalty but a quick check of the Robots.txt file revealed the mistake. A detrimental mistake for this company.

No Follow Tag In The Meta Tags

The "Nofollow" is a no-brainer in Meta tags, but recently I have seen many websites designed in WordPress get deindexed because they activated the WordPress Privacy Mode. When this is checked it sets all the pages to noindex, nofollow which equals blocking it in the robots.txt. file and tell the search engines to remove any mention of the website.

Duplicate Titles and Descriptions Tags

When your site uses the same or a very similar page title and description for every single page, it's no wonder most of them won't show up very well in search results. This really isn't a penalty. It's just logical. Every page should have a unique Title and Description Tags. The Title Tag should contain only a keyword for the page. The description should contain a good description with the keyword for the page embedded in the description in less than 170 characters.

Google Shopping Recommendations

Google shopping all starts at **base.google.com**. Submission to Google Product Search are free and has no bearing on if you use AdWords or have a high website page ranking. With Google Product Search, customers can research products, get descriptions and reviews, and your products show up just before the organic results as seen a few pages back in Figure 14.5.

Results can show up in Google's universal search results on the main search engine. This can occur in either the "onebox" shopping result (in the US, UK, and Germany) or a product search link called "Shopping." When a user clicks on this, they can see product pages that show reviews, specifics, and seller ratings.

Figure 14.6

Google Product Search shown in Figure 14.6 is supported by Google Base. To get your products into Google Base, you can submit them in one of four ways:

To start Go to Google Base (base.google.com) and submit your items. Google only recommends this for if you have five items or less. If you have more you need to use their template to submit what are called product feeds using either atab-delimited text or XML files.

NOTE: There are also store connectors for uploading existing products at an online store such eBay for example.

There is a video to learn more about how to get started and how to use the Google Shopping API in about 5:00. It explains a lot of best practices for submitting your feeds to Google Base. I have a list of my own best practices and tips below:

1.   Product Title - Very Important. Primary keywords should be in title, not more than twice.
2.   Product Description - Very Important. Again, repeating keywords more than once may lead to penalties.
3.   Freshness of feed - Very Important. Products that are new and uploaded on a regular basis are listed above stale products. Upload product feed at least once a week, preferably 2x a week.
4.   Keywords - Place keyword someone would use to find the product in the URL of product of the product page.
5.   Offering Google checkout improves position.

6.   ALT Tags - Also add the complete brand and model name in ALT tag of your images on product pages.

7.   Reviews - Positive (or any) store ratings improve position. I recommend to my clients that when they get started that they buy two of their own products through Google Checkout so they can post a couple of positive reviews to get started. Otherwise you will never show up.

8.   Competition - Research your competitions products at base.google.com.

9.   Price Matching - If you are doing feeds to Google make sure the prices exactly match the prices on the product pages on your website.

Just so you know, SERP rankings have no effect on Google Shopping/Google Products.

Optimization for Bing, MSN, & Microsoft Live

MSN and Microsoft Live are powered by Bing and there is now a new term for optimization of Bing. The term is DAO which stands for Decision Engine Optimization. In a short time Bing has become one of the top three search engines, and it's definitely not one that you should ignored but in my book last year, Bing was not only supplying sponsored results but the organic results matched the Yahoo! results as well. In this book I have returned the Yahoo! section because Yahoo! is back to supplying different results and similarly its previous requirements.

This is one section that gives you a good reason to throw last year's SEO books away for sure! As with other search engines, the basic optimization techniques that you have learned are the best way to get your site listed in Bing's database. Bing does not allow paid rankings, so your organic efforts will be the deciding factor for your rankings.

The one difference with Bing is that this search engine puts more emphasis on the freshness of content than other search engines. Specifically, sites that update high-quality, relevant content on a regular basis have a better chance of ranking high with Bing. Therefore, if you have not yet implemented a content renewal strategy and you want to rank well with Bing, you should plan and implement a strategy as quickly as you can.

The following are factors weighing more heavily in Bing's algorithms:

- Location Meta Tags in Long-tail Searches.
- Content and keyword density of around 6%.
- Excellent and continuously renewing content.
- Rich content (even more important on Bing than just about anything else).
- Keyword placement. Making sure you have your keywords in all the right places is imperative with the Bing search engine, especially page titles, H1 tags, and link text. They must all use matching trophy keywords.
- Authoritative inbound links. News organizations are especially ranked higher for inbound links. Inbound links are important for any major search engine, but Bing appears to act even more favorably toward inbound links, particularly those that are from sites that are news-oriented and have a high number of links.

- A technically sound, well-built site. Validating your code is important. You are penalized heavily for broken links.
- An XML Sitemap is absolutely required, as is a link to it placed under the website's listing in the Bing Webmaster Center.
- Bing recommends you create a Bing-specific mRSS feed through Bing Webmaster Tools for maximal indexing.

Bing offers quite a few Websites and tools to help site owners ensure their sites are well positioned for indexing within the engine. Bing Webmaster Center, which we explained earlier in the book, provides lots of helpful documentation and tools, including technical and content guidelines similar to Google's Webmaster Tools.

There's also a Webmaster blog, which contains a useful section on search marketing. As part of the Webmaster Center, Bing offers "Guidelines to Successful Indexing" to help Website owners ensure that the MSNBot can index all of your website's content.

Optimization for Yahoo

Figuring out Yahoo!'s new algorithm has been a task that two of our best SEO technicians here have been solely devoted to. More emphasis was given to this project than usual because recently Bing appears to have stopped providing results for Yahoo!. In the next section Jason McCormick a Senior Search Engine Optimization Expert reports his findings:

Over the past month and a half I have done experiments with our test websites to figure out the key weights that Yahoo uses to decide rankings and return results from user searches. I have determined the following factors weigh more heavily in Yahoo!'s algorithms:

Use Keywords in the Title Tags of Your Web Pages

A web page's title tag is one of the most important factors for how that page will rank in the search engines. Each page at your site should use a title tag that matches the search term you are trying to get the page ranked for. This is especially important at your main page. The title tag should also describe the content of the page in a concise and accurate manner. This helps the search engines decide how relevant the page is to a particular search term. The more relevant a page is, the higher it will rank in the results for that search term.

Use Your Keywords in Your Domain Name

I have done a lot of research on this and even though not everyone agrees, I have found clear evidence that websites with exact match domains get top ranking easier than non-keyword domain sites. In other words, once you know your best keyword phrase for your niche, see if you can get the domain name that matches that phrase exactly. Go for .com then .net, then .org. If none of them are available, use a hyphen (-) between your best keywords.

Use Your Keywords in the HTML Heading Tags

Heading tags (e.g. H1, H2, H3, etc.) give the search engines more info about how relevant the web page is to certain search terms. Make sure to use heading tags containing your keywords at each page of your site. As a bare minimum, every web page should have one H1 tag that includes the same keywords that are in your title tag.

Check the Keyword Density in Your Website Text

The number of times your keywords appear in the text on your web page or blog helps Yahoo! match the content to the appropriate search terms. As a general rule, for a web page that has about 400-600 words of body content, use the main keyword once in the first paragraph, once in second paragraph, once in the last paragraph, and once somewhere in between.

Setup Your Website's Internal Linking Structure Properly

When you are planning your website or blog, make sure you have at least one text link on every page that links to your main URL. The text link should contain your best keyword or keyword phrase. As your site grows in size, so will the number of web pages that point to your main page, increasing the popularity for that page based on your best keywords. Also, when adding blog posts at your blog, be sure to hyperlink to other posts on your blog when appropriate. (Each time you do this, be sure to use the keywords you're working on and they getting ranked!)

Slowly Grow the Number of Incoming Links from a Wide Variety of External Sites

Of all the factors in SEO, one of the most important is the number of web pages that link to the target page you are trying to get ranked well. In other words, if site A and site B are virtually identical, site A will outrank site B if there are more web pages linking to site A.

> **NOTE:** Of course getting lots of links to a site can be time consuming. That's why you may want to outsource this task.

Grow the Number of Incoming Links From External Sites Slowly and Consistently

Don't go too fast with your link building campaign. Getting a few dozen links a week or even 10 a day is OK, but if Yahoo! sees 1000 new incoming links to your site the next time they update their database, you'll likely move down the SERPS, and not up.

Chapter 15 – Targeting Many Keywords

Most websites selling anything need to target more than three keywords. Even if you just sell a single product or service. So what do you do to promote your website and focus on many keywords since many of the major search engines only allow a web page to be relevant for three keywords.

The answer is a simple one but the execution is about the most complex of any part of your website's code. The answer is that you need to create a perfectly optimized landing page for every three keywords you want to focus on. You then have to have the search engines index all those additional pages separately as separate landing pages.

Now, here is the hard part. Google and the other major search engines require a site map to tell them the landing pages you want to index. Not just any, there is a standard called Sitemap protocol 0.90.

> **WARNINGS:** *There are so many websites and web developers on the Internet that claim they can create a sitemap. Many just create pages with links and call them a sitemap. Also, there has been many updates to the Sitemap Protocol and many websites still push older versions. I highly recommend that if you are not a professional developer you go to a trusted source such as SMMaker.com or SMCreator.com and have them professionally create and install a Sitemap for your website.*

In this chapter I am going to tell you how to make a Sitemap specially formulated to Google and Bing. And then how to tell Google and Bing where to look for your site map. As you saw from the warning above, it is a lot of work to create a site map and test it to see if it is working. It is so much easier to just visit either one of these sites and pay less than $15.00 to have it created for you at either of these websites:

> http://www.SMMaker.com
> http://www.SMCreator.com

So let's take a look at how to create a site map.

Sitemaps XML format

Informing search engine crawlers This document describes the XML schema for the Sitemap protocol. The Sitemap protocol format consists of XML tags. All data values in a Sitemap must be entity-escaped. The file itself must be UTF-8 encoded.

The Sitemap must include the following:

- Begin with an opening <urlset> tag and end with a closing </urlset> tag.
- Specify the namespace (protocol standard) within the <urlset> tag.
- Include a <url> entry for each URL, as a parent XML tag.
- Include a <loc> child entry for each <url> parent tag.

All of the other tags are optional. Support for these optional tags may vary among search engines. Refer to each search engine's documentation for details. For Google you must include this tag:

<urlset xmlns="http://www.sitemaps.org/schemas/sitemap/0.9">

Let's look at an example which shows a Sitemap that contains just a single URL:

```
<?xml version="1.0" encoding="UTF-8"?>
<urlset xmlns="http://www.sitemaps.org/schemas/sitemap/0.9">
  <url>
    <loc>http://www.MikeMonahanSEO.com/</loc>
    <lastmod>2005-01-01</lastmod>
    <changefreq>monthly</changefreq>
    <priority>0.8</priority>
  </url>
</urlset>
```

All XML Tags

Here are all the tags that can be used in your site map and their syntaxes and descriptions.

<urlset> (required)

Encapsulates the file and references the current protocol standard.

<url> (required)

Parent tag for each URL entry. The remaining tags are children of this tag.

<loc> (required)

URL of the page. This URL must begin with the protocol (such as http) and end with a trailing slash, if your web server requires it. This value must be less than 2,048 characters.

<lastmod> (optional)

The date of last modification of the file. This date should be in W3C Date/time format. This format allows you to omit the time portion, if desired, and use YYYY-MM-DD.

<changefreq> (optional)

How frequently the page is likely to change. This value provides general information to search engines and may not correlate exactly to how often they crawl the page. Valid syntaxes are:

- always
- hourly
- daily
- weekly
- monthly
- yearly
- never

<priority> (optional)

The priority of this URL relative to other URLs on your site. Valid values range from 0.0 to 1.0. This value does not affect how your pages are compared to pages on other sites—it only lets the search engines know which pages you deem most important for the crawlers.

NOTE: *The default priority of a page is 0.5.*

The priority you assign to a page is not likely to influence the position of your URLs in a search engine's result pages. Search engines may use this information when selecting between URLs on the same site, so you can use this tag to increase the likelihood that your most important pages are present in a search index.

> **WARNING:** *Assigning a high priority to all of the URLs on your site is not likely to help you. Since the priority is relative, it is only used to select between URLs on your site.*

Here is an example using the different tags:

```
<?xml version="1.0" encoding="UTF-8"?>
<urlset xmlns="http://www.sitemaps.org/schemas/sitemap/0.9">
<url>
<loc>http://www.MikeMonahanSEO.com</loc>
<lastmod>2010-05-20</lastmod>
<priority>0.5</priority>
</url>
<url>
<loc>http://www.MikeMonahanSEO.com/TA.php</loc>
<lastmod>2010-05-20</lastmod>
<priority>0.5</priority>
</url>
<url>
<loc>http://www.MikeMonahanSEO.com/SEO.php</loc>
<lastmod>2010-05-20</lastmod>
<priority>0.5</priority>
</url>
<url>
<loc>http://www.MikeMonahanSEO.com/SEM.php</loc>
<lastmod>2010-05-20</lastmod>
<priority>0.5</priority>
</url>
</urlset>
```

Saving your Site Map

Search engines know to look for a plain text site map at the root directory of your website where your Index page resides. It should be named "Sitemap.xml"

For instance it should be accessible using your site URL. If the Sitemap is located at http://www.MikeMonahanSEO.com/sitemap.xml and it can't include URLs from http://subdomain.MikeMonahanSEO.com.

You can submit a sitemap using a port. If you submit a Sitemap using a path with a port number, you must include that port number as part of the path in each URL listed in the Sitemap file. For instance, if your

Sitemap is located at:

http://www.MikeMonahanSEO.com:100/sitemap.xml

Then each URL listed in the Sitemap must begin with:

http://www.MikeMonahanSEO.com:100

Submit Your Site Map To Google And Bing

You can submit your website's site map URL to both Google and Bing. To do this go to the following websites and login with the Google and Bing ID's you used in Chapter 3. For Google go to:

https://www.google.com/webmasters/tools/

(Go to **Site configuration**, click **Sitemaps**)

For Bing.com go to:

http://www.bing.com/webmaster

Where to go for more information

For more information on how to configure a site map visit:

http://www.sitemaps.org/schemas/sitemap/0.9/siteindex.xsd

There are a number of tools available to help you validate the structure of your Sitemap based on this schema. You can find a list of XML-related tools at the following websites:

http://www.w3.org/XML/Schema#Tools
http://www.xml.com/pub/a/2000/12/13/schematools.html

Chapter 16 – Getting Professional SEO Services

After reading this book you may have come to the conclusion that you don't want to or have the time to invest on optimizing your website. Or maybe you have investigated the competition and found that the amount of competition is too much for you to handle on your own. Whatever the reason, you may come to a point where you feel that hiring a professional is what you need to do.

I could just stop the chapter right here and say hey, e-mail me at:

Mike@MikeMonahanSEO.com

We will take care of you. If that is not what you want to do, let me give you some pointers to help you out. There are a lot of scam artists, cons, and the like which want to separate you from the money in your bank account. In fact I think it is easier to find the scam artists peddling SEO than the real thing.

If I were to guess on a ratio. There is probably 100 scammers for every one SEO consultant that knows enough to get you listed at the top of the search engines. The information in this chapter is crucial to learn to keep you from falling victim to scams.

Hiring the Right Professionals

In this business cutting corners is not an option, because the wrong SEO practices can be far more detrimental to your website than doing nothing at all. Virtually everyone of my major clients was first scammed by an SEO scammer before coming to me. In fact, it is not at all unusual to hear about a company or website owner that's been scammed by a supposed SEO consultant who guaranteed them top placement in hundreds of search engines in just days and they actually sent the fraudulent company money.

One of the first clues is the absolute guarantee part. It's just not possible for anyone, even an SEO expert, to guarantee that your site will appear at number one of search engine rankings all the time. Nonetheless, many people claiming to be SEO experts will tell you they can do just that and in just days. Don't believe them. Good organic rankings for keywords worth using takes months to achieve.

In most cases, what happens is this: A website designer or owner who has had to create a website for SEO decides he or she can implement SEO for others to make a profit. However, just because these people have done SEO on their own sites doesn't mean they can plan SEO and implement optimization techniques on your website in the most effective manner possible. Every site, company and industry have different optimization needs.

In most cases, it takes a team of people to perform proper SEO techniques for a business website. That team might include someone to submit your website to different directories and search engines, someone to create and submit articles to online resources, someone to design and implement SEO elements, someone else to code the website to make it attractive to search engines, and a project manager to manage the whole SEO program from beginning to end.

Recognizing SEO Scammers

There are certain things you should check or look for when choosing an SEO company. These are the following:

- Get references from them. See where their customers rank. Go one step further, though. If at the bottom of the referral website's homepage it does not show that the SEO company you are checking out does their web design or SEO work, call or email the company and verify that their SEO work is handled by them.

  It is not uncommon for scammers to find a highly-ranked site and claim it is their work. Whenever possible I keep a link at the bottom of their homepage that states, "SEO Services Provided By: MikeMonahanSEO.com" and a link to our page. It makes it easy for our customers to see we really do the work we say we do.

- Be wary if the prospective company says that they guarantee that your site will show up in the first page of results or even as the number one result every time! Time for a reality check: the algorithms that the search engines use are closely guarded trade secrets meaning that no one outside of a few people at the search engine companies knows exactly how it all works. Guaranteeing a certain page ranking is a sign of inexperience at best – and much more likely, indicates a scam.

- If you hear an obviously busy call center in the background, run. If their sales department is a room crowded with telemarketers trolling for business around the clock, it's a big red flag that you are being scammed.

- They promise to secure you top rankings for long-tail keywords which strikes you as unlikely to be used by anyone. For starters, they are trying to sell you a guaranteed page ranking (but we know better, don't we?). If the keyword they are offering you great placement for sounds a little fishy to you, look up its popularity with the free Google Keyword Tool we discussed in earlier in this book. See what its popularity is and compare how much competition there is for it. Keywords that no one ever searches for are easy to main on page one of a Google search.

- If their services are offered at unrealistically low prices be weary. There are some SEO scammers who lure victims by offering to optimize your site and run promotional campaigns for prices that sound entirely too good to be true. Usually they want the amount upfront and from a checking account rather than a credit card.

- RED FLAG: "We can give your website and SEO tune up for $499.00."

- RED FLAG: "Results in 48 hours (or less). " If this could be done it would save everyone a lot of money and time. Everyone would be number one. Oh wait. They can't be.

Again, do your due diligence. Look at their credentials, find out who's used their services in the past and what they have to say about the company. You should expect regular weekly reports on how your keywords are performing and you should be able to easily get in touch by phone and speak to one of the SEO consultants to get their advice and input as needed. It needs to be an interactive process. If the reports are only monthly or quarterly that is not enough time to get notified when a keyword drops and take immediate action to correct the issue.

The best SEO companies have years of expertise in the field and know the most effective SEO methodologies inside and out. When algorithms change they also know how to determine the changes and react and have a process in place to notify their customers. Your placements on the major search engines may change from month to month but will return to normal as your professional SEO company does what is necessary to get you back to the top.

SEO Company Expectations

When you find an SEO firm that offers the services that you need, you can expect to receive certain specific services from them. The services vary from firm to firm, but here's a list that you can use as a good rule of thumb:

- You should be provided with an initial professional SEO audit. The audit should thoroughly examine your sites URL properties, current SEO elements, problems with the current design and structure of your existing website, provide keyword and competitor research, and look at the mechanics of a website as a whole and include recommendations.

- If you are trying to employ an SEO company that is a one man show who does the auditing, the optimization, the linking, the articles, the research, the social media, the web changes, monitors the analytics, does the billing, and everything else, you will soon learn that no one can be an expert at everything and you will soon be lost amongst his many clients.

  At MikeMonahanSEO.com everyone wears their own hat and focuses on just one part. That means there is a team assigned to every client.

- The company you hire should employ a project manager who tracks all the needs of your company's website(s) and follows the reports. This person needs to be able to bring in the experts needed at a given time they are needed and always be available by phone. If your SEO expert says he is only available by e-mail that is a red flag!

- You should be provided with recommendations for keywords and a plan to optimize your website. This report should indicate how each page of your website is optimized including what on-page SEO elements such as HTML tags, keywords, and content needs to be changed on your website on an ongoing basis.

- You should be provided with information on how the SEO company plans to perform the optimization of the internal site navigation. Your internal navigation can have a serious effect on how your site performs in search results, so a good SEO will examine and optimize that navigation structure.

- Your SEO company should be able to scan the Internet weekly for mentions of your domain name in Blogs and other social media and provide this in a weekly report. This is now known as "Reputation Management" and is a critical piece of any online presence. And should be part of your weekly SEO Report.

- The SEO company should be able to scan your website weekly for design changes made that inadvertently broke links or strayed from the SEO goals set in place. These warnings should also be in your weekly SEO Report.

- A plan on how the SEO company intends to perform link building for your domain and verify they are only white hat techniques to sites relevant to your industry or follow guidelines set at http://angelasandpaulsbacklinks.com/.

- The company you choose should have procedures and the ability to test the different search engine algorithms to detect changes. They should be able to immediately make changes to your website to combat those changes.

- A plan on how the SEO company will show their progress and the monitoring of your SEO efforts and keyword statistics. They should also be able to give you statistics on your major competitors as well. If the SEO company cannot provide you this information on a weekly basis, especially in the beginning, find another company.

- SEO requires ongoing efforts. The SEO company must be able to train your staff with the most successful methods for maintaining optimization and providing news articles and suggestions.

Professional SEO firms can offer a lot of benefits to your website. After all, your core business is not likely SEO, but an SEO firm's is. The good ones can properly optimize your site, and your services, in less time than you can. For that reason alone, it should be enough to make you consider hiring an SEO firm, whether or not you end up doing so.

Chapter 16 – In-house I.T. Education

In most large companies I have come in to contact with over the years, the website is part of the Information Technology (IT) department and changes go through multiple layers of approvals for changes and the SEO company is usually hired by the Marketing Department.

Soon the Marketing Department is asking for coding changes and things that go completely against the nice esthetically pleasing website and friction starts to mount. One of the things must be done to create a good SEO campaign is changes to the on-page coding, keyword density, and many other aspects. It is impossible to do SEO without making at least some changes on-page, and that means eventually you'll need to enlist the services of the IT Department.

Even though we are working for the same, the SEO/IT relationship has historically been fraught with mistrust: you feel misunderstood, they worry you will break the website, and you're both operating with two very different ideas of what a "simple change" is.

Lend a Hand, Don't Reprimand.

Education is the best tool in an SEO's arsenal. Don't worry about guarding your preciously held secrets; we've come too far for that. most of the good stuff is stuff you won't need IT for anyway, am I right?.

It's easy for SEO projects to get stalled because not everyone involved understands what is going on or why it's important. Make sure IT gets an education in SEO basics (especially relating to site architecture/back end issues).

It accomplishes two things: it gives everyone a frame of reference for your future projects, and it gets a whole lot more eyeballs looking out for back-end changes that could have catastrophic SEO consequences.

Feel Their Pain

You know how sometimes, someone wants results on an SEO project right away, and you say, "You just don't understand how long that takes" IT's life is like that, only times a million.

Be appropriate with your requests and reasonable with your expectations and you'll make everyone's life a lot easier.

If you get pushback on a project, work with the team to find a solution rather than going over their heads right off the bat. Same team, people. Same team.

Be Realistic

Nobody expects you to be completely aware of all of IT's projects, but sometimes your changes just are not as important as other stuff they've got in the hopper – your title tag changes aren't going to get priority over a security flaw in your SaaS product.

Additionally, the benefit for some SEO tasks won't be worth the time and effort it will take to complete them, and you should try to learn and accept that when you have to.

That said, if there are things you feel are actively hurting the website, make sure everyone knows the ongoing costs of leaving them unfixed. If you can tie a dollar amount to it, you can bet it will get fixed eventually.

Be Available

If you submit a list of changes and then wander off, don't be surprised if IT doesn't want to meet up at the flagpole after school anymore.

Part of being BFFs with IT is making yourself available for follow-up and clarification questions. Yes, as many as it takes.

Do NOT take the attitude that once you hand off the tasks to IT, they become IT's problem. If the site SEO fails because your project was implemented incorrectly, you will look bad, not IT. That means that your projects continue to be your projects and you're available to provide them with all the TLC they need until they're completed.

A 2 Pound XXXL Bag of M&M's Would Be A Good Gift Here

Make sure IT doesn't just see your face when you need something right away. Take some time to hang out with the team – bring M&M's, cookies or doughnuts to their team meetings once in a while, or get everyone out to happy hour, and then talk about the website.

This is a great time to revisit some of the SEO basics you have already taken time to teach them about. If anyone on the team expresses an interest in learning more about SEO, for God's sake make them your lunch buddy.

Sooner or later you're going to need a favor from these people. Wouldn't you rather be their pal who brings cookies than that needy annoying person from the Marketing department?

Give Them Tools To Help Them

This book is obviously a place to start but you can also send the I.T. Department articles educating them on why they need to make each change. Another item to consider is sending the person responsible to make the changes to a training class. I offer classes both one on one or in large groups. Visit **http://www.MikeMonahanSEO.com/training** for more information.

Appendix A - Major Search Engine On-Page Recommendations

- Google On-page Recommendations
- Bing and MSN On-page Recommendations
- Yahoo! On-page Recommendations

Google On-Page Recommendations:

- ✓ Create or convert your website to WordPress if at all possible.
- ✓ Focus on only 1 keyword on a page.
- ✓ Keep the keyword density for the word around between 6-6.5% but don't go over. Use http://www.gorank.com/analyze.php to check your keyword density. No other word should be on the page more than 2% of the time unless it is a common word such as "and" or "for".
- ✓ Put relative content including links to your social media accounts in the top 800x600 viewable screen for users to help Google Caffeine indexing.
- ✓ Make sure your domain name is registered for at least 5 years or more.
- ✓ Install Google Analytics to measure traffic to increase rankings.
- ✓ Use Google Webmasters Tools and follow all suggestions.
- ✓ Match the first three keywords on the Title tag, Meta descriptions tag, Meta keyword tag.
- ✓ Validate your HTML code by using either **SEOAudits.com** or **AccuQuality.com** report. Fix all critical or major issues found in the report related to browser or mobile devices, broken links, html coding issues, etc.
- ✓ Avoid broken links.
- ✓ Ensure that you have allowed the GoogleBot to crawl your site and employ Robots.txt.
- ✓ Use static URLs wherever possible rather than dynamic URLs with multiple extensions.
- ✓ Interact with Google owned sites such as Blogger, BlogSpot, and YouTube.
- ✓ Don't use a newly registered domain name if possible.
- ✓ Create valuable content.
- ✓ Use visible on-page text, include a high keyword density.
- ✓ Keep pages down to a reasonable file size under 180K.

- ✓ Try not to cover more than one topic per page.
- ✓ Use static text links.
- ✓ Put keywords in text rather than in images.
- ✓ Don't hide text on a page.

Bing On-Page Recommendations:

- ✓ Validate your HTML code by using either **SEOAudits.com** or **AccuQuality.com** report. Fix all critical or major issues found in the report related to browser or mobile devices, broken links, html coding issues, etc.
- ✓ Avoid broken links.
- ✓ Set up redirects from old pages to new ones.
- ✓ Ensure that you have allowed the MSNBot to crawl your site and employ Robots.txt.
- ✓ Keep the keyword density around 6%.
- ✓ Keep pages down to a reasonable file size under 150K.
- ✓ Use static URLs wherever possible rather than dynamic URLs with multiple extensions.
- ✓ Create valuable content.
- ✓ With visible on-page text, include keywords.
- ✓ Keep pages down to a reasonable file size.
- ✓ Try not to cover more than one topic per page.
- ✓ Use static text links.
- ✓ Put keywords in text rather than in images.

Yahoo! On-Page Recommendations:

- ✓ Validate your HTML code by using either **SEOAudits.com** or **AccuQuality.com** report. Fix all critical or major issues found in the report related to browser or mobile devices, broken links, html coding issues, etc.
- ✓ Ensure that you have allowed all robots to crawl your site and employ the Robots.txt file properly.
- ✓ Setup a good internal linking structure with plain text anchor text links.
- ✓ Keep the keyword density around 5%.
- ✓ Use static URLs wherever possible rather than dynamic URLs with multiple extensions.
- ✓ Create valuable content.
- ✓ With visible on-page text, include keywords.
- ✓ Keep pages down to a reasonable file size.
- ✓ Try not to cover more than one topic per page.
- ✓ Use static text links.
- ✓ Put keywords in text rather than in images.

Appendix B – SEO Checklist for New Non-Ranking Sites

If your new to SEO, I have created a quick little list to help you start ranking quickly. I have also included recommendations on how to make your website overcome each issue. Keep in mind that I am assuming you have already completed all the steps in Chapter 3.

Accessibility

Users and search engines both need to be able to reach all of the pages, you also need to make sure you don't have any dumb mistakes that can harm your SEO. These are things like 404s and 500 errors, and 302s instead of 301s, missing title tags, or thin content where there is not much material on the page for the search engines to grab on to and maybe for users as well. Get an AccuQuality.com or SEOAudits.com report done to help you eliminate these issues.

Keyword Targeting

Choosing the right keywords to target. You might not be able to target high value terms because you are also looking for low difficulty when you are first launching a site. You can look at search volume, the relevance to the website, and low difficulty.

Content Quality and Value

If you have users coming to this page and they are thinking this does not really answer my question or maybe only one part of my question, but I wish there was more detail. If you can change that to "I like this site, it makes me happy!" This kind of satisfaction from your users with the quality of the content that you produce, you are going to do much better in the search engines. Google has gotten so much better about noticing the true quality and value with results.

Design Quality, User Experience, and Usability

Unless you have a professional designer or you have a professional design background, you almost certainly need to hire someone or go with a very simple, basic design that is very user friendly. Then take a survey from friends and people in your company, see how they react to the site. Their reaction will tell you if the design works and if the usability is easy to understand. There is really no point in ranking unless you are nailing these two, because you are not going to get many more customers. People are just going to be frustrated by the website.

Social Account Setup

Because social and SEO are coming together like never before, Google is showing plus ones and things that people share by default in the search engine rankings. It really, really pays to be in social and social signals help search engines better rank things as well as having a nice second order effect on user and usage data, on branding, on the impact of people seeing those sites through social sharing and potentially linking to them.

For your social account set up you will want to have these four: Facebook, Twitter, LinkedIn and Google+. LinkedIn, Twitter, Facebook are all over 150 million users right now and growing every day. Twitter is at 200 million and Facebook is at 750 million, their numbers are growing quickly. While having your accounts spread throughout these social accounts you will want to keep them looking consistent so when people log on they know it is your site. Things like logos, colors, and photos help people to feel comfortable as they get to know you.

Once you have got these social accounts set up, you can feel good about sharing the content that you are producing through those social accounts, finding connections, building up in that world, and spending the appropriate amount of time there depending on the value you are feeling back from that.

Link Building

When you don't have any trustworthy quality links to boost you up, this is when low quality links can hurt your website the most. So, start with your business contacts and your customers to see if you can exchange links. If the contacts that you have in the business world are willing to say, "hey, my friend Steve just launched a new website, boom, that is a great way of getting a link". All your email contacts, your LinkedIn contacts, the people that you know personally and professionally, if you can ask them, hey, would you support me by throwing a link to me on your "About Page" or your Blog Roll or your list of customers or your list of vendors, whatever it is.

High quality resource lists are great too, this would be things like the Better Business Bureau. If you are a startup in the technology world, you definitely need to have a CrunchBase listing. You might want to be on some Wikipedia lists, it is a good place to start getting some visibility. Another great way is talking to the press, let them know when you are launching a new site or changing a branding, anything that could draw attention to the company and bring about publicity.

Social Media Link Acquisitions

This is where you spend time on Twitter, on Facebook, on LinkedIn, Google+ connecting with people and over time building those relationships that will get you the links possibly through one of these other forms or just through the friendliness of them noticing and liking, and enjoying your content. That is what content marketing is all about! All of this is very important and are really great ways to start, but they are not short-term wins. Most of these things require effort, investment of time, energy, creativity, good content, and some authenticity in your marketing versus a lot of the stuff that tempts people very early on. It is not like you will just go out there and instantly link up with 500 links and all of a sudden everyone is working together happily, there is much more work than that. Almost all low quality directories have spammy manipulative link profiles. Plus, they will not even show the brand names on the list.

Stay away from the low quality directories they will not help you with your business. You might want to also avoid article marketing or article spinning, unless you know how it really works it can hurt you way more than help you in the links world. One last thing to be cautious about are the forums, open forums, be careful of where you decide to leave a link. Google looks at sites that are grouping with a bunch of bad sites and will penalize them for their actions. A term for this is link farms, essentially this is when people are setting up all these different systems of links that point to each other across tons of domains that are completely artificial or link for no human reason, they are there merely to manipulate the engines, Google does not look onto these very nicely.

Appendix C – Resources For SEO

There are many free resources for SEO on the Internet. Here is a few of them that I find most valuable, productive, or unique.

Best SEO Blogs

The world of SEO is constantly changing because search engines constantly change their algorithms. These blogs help you to keep up on the latest news, information, and tips about SEO.

1. Search Engine Land (SearchEngineLand.com) – One of the most well respected search engine and SEO news website.

2. Search Engine Guide (SearchEngineGuide.com) – A blog with a heavy focus on SEO for small businesses.

3. Search Engine Watch (SearchEngineWatch.com) – One of the oldest blogs out there.

4. Online Marketing Blog (TopRankBlog.com) – A great mix of SEO, PR, and social media articles.

5. Matt Cutts (MattCutts.com) – This is a blog by the head of Google's Web Engineering team. When he talks, you better listen.

6. Search Engine Journal (SearchEngineJournal.com) – This is one that I personally follow.

7. Google Blog (GoogleBlog.BlogSpot.com) - Google's official blog however they only discuss everything related to Google.

8. Traffick (Traffick.com) – A blog with a strong focus on PPC.

9. Google Blogoscoped\ (Blog.Outer-Court.com) – This blog is also all about Google. But the difference is, this one is written by a third party.

SEO Information Resources

Blogs can be your main source of information, however they don't cover everything. Usually the latest changes. If you are going to start from the beginning of SEO, here are some good resources as well as some unique resources.

1. Marketing Terms (MarketingTerms.com) – This site has a dictionary which will help you understand all of the marketing terms you run into.

2. Google's SEO Guidelines (google.com/webmasters/seo) – Google's take on SEO as well as their rules and a starter guide.

3. SEO Chat (SEOChat.com) – Here you can find a weekly SEO video and more information.

4. Search Engine Colossus (SearchEngineColossus.com) – Here you can learn that there is a lot more search engines than you may know of. This is a place where you can find them all.

5. Web Pro News (WebProNews.com) – Information and video interviews from SEO expert.

6. SEO FAQ (HighRankings.com) –This resource answers the majority of newbie questions.

SEO Tools

If you are not cheating and doing SEO right it is a very time consuming process. These tools will not only make your life easier, but they'll help you understand what you need to do and how to rank well on search engines.

1. SEOAudits (SEOAudits.com) – A tool to check your website for mechanics issues, browser compatibility, SEO issues and much more.

2. AccuQuality (AccuQuality.com) – Best website analysis tool I have ever used. They run 450 tests on every page which in include W3C compatibility, errors, code violations, browser compatibility, link problems, SEO, and they even spell check every page and provide a report.

3. Submission Complete (SubmissionComplete.com) – A very affordable tool to submit your website to all the major search engines and directories.

4. Website Submitter (WebsiteSubmitter.org) – Another affordable tool to submit your website to all the search engines and major directories.

5. SpyFu (SpyFu.com) – This site will help you understand what search terms your competition is using or is advertising with and how well they are doing.

6. Wordtracker (WordTracker.com) – You don't have to wonder how popular keywords and phrases are.

7. Google Toolbar (toolbar.google.com) – This toolbar will show you what your Google PageRank number is and much more.

8. Google Webmaster Tools (Google.com/webmasters/tools) – It seems this tool gets more and more important. You can now see the keywords people find your site with, errors on your website, submit an XML sitemap, and soon you will be able to see if your website has duplicate content somewhere on the Internet.

9. Digital Point SEO Tools (DigitalPoint/tools) – A collection of 17 different SEO tools.

10. AdWords Keyword Tool (adwords.google.com/select/KeywordToolExternal) – Although you might not be looking to pay for traffic, this tool will give you a good idea of how many clicks you can get from Google and help you with your keyword research.

11. DIYSEO (DIYSEO.com) – Tools to help you keep track of your SEO progress.

12. Backlink Checker (iwebtool.com) – See how many websites link to your website VS your competition.

SEO Forums

Sometimes you are going to be unsure of what to do. The best thing to do when this happens is to ask someone for advice. Through forums you can communicate with other SEOs or ask questions..

1. High Rankings Forum (HighRankings.com/forum) – A good community with a lot of friendly SEOs to help you.

2. Webmaster World (WebmasterWorld.com) – By far one of the oldest and well known SEO forums.

3. Digital Point Forum (forum.digitalpoint.com)– One of the larger forums in the SEO world.

4. Search Engine Watch (forums.SearchEngineWatch.com) – Almost 60,000 SEOs discuss search related stuff here. This is one that I use and highly recommend.

SEO Conferences

A good way to learn SEO is in person. Going to conferences won't just keep you up-to-date on the SEO world, but it will allow you to learn from some of the most successful SEOs.

1. Search Engine Strategies (SearchEngineStrategies.com)– Many conferences all over the world throughout the year.

2. PubCon (PubCon.com) – This conference started from the Webmaster World forum. Not only will you learn about SEO. It is held in Las Vegas and Austin Texas once per year. Usually November in Las Vegas and in Austin in March.

3. SMX – This is by far the largest of the conferences and are held all over the world.

Appendix D – IIS/.Net SEO Server Issues

This part of my presentation deals with Microsoft's Internet Information Server (IIS) and how to improve technical SEO on the Microsoft server stack.

After completing technical SEO assessments on numerous sites running on IIS and .NET using both SEOAudits.com and AccuQulaity.com, I believe that it is a very scalable and production-worthy platform, but I have found that its default settings are far from optimal for SEO of any website that the server is hosting from a technical SEO point of view.

Oh, and here is a second caveat: Please be sure to test any changes on a staging server *before rolling them out* to production. I would hate for something to happen to your website because I made a typo, worded something unclearly, or these don't apply to your current configuration.

Default Pages (Default.aspx)

Directory pages are available at two different URLs, one with and one without the default page. For example, these two URLs would lead to the same page:

> http://www.MikeMonahanSEO.com/home

> http://www.MikeMonahanSEO.com/home/Default.aspx

In this example, the default page is Default.aspx, though it could be configured to be a different name.

To Google this is duplicate content. Google can get to the website on two different URL's. The same problem occurs without a proper 301 redirect. If your domain comes up by using www.MikeMonahanSEO.com as well as if you just typed MikeMonahanSEO.com and doesn't redirect to one or the other, the to Google you have two different pages with identical content. Also inbound bound links to the page could point at either of these two URLs as well. You should focus all inbound links to a single URL for the page.

Creating Case Insensitive URLs

The issue with this, is the path portion of the URL which is served by IIS is case-insensitive. So any of these URLs will usually lead to the same page such as you see below.

http://www.MikeMonahanSEO.com/home/default.aspx

http://www.MikeMonahanSEO.com/home/Default.aspx

The fact that the case creates a different URL to Google, it creates a major crawler inefficiency. Google and Bing will crawl all of the different case variations that it sees in links and believe there is duplicate content on your website although all the links are going to a single web page.

So how do I fix this issue? Again, you can solve this issue by using canical tagging such as the rel=canonical tag that points to the URL with the correct capitalization or all lower case which I recommend.

I usually create a rule that rewrites the URL to all lower case that will work with a tool I use called URLRewrite:

```
<rule name="LowerCaseRule">

<match url="[A-Z]" ignoreCase="false" />

<action type="Redirect" url="{ToLower:{URL}}"
appendQueryString="true" />

</rule>
```

TIP: The Bing authorization file *BingSiteAuth.xml* is a case sensitive file name. You can add an exception for URLs which need to be case sensitive.

Error Page Responses in ASP.NET

The default configuration for ASP.NET handles errors such as if a page is not found by using only a 302 temporary redirect to an error page, which usually returns a 200 response.

A 302 redirect is only a temporary redirect notification to the search engines. This means they will continue to check that URL when they come to visit to see the new page when it finally appears. Some search engines still index the URL.

This issue also occurs if you have a server issue such as a database problem. In this instance many of your pages will default to the same 302 URL leading the search engines to believe you have a lot of doorway pages.

So how do I fix this issue? To fix this you need to modify **web.config** file. Here is code portion from the web.config file that prevents these redirects:

```
<customErrors mode="RemoteOnly"
defaultRedirect="GeneralErrorPage.aspx"
redirectMode="ResponseRewrite">

<error statusCode="404" redirect="404ErrorPage.aspx" />

</customErrors>
```

The attribute *redirectMode* needs to be changed to *ResponseRewrite* instead of its default value of *ResponseRedirect*.

NOTE: If the *redirectMode* option is not available, you will need to upgrade your version .NET.

Browser Dependent Code Issues

.NET has some features that makes it easy to rewrite the page code so that a page changes based on the user agent requesting it. From a technical SEO perspective this is a problem because it leads to unintentional cloaking of the content on the page. Google places penalties on any pages or sites that have any hidden content.

By default, there is nothing to fix. However, since this functionality is there, it is possible that browser-dependent code exists in your site right now.

How can I fix this? Well, tell your web developers not to use these code options on pages they create. But you should evaluate all the code for potential browser-dependent code issues.

Appendix E – The Google Toolbar

The Google Toolbar

Google makes it easy to see when its Googlebot has last visited a webpage. All you need is the Google Toolbar to find out. The Google toolbar is available free of charge at **http://toolbar.google.com**. You download a small program, and you are ready for some easy searching. The toolbar works with Microsoft Windows NT, 2000, XP, Vista, 2003 Server, 2008 Server and Windows 7. You must also have Microsoft Internet Explorer version 5.0 or greater installed. There is also a similar version available for Firefox users. Unfortunately, Mac users are out of luck.

> **NOTE:** Per Google's own words, "You get the best of the Google Toolbar built right in to Chrome." So you already have the PageRank Tool in Google Chrome.

If you have the Google toolbar installed there is a plethora of additional tools and options you can configure including a tool called "PageRank." When you hit the check mark to place the PageRank box on the toolbar as shown in the screenshot below you see a small but very powerful rectangular box that is added on the Google Toolbar right next to the Bookmarks button.

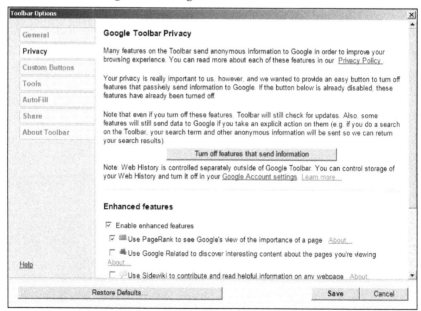

On some versions of the Google Toolbar it can be found under tools as shown in the next screenshot.

The PageRank is in essence the term *quality scoring.* Google's PageRank is a score of a website from zero to ten (0-10). Ten is the highest and zero is the lowest. If you are competing against another website on the same keywords, the website with the higher PageRank will be higher on the SERP page when a search is performed. When you are higher on a page due to your Google page ranking, you have obtained this search.

Google makes a ranking of a website based on the factors we have already discussed and some we will discuss later in this book. After the crawlers, spiders, and robots have gathered data from all the sites known on the web, it uses this information to determine a sites page ranking. This ranking or scoring determination is one of the most secretive parts of SEO.

 The goal is to score pages based on the quality and relevance that site visitors derive from each page they visit. How good it looks visually has virtually no effect on what the crawler, spiders, and robots gather from a website, as shown on the Google PageRank tool below.

Note: *There once was a time when the keywords in the Meta tag made up the rank of a page and was the most important factor. Now they make up about one percent of the Google page ranking. Keywords are still important in web page rankings. However, they're just one of a hundred or so elements that are taken into consideration.*

I know the major influences of this score from experience and from information provided by Google and other search engines. Google as well as the other major search engines are masters of changing their algorithms and the elements that weigh in to their algorithm used to determine the PageRank of each URL. It changes so often that there will probably be a SEO Secrets Book 2012, 2013, and so on.

Google looks at more than the sheer volume of visits a page receives or the number of links to that page from other websites. It also looks at the pages that direct traffic or have links to your site. If you looked at it from a point system, certain types of websites such as; news sites, government sites, education sites, and sites Google has already ranked highly, give your website more points. Accumulate enough points and Google starts to rank your page highly. Accumulate more and Google increases your page ranking. Links are a heavily weighted item but it is only one part of hundreds of items that will be required to make your website rank highly.

A web page that has multiple links to it might rank lower than a page that has just a single link from a "more important" page. It is always good to create pages visitors like, but be mindful of search engines.

Want to know how your page ranks? Let's take a look at how we can view this information and much more using the PageRank Tool from the Google Tool Bar.

Google Toolbar PageRank Tool

Now let's get to the Google PageRank tool and see how useful this tool really is. It has 4 main features. Let's take a look at each one. The first really cool feature is the rectangular box. It feels like a gauge every time you visit a new website and if you hover over the PageRank box with your mouse, it shows you the site's Google PageRank.

The second feature actually has two parts to it. This is where you can tell on any website that Google has come to visit the site. If you click the little down arrow next the PageRank box you will see the first of three options—"Caches Snapshot of The Page." Every time the Googlebot visits, it takes a picture of the page as shown on the next page.

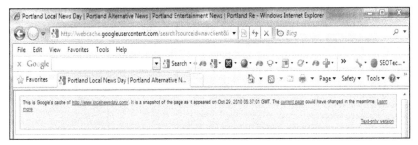

Along with a picture of the website, the time and date of the snapshot is also logged. You also have one other important tool here! Notice to the right a little link that say "Text-only version." Click this and see what the spiders, crawlers, and bots really see in the screenshot below.

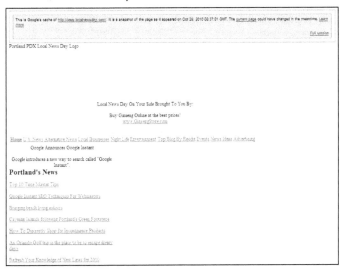

It is amazing to see how little text relating to their website is found on some web pages. All the text on the site is contained in the pictures. I have one customer who had the one of the best looking websites. It was all done in Flash. However, she had a PageRank of zero, even though she had the website up for 8 years. Her website was better-looking and more interactive than all of her competition.

Nonetheless, her competition was at the top of the organic searches and winning all the clicks, whereas she was on page 43 for her best keyword.

Since the Panda/Farmers update as it was called when Google's Algorithm changed in 2010, you need to have more content. The bare minimum is now 300 actual words in text on the page. The more original the content the better Google will index it and let it perform.

Once the company, that had their site done in Flash, became a customer, you can't even imagine how upset she was when I told her we would have to limit

the Flash and include text instead to get her rankings up.   It is hard for some
people to understand why Flashy isn't always better.

The third feature is called, "Similar Pages" as shown below

The "Similar Pages" option provides you with links to pages which Google
deems similar; these links are prime candidates for link exchanges which we
will talk about later in this book. Since Google already believes they are
related to your industry. The more relevant the links to and from your
website are, the higher Google will make your PageRank score.

The last feature you will find on the Google PageRank Tool is the
"Backwards Link" shown in the next screenshot.

The Backwards Links option takes you to a list of links that the Googlebot has found that link directly to your website. These are very important to know. The more of these from relevant sites that Google knows about, the higher your PageRank will be.

There is a lot to cover in this book, so let's get started in the next chapter with understanding Meta tags

NOTE: *Here's a link to the Google Toolbar for Mac.*

http://www.google.com/mac

Index